THE IRISH QUESTION AS A PROBLEM IN BRITISH FOREIGN POLICY, 1914–18

THE IRISH QUESTION AS A PROBLEM IN BRITISH FOREIGN POLICY, 1914–18

Stephen Hartley

Palgrave Macmillan

ISBN 978-1-349-18548-1   ISBN 978-1-349-18546-7 (eBook)
DOI 10.1007/978-1-349-18546-7

© Stephen Hartley 1987

Softcover reprint of the hardcover 1st edition 1987

All rights reserved. For information, write:
Scholarly & Reference Division,
St. Martin's Press, Inc., 175 Fifth Avenue, New York, NY 10010

First published in the United States of America in 1987

ISBN 978-0-312-43618-6

Library of Congress Cataloging-in-Publication Data
Hartley, Stephen.
The Irish question as a problem in British foreign policy, 1914–18.
Includes index.
1. Great Britain – Foreign relations – Ireland.   2. Ireland – Foreign relations – Great Britain.   3. Irish question.   4. Ireland – Politics and government – 1910–21.   5. World War, 1914–18 – Diplomatic history.   6. Great Britain – Foreign relations – 1910–36.   I. Title.
DA47.9.I73H37   1987   327.410415   85-27828
ISBN 978-0-312-43618-6

For My Father

Contents

	Preface	ix
	Abbreviations and References	xi
1	Ireland and Pre-War British Foreign Policy	1
2	'The One Bright Spot' (August 1914–May 1915)	18
3	The Asquith Coalition; the Worsening Irish-American Situation (May 1915–April 1916)	33
4	The Easter Rising and its Aftermath (April–November 1916)	50
5	Sir Roger Casement's Trial and Execution (April–September 1916)	79
6	The Home Rule Negotiations; the American Presidential Election (May–November 1916)	96
7	Lloyd George Takes the Helm (December 1916–April 1917)	117
8	America Enters the War; the Balfour Mission (April–June 1917)	133
9	The Northcliffe Mission; the Irish Convention and British Propaganda in the United States (June 1917–April 1918)	151
10	The Conscription Crisis; the Last Months of the War (April–December 1918)	174
11	Conclusion	193

Appendix: Organisation and Personnel of Relevant Sections of the Foreign Office, Department of Information and Ministry of Information	200
Notes	203
Bibliography and Sources	228
Index	237

Preface

This work arose from a long-standing interest in the repercussions of the Irish Question on British foreign policy and in the influence of foreign pressure on British handling of Irish affairs. Before August 1914, the Irish Question may have affected the diplomatic calculations of certain European powers, but, once war had broken out, the most serious reverberations were felt in Anglo-American relations. There are many studies of the Irish-American community and its role in American politics, while several works purport to analyse the effect of the Irish Question on Anglo-American diplomacy. However, the great majority of these focus attention on the aspirations of Irish Nationalists and their American supporters, with the result that insufficient attention has been paid to the problems of opposing British diplomats and politicians. This study attempts to remedy the general deficiency by focusing primarily on British reactions to American pressure and particularly on the opinions of Foreign Office officials, Cabinet ministers and Unionist opponents of Irish Home Rule. Evaluation of American opinion is, of course, essential, but is included only where it provoked British comment or inspired British action.

Grateful acknowledgement is made to the following for permission to quote from archive material (see Bibliography for details): Her Majesty the Queen, for her gracious permission to quote from papers in the Royal Archives at Windsor; the Controller of Her Majesty's Stationery Office, for papers in the Public Record Office; the Deputy Keeper of the Records, Northern Ireland Public Record Office; the British Library Board; the Clerk of the Records, House of Lords Record Office; the Beaverbrook Foundation and A. J. P. Taylor, for the Lloyd George, Bonar Law and Beaverbrook Papers; Times Newspapers Ltd; the *Spectator* for St Loe Strachey material; the Bodleian Library, Oxford; the Co-operative Library of the Plunkett Foundation for Co-operative Studies, Oxford; the Master, Fellows and Scholars of Churchill College, Cambridge; the Cambridge University Library; the Warden and Fellows of New

College, Oxford, for the Milner Papers; the University of Birmingham Library; the Wiltshire County Record Office; the Kent County Archives Office; the Ulster Unionist Council.

I must also thank the following private individuals for their kind permission to quote from collections in their ownership: Mark Bonham-Carter; Captain Peter Montgomery; Miss Sylvia M. Duffin; Lord Monteagle; the Marquess of Reading; Lady Elizabeth Arthur; Mrs Joan Longden.

The following were generous enough to supply private information to the author: the Mount Stuart Archives, Rothesay; Sir Cecil Dormer; Sir Colville Herbert Barclay; Major Graham Curtis Lampson; Lady Hilda Salisbury-Jones; Mrs C. E. Emery.

In those cases where it has not been possible to trace the holder of copyright, or where it may have been overlooked, the author offers his apologies.

Finally, I must thank Dr M. L. Dockrill of King's College, London, for his advice and assistance, and my father for his patient help in manuscript adjustments and proof-reading.

S. HARTLEY

Abbreviations and References

APR	American Press Résumé
Cab	Cabinet
DMI	Director of Military Intelligence
D of I	Department of Information
FO	Foreign Office
M of I	Ministry of Information
PRO	Public Record Office
WO	War Office
WRO	Wiltshire Record Office

Hansard references:

HC represents House of Commons Debates; HL represents House of Lords Debates.

The notes do not show the locations of papers cited, since these can be found in the Bibliography and Sources.

1
Ireland and Pre-War British Foreign Policy

I

At the start of his mission to Germany in November 1914, Sir Roger Casement noted in his diary the conviction that

> the blow struck today for Ireland must change the course of British policy towards that country. Things will never be quite the same again. The Irish Question will have to be lifted from the mire and mud and petty false strife of domestic politics into an international atmosphere. That, at least, I shall have achieved.

In visiting Berlin, Casement was taking advantage of Britain's involvement in the European War in order to continue a tradition of Irish nationalism – the quest for both moral and military support from any foreign power willing to exploit Britain's recurring difficulties in Ireland. Many centuries earlier, for example, Irishmen had looked to Spain as an ally against Elizabethan England, while revolutionary France had figured prominently in subsequent Irish rebel thinking. The Entente Cordiale (1904) precluded any possibility of further French support, but, in the build-up of Anglo-German tension after 1905, Irish extremists saw growing potential in imperial Germany as a sympathiser towards the Irish cause.[1]

As early as 1908, Casement, then in the middle of an illustrious career with the British Consular Service, had dreamed of a German liberation of Ireland from British rule, and this dream assumed firmer proportions when his friendship with certain Foreign Office officials convinced him that an Anglo-German war was inevitable in the near future.[2] From 1912 onwards, Casement began to expound his views in anonymous articles for Irish periodicals, culminating in 'Ireland, Germany and the Next War' for the *Irish Review* of July

1913, which analysed Ireland's role in a post-war peace settlement. Casement considered that, if a 'foreign ruler' was obligatory for Ireland, Germany would be preferable to Britain, since it would be in the German interest to govern Ireland beneficently. However, he argued that such an annexation was extremely unlikely, since 'a German-owned Ireland could not but provoke universal alarm and a widespread combination to forbid its realisation'. Casement predicted that, instead, Ireland would be 'erected into a neutralised, independent European state under international guarantees' – an ambition which subsequently played an important part in Irish extremist thinking – and he added,

> An independent Ireland would, of itself, be no threat or hurt to any European interest. On the contrary, to make Ireland an Atlantic Holland, a maritime Belgium, would be an act of restoration to Europe . . . that a Peace Conference should, in the end, be glad to ratify at the instance of a victorious Germany.[3]

Although the article is unlikely to have created much interest in either the Wilhelmstrasse or Whitehall, it was none the less of far-reaching importance to Irish history. First, it indicated Casement's philosophy when subsequently negotiating with the German Foreign Office for a statement of Germany's intentions towards Ireland. Secondly, and more significantly, although Casement was by-passed by the rebels who planned the Easter Rising, his political theories permeated much of their thinking on international affairs and exercised a strong influence over later Sinn Fein policies.

Although various European powers had successively figured as a potential ally for Ireland, the strongest and most constant support from the mid nineteenth century onwards came from the United States. This was particularly so following the influx of Catholic immigrants from Southern Ireland to America during and after the Great Famine. As the political power of the Irish-Americans grew, British governments were forced to recognise the threat they posed to Anglo-American relations by their influence over US foreign policy and their ingrained hostility towards England. In 1900, Arthur Balfour, then leader of the House of Commons, admitted to the American diplomat Henry White that 'harmonious cooperation between the two great Anglo-Saxon states' would be difficult to attain since 'large numbers of the most loyal citizens of America . . .

come from that part of Ireland which has never loved England'.[4]
Many Irish Nationalists used this Irish-American animosity as a lever to demand Home Rule – especially after the General Election of November 1910, when it became clear that the Liberal Government (which held power by virtue of support from John Redmond's Irish Parliamentary Party) would relentlessly push a Home Rule Bill onto the Statute Book. Early in 1914, for example, Joseph Devlin, the MP for Belfast, privately urged Lloyd George that American public opinion, 'as evidenced by forty-seven state legislatures of the American Union', was strongly in favour of Home Rule. John Dillon, Redmond's deputy, persistently warned of the serious consequences for Anglo-American relations if Home Rule failed to materialise. Provoked in a House of Commons debate by derision towards Irish-Americans, he retorted that they were 'a great element of power' and scolded his Tory opponents, 'We are endeavouring, in spite of your sneers and your hostility, to win the Irish race at home, in Ireland and in the United States to friendship with England. Why should you make that a matter of reproach?'[5]

Unionists had always decried this line of argument and professed doubts as to whether Irish-Americans would be satisfied with a Home Rule parliament subordinate to Westminster. Philip Cambray of the Unionist Defence League argued in a propagandist pamphlet that the Irish-American conception of Home Rule was, in fact, complete independence and that 'no one who has an acquaintance with the speeches and literature of the Irish-Americans can fail to be struck by their anti-British spirit'. While most Unionists shared Cambray's sentiments, a few had misgivings. As early as January 1910, J. L. Garvin, the influential editor of the *Observer*, displayed a prescience unequalled by any of his fellow Tories when he wrote to Balfour's secretary, Jack Sanders,

> What we need is better relations with America. The new alliance between the Irish and German vote in the United States is a more important thing than almost anybody here seems to realise. It is one of the greatest dangers that ever threatened the Empire. Yet if some sort of Home Rule made the relations of England and Ireland better, and the relations of the Empire and the United States better also, the Irish at home would not only stand by us to a man against Germany, but would be foremost in our fighting line.[6]

Garvin, although a strong imperialist, was less obsessed than many Tories with preserving the almost sacrosanct Act of Union, and, faced with what he regarded as a necessary choice between changes in the structure of the Union or irreparable damage to the Empire, he reluctantly advocated the former. In October of the same year, he reiterated his ideas to another leading Tory, Austen Chamberlain, urging that the Irish problem presented 'graver dangers than limited Home Rule can ever involve. . . . It prevents any firm entente with the United States and is a valuable help instead to German purposes at Washington.' Chamberlain, however, would not acknowledge that the maintenance of the Union and the security of the Empire were in any way incompatible. Although, like his father, he was a staunch supporter of an Anglo-American understanding, his reply to Garvin expounded the traditional Tory viewpoint that foreign considerations should not affect the framing or execution of domestic policy:

> I think it unwise to lay too much stress on the American side of the case. We never have done any good, and we never shall do any good, by touting American sympathy and kowtowing to American opinion, and if our domestic policy appears to be directed by a desire to secure an American entente or alliance, it will only earn the amused contempt of the American people. Let us do the right thing because it is the right thing and not to please foreign, even American, opinion.[7]

Although rejected summarily, Garvin's predictions foreshadowed with surprising accuracy important developments in the Irish Question – especially during the 1914–18 war. Moreover, the divergence of opinion between the traditionalist stance of Chamberlain and the new pragmatic view advanced by Garvin was one of the first indications of a subsequent rift in the Unionist Party over America's role in the Irish Question.

Unionists were not alone in resenting American pressure. In March 1913, when the American Secretary of State, William Jennings Bryan, publicly referred to the 'degradation of the House of Lords' in having opposed Irish Home Rule, Lord Morley, Lord President of the Council in the Liberal Government, 'commented with great severity on the extreme impropriety of the Secretary of State of a friendly nation using such language'. Indeed, Morley spoke so strongly that a colleague, Sir Almeric Fitzroy, wrote in his diary, 'I realised the force of Lord Acton's remark, "there is a Conservative inside him [Morley]".'[8] The Conservative reaction of Morley (a Liberal) and the progressive views of Garvin (a Tory) underline the fact that the international aspect of the Irish Question was not merely a pawn in the tactical thrust of party polemic. Opposing attitudes often resolved themselves into a clash between traditional principles and pragmatism. There were those who insisted that external pressure over the Irish Question had to be accepted as a fact of life, whereas others believed that the principle of domestic sovereignty should not be sacrificed to expediency in foreign affairs and that outside opinions should not influence domestic problems. Thus, the seeds were sown of a controversy which was later to provoke great dissension, not only at Cabinet level, but also in Parliament, at the Foreign Office and in the realm of public debate.

II

When Garvin warned Chamberlain that the Irish problem would prove a 'valuable help . . . to German purposes at Washington', he pinpointed its dual importance in British foreign affairs at that time. Indeed, before the First World War, Ireland not only affected Anglo-American relations but may well have influenced European – and especially German – calculations regarding Britain's reliability in an international crisis.

This possibility would have increased when, as part of a growing campaign against the imposition of Home Rule on their province, Ulster Unionists under Edward Carson formed a powerful paramilitary force known as the Ulster Volunteers and some of Carson's lieutenants made impassioned statements favouring German rule in preference to that of Dublin Catholics. Their deputy leader, James Craig, proclaimed that the German Emperor would be preferable to 'the rule of John Redmond', while another prominent Ulster organiser, Major Frederick Crawford, declared that, if Ulster was excluded from the Union, he would prefer to change his allegiance 'right over to the Emperor or anyone else who had got a proper and stable government'.[9] To the fury of Liberals, British Tory leaders fully sympathised with the Ulster Unionist stance. When, in January 1913, Andrew Bonar Law, the new Conservative Party leader, echoed these warnings, Winston Churchill, amidst general uproar, taunted his opponents that 'Ulster would rather be annexed to a foreign country than continue her allegiance to the Crown. This, then, is the latest Tory threat. Ulster will secede to Germany.'[10]

In November 1913, a Belfast Protestant journal, the *Irish Churchman*, added to the speculation by claiming that 'We have the offer of aid from a powerful monarch who, if Home Rule is forced on the Protestants of Ireland, is prepared to send an army sufficient to release England of any further trouble in Ireland by attaching it to his dominion.' It is clear, however, that neither the Emperor nor the German Embassy in London was sympathetic towards Carson or the Ulster cause. The German Embassy frequently criticised both Ulster's stand and the Liberal Government's weakness in tolerating it, while the Emperor himself dismissed one of Carson's most famous attacks on the Home Rule Bill as 'rubbish'. Nor was Ulster talk of German aid taken seriously by the British Ambassador in Berlin, Sir Edward Goschen, who considered the *Churchman*'s claim to be 'the only thing that strikes me as amusing in that distressful Irish Question'. Many writers have taken a more sinister view of Ulster's pro-German declarations. Of one such statement in early 1914 – which threatened to seek the aid of 'the greatest Protestant nation on earth, Germany' – the poet and wartime publicist Alfred Noyes wrote, 'This was on the very eve of war with Germany and these suggestions could not have been made unless that war were already envisaged. There is not the slightest doubt that this manifestation gave "aid and comfort" to the enemy in its war plans.' Sensitive to such criticisms, Sir James Stronge, a former Secretary of the Ulster Defence Union, subsequently admitted to a colleague,

> Of course one was (and is) ashamed of the pre-war Germanizing speeches made by a few members of our party (I think that James Craig is the only one of them who can be said to be of any political importance). If they had then known the Germans as they now know the Germans, they would have sought a more legitimate illustration for their argument. We all believed (and still believe) that Home Rule implies eventually an Irish Republic, anti-British in sentiment, and I can't, even now, say that I would prefer to live under an Irish Republic to living under a German Empire. I would emigrate rather than live under either.[11]

Although Ulster's infamous flirtation with Germany was largely bravado, designed to intimidate the Liberal Government, informed commentators agreed that the defiant speeches of the Ulster leaders were 'taken very seriously by the grim Puritan rank and file in Northern Ireland, to whom they were addressed'.[12] This clearly affected Ulster's recruiting during the early stages of the war. Edward Carson later stated that at the outbreak of war Protestant feeling was so high that many Ulstermen saw no reason to fight Germany, a Protestant power, while in November 1915 the Nationalist MP Tim Healy wrote to his brother, 'Outside the towns few Protestants have enlisted as privates, nor will they do so. They say the Kaiser is a good Protestant.'[13]

III

Ulster's 'Germanizing speeches' were probably given little credence in Europe, but its campaign against Home Rule attracted considerable attention. In 1912, the German Embassy's Counsellor in London had reported to Berlin that the resurgence of the Irish Question 'would weaken England as a world power because of the influence the Irish exercise in America', a development which the Emperor considered 'would be a great boon'. In November 1913 the Embassy reported further, 'So long as Ireland is in the foreground of internal policy, England's parties will be compelled to manage their foreign policy cautiously and with discretion.' It argued that it would thus be in the interests of German foreign policy if the Unionists were to succeed in impeding the Liberal Government's efforts to pass Home Rule.[14]

Some British officials at the Foreign Office and in the diplomatic service were concerned at the effect which the Irish imbroglio might have on their country's position abroad. Arthur Nicolson, Permanent Under Secretary at the Foreign Office, was a fervent Unionist and Ulster sympathiser, both by temperament and by family connections, and he was more concerned than most with the Ulster problem and its possible repercussions abroad. In common with most Ulster partisans, Nicolson believed that the Liberal Government had cynically resurrected Home Rule for party gain and had thereby provoked righteous resistance. Indeed, he frequently expressed this opinion to diplomats such as Sir Louis Mallet, the Ambassador at Constantinople: 'I cannot find words strong enough to express my opinion of the conduct and attitude of the Government. What distresses me is the pitiable exhibition which we are presenting to foreign powers and the fact that it must before long seriously affect our position in Europe.'[15]

Towards the end of March 1914, there occurred the infamous Curragh Mutiny, which probably had considerable influence on Continental assessment of Britain's credibility in any European crisis. Immediately prior to the 'Mutiny', Sir Henry Wilson, the Director of Military Operations and one of the leading mutineers, warned Colonel Seely, the Secretary of State for War, that any Government order for army action against Ulster would result in 'regiments depleted of officers, a hostile Europe, our friends leaving us because we have failed them, and our enemies realising that we had lost our Army'. According to Wilson, this warning made little impression on Seely and the Government proceeded with the troop movements which culminated in the Curragh resignations. With the crisis 'attracting a good deal of attention in France and, indeed, all over the Continent', Wilson was compelled to visit Paris to reassure the French military authorities that the British Army's reliability would not be impaired.[16]

Arthur Nicolson also foresaw repercussions on British standing in Europe, particularly the effect on Anglo-Russian relations. As an ardent Russophile, he feared that conservative and autocratic Russia would shrink from Britain's 'revolutionary or ruinous course' and would 'gravitate' towards Germany, which at least had 'the appearance of stability'. In early April, Sir George Buchanan, the British Ambassador to Russia, confirmed many of Nicolson's suspicions when he reported a growing feeling that, 'as we cannot be counted on to stand by Russia in the event of war, an understanding with us is of but little value'. The Tsar and the Russian Foreign Minister, Sazonov, had both voiced fears concerning the 'dissensions and disaffection' within the British Army, but Buchanan had reassured the Tsar (who professed difficulty in comprehending the Ulster problem) that the Curragh incident had arisen from misunderstandings, with no question of disobedience among officers. Nevertheless, Nicolson had become so convinced that the Liberal Government would have to resign over the Home Rule issue that he came to doubt the advisability of new initiatives in foreign policy – including even his cherished aim of an Anglo-Russian alliance. On hearing that the Russians were sounding out Edward Grey regarding a firmer understanding, he wrote to Buchanan that 'it may be as well to defer going into the matter until the political outlook here is clearer and more settled'.[17]

Nicolson's scathing criticism of the Government's Irish policy greatly irritated Grey – the Foreign Secretary of a Liberal Government committed to Home Rule – and relations between the two men became increasingly strained. By May 1914, Valentine Chirol, a close Foreign Office observer, was convinced that Nicolson's position had become 'quite impossible' and that 'perhaps because he talks too much about Ulster . . . , he has absolutely lost Grey's confidence and does not conceal the fact that he is sick of it all'. According to Zara Steiner, Nicolson had become 'Grey's chief adviser in name only' and was by-passed on most major issues. This must have hindered the working of the Foreign Office, since 'differences of personality and diplomatic inclination were coming into the open and becoming relevant to the actual making of policy'.[18]

Nicolson was not the only senior figure to express doubts as to the Government's future. At the height of the Curragh crisis, Lord Hardinge, Viceroy of India and Nicolson's predecessor as Permanent Under Secretary, wrote cynically that he had hitherto believed that ministers would 'hang on to their posts and to their emoluments to the very last moment', but now considered them to be 'in such an awful mess that they will not feel in a position to carry on government any longer unless they obtain a fresh mandate from the people'. Hardinge had earlier berated the 'sickly' Liberal Administration for its 'deplorable' mismanagement of the Irish Question, but was equally severe towards the Unionists, whom he dismissed as 'hopelessly feeble' and 'rent by internal dissensions'. This frustration with the existing political system led him to see 'ample room for a Centre Party which will comprise the best elements of the two existing parties'. Unlike Nicolson, Hardinge was by no means opposed to the principle of Home Rule, having already observed a similar system operating satisfactorily in India. Consequently, when the Irish imbroglio threatened open conflict in 1914, he took the pragmatic view that Home Rule with Ulster exclusion offered the only chance of averting civil war. However, Hardinge was not an Ulster sympathiser and considered that Carson's defiant rhetoric was 'very aggressive and, as an example, does much harm elsewhere'.[19]

Most British politicians, although aware that the Irish situation was undermining their country's influence in Europe, were too immersed in domestic party strife to recognise the need for compromise. Liberals contended that Unionist support for Ulster was responsible for these diplomatic difficulties, while Unionists retorted that the blame lay with the Government, which was undermining the constitution for mere party gain. A more realistic awareness was shown by Austen Chamberlain, who, after returning from a European holiday in 1913, 'convinced that British domestic difficulties were encouraging Germany in her policy of aggression', suggested a federal solution of the Home Rule question.[20] Chamberlain's initiative was an ironic twist when one recalls that he rebuked J. L. Garvin in 1910 for proposing federalism as a means of improving Anglo-American relations. Despite his rejection on that occasion of 'kow-towing' to Irish-American pressure, he was now prepared to modify his attitude towards Home Rule in the light of the European situation.

Chamberlain was not alone in his fears. Lord Cromer, former High Commissioner of Egypt, wrote to *The Times* urging all parties to consider the possible connection between the Ulster crisis and developments in Europe, and to avoid any controversy which might 'prevent the Government of this country from speaking in the Councils of Europe in the name of a united people'. Cromer also wrote privately to Lord Milner, his former protégé in Egypt and a leading English supporter of the Ulster campaign, 'The Germans are always on the look-out with a view to taking advantage of any dissensions which may occur in this country. I hope this point will not be forgotten.'[21]

However, Cromer's appeal fell on deaf ears, for it was quickly followed first by the divisive Curragh Mutiny, and then, in late April, by the landing at Larne of arms for the Ulster Volunteers from a Hamburg dealer. Ulster's principal gun-runner, Frederick Crawford, at first attributed the Larne success to the deliberate inactivity of the German customs authorities, but later denied that this was so, while Hugh Montgomery, another leading Ulster Unionist, assured a correspondent that 'Germany did not supply the Ulster Volunteers with either gold or arms. Their arms were purchased from a dealer . . . and the German Government knew nothing of the transaction.'[22]

The Larne episode further underlined the divisions at the Foreign Office. While Arthur Nicolson was writing jubilantly to Goschen, 'I hope you were amused by this "coup" . . . so wonderfully organised and so beautifully carried out', Grey was instructing the consuls at various European ports (including Hamburg) to watch for any more gun-running and, where possible, to obtain information from local authorities. By this time, the diminution of British standing in Europe had come more to the fore in public debate. In the House of Commons, Arthur Balfour warned that 'we are going for a long time to suffer in the councils of Europe by what has occurred', while, from the Government benches, Winston Churchill – previously one of the most bellicose towards the Ulster agitators – appealed for a spirit of compromise, since 'the high mission of this country seems to be in abeyance and the balance of Europe appears in many quarters for the time being to be deranged'.[23]

IV

The gravity of the Irish situation intensified with the growth of another paramilitary force as a counterweight to the Ulster Volunteers. Disillusionment with Redmond's Home Rule Party and its fruitless constitutionalist activities had produced a new breed of Irish Nationalist who channelled his sense of frustration into bodies such as Sinn Fein and the revived Irish Republican Brotherhood. In November 1913, leaders of these new organisations formed the Irish Volunteers and induced John Devoy and his Irish-American extremist society, the Clan na Gael, to set up an Irish Volunteer Fund on their behalf. The British Ambassador in Washington, Sir Cecil Spring-Rice, could only speculate as to the plans of the fund-raisers, and at the height of the Curragh crisis he telegraphed Sir Edward Grey that, in the event of fighting in Ireland, 'men and guns will almost certainly be sent from America'. Grey considered the message too vague to warrant action, pointing out that it was 'not clear to whom the men and arms will be sent', and Spring-Rice was merely informed that his warning would be borne in mind. Obviously dissatisfied, the Ambassador wrote again that, should the situation in Ireland worsen, 'American unfriendliness to England' would probably have serious results. As an illustration, he enclosed a vitriolic article from an Irish-American newspaper, the *Irish World*, which advised 'the shooting of a few hundred of the bumptious and bigoted bullies of Ulster' and urged that a future Irish Parliament should compensate Ulstermen for their land and then 'get rid of them'.[24]

Lukewarm reaction to such warnings was illustrated by Lord Eustace Percy, a Foreign Office specialist in American affairs, who, on hearing of Clan na Gael subscriptions for the Irish Volunteers minuted, 'It is so impossible to keep any proceedings secret in the US that I doubt if we can stand in much danger of arms from New York.' Similarly, when Courtenay Bennet, the British Consul at New York, sought permission to employ a Pinkerton detective to augment the meagre information on gun-running activities, Augustine Birrell, the Chief Secretary for Ireland, quashed the idea on grounds of expense.[25]

The danger that conflict in Ireland might foment unrest in the United States became more apparent when Spring-Rice reported that, as a result of the 'threat' to Ulster, the hitherto apolitical Orange lodges had become increasingly active. 'The ultra-Protestant papers here are fully as violent as "The Irish World" ', he added, 'and the Presbyterians of America are now, as they always have been, good at a fight.' Moreover, the sympathies of the US Secretary of State, William Jennings Bryan, were 'strongly Protestant' and he seemed to favour 'local Home Rule' for the Unionist countries of Ulster as part of an overall federal solution. However, whilst 'a good many' of the American Cabinet were solid Presbyterians, Catholics were very influential in the Democrat Party as a whole and would pressure the Government to 'condone infractions of neutrality'. As a result, the Ambassador advised,

> It will require great pains and care to avoid occasions for offence, but at the same time, American opinion, though generally inclined to be hostile to Britain, will be to some extent divided on the Irish question, which will appear to be a struggle of oppressed Protestants against oppressing Catholics.[26]

Spring-Rice probably overstated American sympathy for the 'oppressed Protestants' in Ireland, for, as the *Times* correspondent, Arthur Willert, wrote a few months later, 'Training and tradition and often origin make the average man over here a Home Ruler.' Moreover, the 'oppressing Catholics' sharply polarised after June 1914, when John Redmond – concerned at the strength of Irish extremists on both sides of the Atlantic – forced a take-over of the Irish Volunteers by his own supporters. In consequence, a bitter factional squabble developed in America between the Clan na Gael and Redmondites, each promoting its own volunteer fund. However, Eustace Percy noted that, although funds could 'still be raised in America for Ireland', the Redmondite collections were small in comparison with former years. In contrast, John Devoy subsequently claimed that Clan funds survived periods of uncertainty and eventually supplied the Easter Rising rebels with 'the means of striking their historic blow'.[27]

Irish-American organisations were also involved in another issue affecting British interests: the Panama Canal tolls dispute. When Congress passed an act exempting US shipping from paying tolls, the British Government protested that this violated an earlier agreement. President Wilson supported the British interpretation and asked Congress to repeal the Exemption Act, thereby provoking the fury of Anglophobe politicians, who attacked any measure favouring British interests as un-American. The President reportedly believed that his opponents were 'composed largely of Hibernian patriots, both in the Senate and out, that always desired a fling at England'. In similar vein, Spring-Rice warned London that the Irish political societies, with Senator O'Gorman as their principal spokesman, had emerged as the main opponents of repeal. Despite this opposition, the President eventually persuaded Congress to repeal the Tolls Act in June 1914. The struggle had been prolonged, for, although Irish-Americans no longer appeared sufficiently powerful to induce American intervention in the Irish Question itself, they had demonstrated their potential influence – albeit a declining one – over American foreign policy. Indeed, while their motives derived from the grievances of Irish history, their principal successes were not in purely Irish matters but in the obstruction of any development beneficial to British interests or conducive to improved Anglo-American relations.[28]

V

The career of Cecil Spring-Rice was illustrious, but, in many respects, tragic in its final chapter. Although he had served in Washington over twenty years earlier as an Embassy secretary and had forged close relationships with many leading Republicans, he had few contacts with the Democrats and found himself temperamentally at odds with Woodrow Wilson.[29] Moreover, the Ambassador frequently irritated American Government officials by taking an oversensitive stance on behalf of British interests, while in his despatches to London he tended to report the American point of view as sympathetically as possible. The result was that he 'found himself in the unenviable position of seeming to Wilson a mere British chauvinist, while in Britain he was regarded by the more traditionally-minded realists of the Foreign Office as too pro-American'.[30]

Spring-Rice's attitude towards the Irish Question produced a similar paradox. By birth he was a Protestant from the landlord class of Southern Ireland, and, while he had little first-hand knowledge of his native country, 'Ireland was in his blood'. However, while his friends were largely staunch Unionists, his family were Liberals and he himself was a confessed Home Ruler. As Ambassador in Washington, he was naturally cautious about expressing opinions on such a delicate subject as the Irish Question – especially since it was, in Arthur Balfour's words, a tradition that 'an Ambassador during his tenure of office must be, like the King, above party politics'. This perhaps explains Arthur Willert's recollection that Spring-Rice 'annoyed Irish-Americans' by being 'non-committal about Home Rule'. However, as an Irishman, he was moved to complain to the Foreign Office in January 1914 of the 'unfairness and misconception in the way in which the Irish have been constituted the sole scapegoats for the half-conscious suspicion and resentment against Great Britain still lurking in most American minds'. The Ambassador saw other factors, such as the American Revolutionary tradition, at the root of Anglo-American friction and reflected 'how skin-deep the hostility of the Irish in this country really is, and how slight an obstacle it will probably be in the future to an understanding between the two countries based on dignity and patience'. Foreign Office officials were generally less charitable, and Walter Langley, an Assistant Under Secretary, minuted sourly, 'The skin-deep hostility of the Irish takes an unpleasant and practical form. It is always a Curley, a Fitzgerald or an O'Gorman who takes the lead in any anti-British measure.'[31]

Since the Ambassador's advice on Irish matters was largely falling on deaf ears, his principal concern when returning home on leave in June 1914 was to convince the Government that the Irish situation might gravely endanger Anglo-American relations should it deteriorate further. He expressed his fears to Asquith, the Prime Minister, and to Arthur Nicolson at the Foreign Office, and doubtless mentioned them at an interview with Grey on the following day. The likely tenor of Spring-Rice's warnings is perhaps illustrated by a letter to Lord Newton, subsequently Assistant Under Secretary at the Foreign Office: 'Both Protestants and

Catholics in the US would look on Ireland as the field where they could fight their battles, and both sides would give what help they could – and in a manner not sanctioned by diplomatists.'[32]

On 21 July, the parties to the Irish dispute met in the Buckingham Palace Conference, convened by the King in a last attempt to avert a civil war. Just before the Conference opened, Spring-Rice wrote to a participant, Lord Lansdowne, the Unionist leader in the House of Lords, imploring him to consider the international implications of Conference decisions. Lansdowne's reply was pessimistic, but he assured the Ambassador that the delegates would 'bear in mind not only the local aspects of the case but their wider considerations to which you refer'. Geoffrey Dawson, who, as editor of *The Times*, was keenly aware of the European situation, wrote in his diary, 'Foreign situation very threatening – an additional reason for supporting King and Conference.' However, the Conference broke down within a few days and, to avoid public panic, an official report of the King's speech to the delegates deliberately omitted 'a very bloodcurdling reference to foreign affairs and a statement that the King's hands were tied abroad by the state of Ulster'.[33]

The worsening Irish situation was being closely monitored by Germany. Information was garnered from an increased number of Germans visiting Ulster on various pretexts. These included the 'German Emperor's chief political spy', Professor Schiemann, and a fellow historian, Professor Kuno Meyer – both with close contacts at the German Foreign Office. 'The British public', wrote Wickham Steed, European-affairs editor of *The Times*, 'was utterly blind to the meaning of these activities; the Irish leaders of all parties gaily played the German game.' Similarly, the private papers of Lord Northcliffe, proprietor of *The Times*, contain a note that the Kaiser's brother, Prince Henry of Prussia, was in Britain in late July in order to 'nose about on the Irish question'. On returning to Germany, Prince Henry asserted that Britain would not intervene in any future war – an opinion which may well have been 'an important factor in determining Germany to go ahead'. The consensus of German opinion was described by James Gerard, the American Ambassador to Germany:

> Undoubtedly, the German Foreign Office believed that Great Britain would remain out of the war. The raising of the Ulster army by Sir Edward Carson . . . was reported by German spies as a real and serious revolutionary movement and, of course, it was

believed by the Germans that Ireland would rise in general rebellion the moment that war was declared.[34]

On the eve of war, the Belgian Ambassador to Berlin, Baron Beyens, advised his government that in German eyes Britain was 'paralysed by internal dissensions and her Irish quarrels'.[35] Lloyd George, then Chancellor of the Exchequer, assured a press confidant that the Foreign Office was 'quite convinced' of German reliance on such 'extravagant and erroneous' impressions. Subsequently, in his memoirs, Lloyd George returned to the theme:

> The long drawn-out and wearisome tragedy of the relations between Great Britain and Ireland played an important part in the World War. There can be little doubt that the expectation on the Continent that Britain had for the moment sunk so deep in the quagmires of the Irish bog as to be unable to extricate her feet in time to march eastward, was one of the considerations which encouraged Germany to guarantee Austria unconditional support in her Serbian adventure.

While such testimony suggests that the Irish situation affected German calculations, the historian Felician Prill argues that it could not have been the pivotal factor between war and peace, since neither the Emperor nor the General Staff would have ordered the invasion of Belgium on a 'vague presumption' that civil war was imminent in Britain.[36]

Until the end of July, the British Government had little time for foreign affairs, being 'preoccupied with the Irish crisis and the danger of civil war, to the exclusion of almost everything else'.[37] The harassed Cabinet, now faced with two crises – Irish and European – moving in tandem towards the brink of catastrophe, suddenly gained temporary succour from one danger and was thus enabled to concentrate on the other. On 30 July, at a private meeting between Asquith, Bonar Law and Edward Carson, the two Unionist leaders suggested that in the national interest the pending Home Rule legislation be postponed, so that a united Britain could give full attention to its European commitments. After consulting his colleagues and John Redmond, the Prime Minister readily agreed.[38] The Cabinet now began to break free of its Irish preoccupations, as Winston Churchill later described in dramatic terms: 'The parishes of Fermanagh and Tyrone faded back into the mists and squalls of

Ireland, and a light began immediately, but by perceptible gradations, to fall and grow upon the map of Europe.'[39] Thus, against all the odds, the likelihood of civil war in Ireland – so ominous just a few weeks earlier – had evaporated with the unexpected turn of European events.

Meanwhile, with war in Europe imminent, Spring-Rice made a personal appeal on 1 August to the Duke of Devonshire, a leading Unionist peer, asking Tory leaders to shelve party conflict for the duration of the crisis. Devonshire arranged a meeting between the Ambassador and Arthur Balfour, who, significantly, spent much of that day impressing upon the French and Russian Ambassadors that his party would be united behind any British decision for war.[40] Prompted by 'ginger groups' advocating a firm stand against the Central Powers, Unionist leaders met at Lansdowne House that evening, following which Bonar Law sent a letter to Asquith offering support for any declaration of hostilities.[41]

On the following day, 2 August, the British Cabinet reached its decision to intervene in the event of a German violation of Belgian neutrality. Although Asquith and Grey subsequently refuted any suggestion that the Cabinet's action was influenced by the Tory letter of support, it is probable that the pledge sustained the Cabinet 'hawks' during the crucial meeting.[42] However, as Britain was sucked into the European maelstrom, the Irish Question entered upon a new and ultimately critical stage, while its international dimension gradually assumed an increased importance for the British Government.

2
'The One Bright Spot' (August 1914–May 1915)

I

On 3 August, Edward Grey rose in the House of Commons to appraise Britain's position in regard to the European hostilities and was able to qualify his otherwise gloomy assessment with the declaration that 'the one bright spot in the whole of this terrible situation is Ireland. The general feeling throughout Ireland – and I would like this to be clearly understood abroad – does not make the Irish question a consideration which we feel we have now to take into account.' Grey's statement moved John Redmond to announce that British troops could be withdrawn from Ireland, since Irishmen would defend their own country against the threat of foreign invasion. This offer came as a particular relief to such Liberal ministers as Winston Churchill and Herbert Samuel, for whom the Irish problem was now dwarfed by the European conflict. As early as 26 July, Samuel had written to his mother, 'How infinitely small, in the shadow of this awful catastrophe, appear the petty troubles of Ulster.' Not all Liberal ministers took this view, for Viscount Morley, a strong pacifist and staunch Home Ruler, resigned as Lord President of the Council following the Cabinet's commitment to war. Augustine Birrell considered that 'the fate of Home Rule for Ireland, if war broke out, lay like a heavy weight on Morley's mind, paralysing his activities. He thought the war would impair the chances of Ireland, whereas it did the very reverse.'[1]

Despite Grey's optimism, the Irish difficulty continued to create party friction. Two main procedures were suggested as a stop-gap solution. On the one hand there was strong pressure from Unionists for a total suspension of all domestic controversy – especially the Home Rule Bill – for the duration of the war; on the other hand there was, as *The Times* had earlier remarked, 'a feeling among moderate Irishmen of all parties that the European crisis should precipitate some sort of settlement'. Indeed, Redmond warned Asquith that this had come to be 'the touchstone to the Irish mind of the sincerity of the promises of justice to Ireland', and that without it he would be 'faced in Ireland and in America by a situation which would be desperate'. Meanwhile, another leading Nationalist MP, T. P. O'Connor, similarly urged Lloyd George, 'We must have the Bill before anything further could be hoped. In America, as in Ireland, any paltering with the question would turn the whole thing the other way, and with the frantic campaign of the Kaiser and the German population in America . . . it would be the end of all things.' O'Connor cited the views of a Cabinet minister, Walter Runciman, the new President of the Board of Trade, who considered that delay in passing Home Rule would be 'one of the greatest blunders any government could make at this time . . . when we need more than at any time in our history the support of Irishmen and keen supporters of Irish Home Rule in Ireland itself, America and the Colonies'.[2]

These views were supported by the Liberal press, notably the *Daily Chronicle*, whose editor, Robert Donald, privately warned Lloyd George that the German element in America was stirring up a strong anti-British agitation. A Home Rule settlement, he contended, would prevent the Clan na Gael from recruiting Irish-Americans to become 'by far the most powerful element working against British interests'. He concluded pointedly that, 'with regard to Home Rule, I am thinking more of the effect on America than of the effect on Ireland'.[3]

These various pressures produced a Cabinet deadlock: Asquith, Grey and Lord Kitchener, Secretary of State for War, wanted to shelve the Bill to avoid party strife, while Birrell threatened to resign unless it was passed. He was supported by Lloyd George and by Churchill, who feared that the alternative was the immobilisation of two army corps in Ireland. The impasse was only overcome when Grey, stressing that American goodwill might be at stake, changed sides and advocated that the Home Rule Bill be placed on the Statute Book immediately. The Cabinet then resolved to pass the Bill, together with a supplementary measure which suspended its application for the duration of the war. In announcing these measures to the Commons, Asquith stressed the Cabinet's concern for the probable effects of postponement on Irishmen at home and 'in the great kindred country of the United States'.[4]

Neither Asquith's 'imperial arguments' nor the subtle device of the suspensory measure placated the Unionists, who believed that the Government had agreed to a cessation of all controversial legislation during the war. Tory leaders angrily denounced Liberal duplicity and a memorandum to the Prime Minister claimed that Conservatives were being compelled to choose between 'an artificial reticence of debate' and a renewal of the Irish controversy which would 'accentuate our differences at home and advertise them abroad'. This, it was argued, was 'unjust' and would have 'lastingly injurious effects on the international situation'.[5]

While some Unionist leaders, including Carson, Walter Long and Robert Cecil, remained intent on contesting Home Rule, the majority reluctantly acceded to Asquith's plea for national unity. Indeed, Bonar Law urged a Carlton Club meeting of Unionist MPs that opposition be postponed until after the war, so that, 'whatever our internal difficulties may be, we shall present to the enemy the front of a united nation'. Most Unionists grudgingly accepted their leader's advice, but the need to satisfy Irish-American opinion remained a highly sensitive subject, as Lord Curzon demonstrated in Parliament by querying, 'Why should the loyalty of Ulster be sacrificed to the loyalty of the Irish in the United States of America?' Party friction on the issue was again illustrated when Austen Chamberlain, who was due to appear on a recruiting platform with Winston Churchill in Birmingham, withdrew a previous offer of accommodation for Churchill's visit. In an attempt at conciliation, Churchill urged Chamberlain to realise 'what an act of recklessness and unwisdom it would be for us – either party – to start a quarrel with Irish Nationalism here, in the Colonies and above all in America at this time of crisis'. Chamberlain's reply was scathing:

> I believe, and I have the best American authority for thinking, that if you had done the obvious thing and announced at the beginning of the war that all domestic controversy must cease till the war was over, you would have had the unanimous approval of America; and even the Irish themselves would have recognised the justice and wisdom of your action. As it is, you deliberately sacrifice the Ulstermen, who have shown an unconditional and splendid loyalty, in order to pay blackmail to the National Volunteers . . . and to their American paymasters, whom I see no more reason to trust now than at any time during the last twenty years.[6]

'The One Bright Spot' 21

The 'American argument' was also contested by Tory journalists. Indeed, while Liberal pressmen were citing American factors in favour of Home Rule, H. A. Gwynne, editor of the right-wing *Morning Post*, urged on Bonar Law an opposing view from his Washington correspondent that 'incredible harm' would be done to the British cause in America if the Home Rule issue was resurrected. The attitude of *The Times*, traditionally hostile to Home Rule, was more complex, since, while its editor, Geoffrey Dawson, was a strong Unionist, its Washington correspondent, Arthur Willert, was a confessed Home Ruler. In early September Willert urged that 'Redmond's fine stand has increased the already strong sympathy with the Nationalists' and any renewed opposition to Home Rule would 'lose not only much of the Irish support which we have but the . . . undiluted respect of numbers of real Americans'. Dawson, however, expunged all references to Irish-American feeling from Willert's despatches to *The Times*, prompting the piqued correspondent to write, 'I shall take it that this is done for reasons of policy and shall not send anything much about Irish-American opinion.' Dawson, meanwhile, assured Carson that, although he hated advertising 'the slightest sign of division in our ranks', he was prepared to do this to show that 'the course proposed by the Government would produce an actual and most serious cleavage'.[7]

The growing rift between Liberals and Tories, which hardened after the passing of the Home Rule Bill on 18 September, doubtless disturbed the harmony of the British war effort. Although working co-operation was eventually restored, the Government's action and its use of the contentious 'American argument' left a lingering resentment among Unionists and set the stage for later and equally virulent disputes over Home Rule and America's involvement in the problem.

II

While British politicians were indulging in mutual recrimination, the Irish situation in America began to undergo significant changes. Initially there was considerable evidence that most Irish-Americans supported Redmond's pro-British stance. In August, for example, Willert informed Dawson,

Roughly speaking, only the Germans and the elder Irishmen are against us. The young college-trained Irish-Americans are, I am told, mainly for us. . . . In fact, things could not be more satisfactory as far as public opinion goes. But always remember that an untoward incident may produce a change. The traditions of a century are not obliterated in a day.

Further evidence was provided when Redmond cited the attitude of Patrick Egan, one-time extremist but now a convinced Home Ruler, who had requested help in opposing Devoy's schemes for a German–Irish alliance against Britain, and who had assured Redmond that the majority of 'reasonable and decent Irishmen in America' sympathised with his House of Commons declaration.[8]

This reassuring situation quickly deteriorated when, in a speech at Woodenbridge, County Wicklow, in late September 1914, Redmond urged the Irish Volunteers to fight with the British forces 'wherever the firing line extends'. The speech was far-reaching in its repercussions. In Ireland, it split the Irish Volunteers; a minority of 12,000 broke away but retained the name 'Irish Volunteers', while the remaining 160,000 stayed with Redmond and became known as the 'National Volunteers'. In the United States, the effect was even more drastic. The speech provoked serious dissension within the American branch of the United Irish League, some of whose members chose to cease active participation rather than uphold Redmond's new recruiting-policy. The most serious defection was the League's mouthpiece, the *Irish World*, which embarked on a 'vicious, villainous campaign of vituperation and misrepresentation against the Irish Party'.[9] Among Irish-Americans in general, it signalled the beginning of a slow drift away from the Home Rule cause, thereby creating an ever-growing pool of disillusioned and uncommitted individuals who could easily be swayed by disturbing events in Ireland itself. Thus a political vacuum was created in America which would ultimately be filled by the growth of the Clan na Gael and its kindred spirits. This transition was detrimental to Britain, since Redmond had identified both himself and the Home Rule cause with the British war effort.

It is perhaps understandable that the British Foreign Office, with greater matters monopolising its attention, was oblivious to the worsening Irish-American situation. Even the British Embassy was not alive to the growing danger, so there tended to be a time-lapse before developments were reported to London and a further period before the Foreign Office appreciated their significance. Indeed, in late September Spring-Rice reported to Grey that the overwhelming majority of Irish-Americans were friendly to the Allies, while six weeks later he assured Grey that 'On the whole, there seems practically no chance of united action between the Germans and the Irish. All attempts that way have failed.'[10] It is not surprising, therefore, that when Spring-Rice and the British consuls in America reported on German–Irish meetings, at which Redmond was bitterly denounced for his recruiting-stance, there was little response at the Foreign Office other than the occasional complacent reference to the overwhelming percentage of Germans present.[11]

Neither the Foreign Office nor Spring-Rice was prepared to consider a counter-campaign against the anti-British propaganda, believing that the risks outweighed the anticipated benefits. Thus, when Lord Newton offered to speak in America for the British cause, Spring-Rice deemed this unnecessary, since, through its excessive propaganda, 'Germany has almost made England popular in America. . . . An Irishman here was asked if he was neutral. He said, Bedad, he was, he didn't care a damn who beat the Germans.' According to Newton, the Ambassador 'had little faith in the value of propaganda oratory', believing that Americans 'resented attempts to proselytise them, and much preferred to form their own opinion'.[12]

The Foreign Office largely shared Spring-Rice's caution, and Hubert Montgomery stressed to Asquith its opposition to emulating 'the orgy of second-rate publicity' in which the Germans had indulged. Consequently, in early 1915, when the Irish Nationalist MP Tim Healy offered to lecture in America, Grey himself vetoed the idea with the warning, 'According to my information, anything like an officially-inspired mission to the USA would be resented here.' This fear was well borne out by the American lecture tour of Wilfrid Ward, a Conservative Catholic and editor of the *Dublin Review*. Ward's visit provoked much ill-feeling among Irish-Americans, partly as a result of an innocent but indiscreet interview which had embarrassed the American Chief Justice. This prompted Spring-Rice to observe that 'it would have been very dangerous for this Embassy to have had anything to do with propaganda among the Catholics, who strongly advise against it', and he suggested that any future missionary should be 'someone who is not connected with the conservative section'. The Foreign Office file on Ward's visit was closed with the comment, 'An unfortunate occurrence, plainly showing the danger of "missionaries" unless they possess great tact.'[13]

Although the Irish situation imposed restrictions on missions to America, the Foreign Office was fully alive to the value of any risk-free propaganda. It therefore strongly supported T. P. O'Connor's idea of an Irish mission to France, which in the past had been Ireland's traditional ally. However, former ties of friendship had been weakened by the Anglo-French Entente and by the Irish clergy's fierce condemnation of the anti-clericalism of successive French governments. 'The young priests hate the French anti-clericals', wrote Tim Healy in December 1914, 'and talk of Austria's Catholicity.' To counter this growing Francophobia, O'Connor, in addition to praising France in public speeches, conceived the idea of presenting an Irish Nationalist address to Cardinal Amette, Archbishop of Paris. His object was 'to indicate to the world that the Irish people are in entire sympathy with the Allies', and in a subsequent article for the *Daily Chronicle* he developed this theme:

> Lies, at once enormous and grotesque, are being scattered wholesale over America as to the state of feeling and the events in Ireland. Men of the Irish race there were told that recruiting in Ireland had miserably failed. . . . We resolved then to proclaim the position of Ireland in such a fashion as would make any further misrepresentation more difficult.[14]

O'Connor's deputation, which included seven other Irish Nationalist MPs, duly presented their address to Cardinal Amette in Paris in late April 1915. Even this mission, like its American counterparts, had its problems, for, as the British Ambassador, Sir Francis Bertie, reported to Edward Grey, parts of the address were 'from an Englishman's point of view open to objection, although acceptable to Frenchmen'; indeed, one passage claimed that, 'in the darkest hours of persecution and of suffering through which we have passed for our faith and our country, we have always continued to dream that help would come to us from France'. However, when the visit was extended to include an audience with the President, Raymond Poincaré, and dinner with the Foreign Relations Committee of the Chamber of Deputies, Bertie queried whether he should attend the latter, since 'Irish speeches may be made which might be rather embarrassing to the person who is supposed to be neutral in political questions'. Grey nevertheless instructed Bertie to attend the function, which passed without incident because some of the offending passages in the address were expunged and, in Bertie's rather pompous phrase, 'The Irish behaved themselves.'[15]

The mission produced mixed reactions in Britain. The *Manchester Guardian*, a fervent supporter of Home Rule, considered that the mission 'cannot fail to have an effect on Irish opinion in the United States', while O'Connor's Nationalist colleague T. P. Gill hailed the visit as 'one of the great world-impressing incidents of the war', which would show 'the great international asset Ireland is thus capable of bringing to the modern policy and diplomacy of the British Empire'. Not surprisingly, Unionist press and politicians were piqued by the venture, and the *Belfast News Letter* commented of the address to President Poincaré that 'its partisan and inaccurate statements are calculated to mislead public opinion in France'. The chief object of the mission, it added sourly, seemed to have been 'to emphasise their claim to speak in the name of "the Irish nation" and perhaps to lay the foundation for a request to the President to interfere when the war is over on behalf of the unconstitutional Home Rule Act'. Bertie, however, judged the mission purely by its effect on Irish recruiting, which by August 1915 he considered to be negligible.[16]

These criticisms overlook perhaps the most important point. Although Home Rulers greeted the Paris mission as a resounding success, it was an indication of their delicate position in America that they were now forced to use Paris as a safe platform from which to influence Irish-Americans. The Foreign Office clearly appreciated this fact and, in order to further British interests, had co-operated with the mission. Subsequently, when the Home Rulers lost further influence in America, the Foreign Office turned increasingly towards Unionist propaganda to fill the void, thereby incurring Nationalist animosity. However, in the winter of 1914–15 the Irish Question was largely dormant in British politics, and this was reflected in the phlegmatic Foreign Office attitude towards Irish-American disaffection with Redmond's movement. Ireland was still generally seen, in Grey's phrase, as 'the one bright spot', and it required further evidence of trouble in the months ahead to disturb this complacency.

III

The thorniest Irish problem for the Foreign Office during the earliest months of the war concerned the activities of Sir Roger Casement, who had gone to the United States in June 1914 to collect funds for the Irish Volunteers. After the war broke out, he embarked on a publicity campaign to dissuade Irishmen at home from enlisting in the British Army. Initially, the Foreign Office was unmoved by his activities – an attitude illustrated by Assistant Under Secretary Eyre Crowe, who minuted contemptuously, 'I do not think he is worth powder and shot.' However, opinions hardened when, on 5 October, Casement produced a notorious open letter to the *Irish Independent*, which appealed to the Irish Volunteers to ignore a war that 'concerns Ireland not at all' and would only burden a people who had 'already been bled to the verge of death'. The letter, with its potential damage to Irish recruiting, irritated the Foreign Office and, on Grey's instruction, Nicolson wrote brusquely to Casement, inquiring whether he admitted authorship of the letter.[17]

Casement, however, had already left the United States on his infamous mission to Germany. His aims were threefold: first, to obtain from the German Government a declaration of good intent towards Ireland; secondly, to form an Irish Brigade from Irish prisoners in Germany (mainly as propaganda against recruitment, but also for use in a future Irish rebellion); and, thirdly, to act as spokesman for the Clan na Gael in requesting arms and ammunition for an Irish rising later in the war. By his mission Casement hoped to accomplish his principal objective of making Ireland an international rather than a British domestic question.[18]

Casement arrived in Berlin at the end of October 1914 and, despite some suspicion of his motives, soon obtained an official declaration from the German Foreign Office, which appeared in the *Norddeutsche Allgemeine Zeitung* and proclaimed,

> Should the fortune of this great war, which was not of Germany's seeking, ever bring in its course German troops to the shores of Ireland, they would land there, not as an army of invaders to pillage and destroy, but as the forces of a Government that is inspired by goodwill towards a country and a people for whom Germany only desired national prosperity and national freedom.[19]

The publicity thus created was just what Casement sought, for, according to the Irish poet Padraic Colum, it 'did a great deal towards making the Irish a European question'. In America, the German Ambassador, Count von Bernstorff, reported that it had made an 'excellent impression', while Patrick Egan noted that it had been 'spread all over the country because it contained a spice of sensation'.[20]

Reports from British diplomats that the declaration had been published in neutral countries created considerable ill-feeling at the Foreign Office in London, where Arthur Nicolson queried, 'Surely Sir Roger Casement should be regarded as engaged in treasonable intercourse?', to which Grey replied, 'He has been so regarded for some time, and I said his pension was to be stopped. What else can we do?' Of the declaration itself, however, British officialdom was, in the main, contemptuous. Lord Kitchener was merely amused by it, while Spring-Rice expressed mock relief that 'the German Army will land in Ireland, not to pillage churches and sack towns (as is falsely though somewhat naturally asserted) but on a mission of mercy and culture. I hope the good news is being spread in Ireland.' Augustine Birrell reflected disparagingly that Casement had 'gone the Whole Hog In Berlin', but added, 'I don't suppose for a moment he will set foot in Ireland where his name is not worth 2^d.' Nevertheless instructions were issued by the Foreign Office to keep watch for Casement should he try to leave Europe through a neutral port.[21]

Casement wrote of his second aim – the formation of an Irish Brigade from prisoners-of-war in Germany – that 'it shames John Bull's Army and it knocks recruiting on the head in Ireland', while Franz von Papen, the German Military Attaché in Washington, assured his Government, 'The moral effect that the Irish are volunteering to fight against England will be great.'[22] By mid December a treaty setting out the objects of the Brigade and the assistance expected from Germany had been drafted by Casement and given the seal of approval by the Chancellor, von Bethmann Hollweg. However, publication was deferred until the scheme showed signs of success. In the event, German reservations proved well founded, for Casement received a hostile reception from most of the Irish prisoners-of-war, of whom a mere fifty or so volunteered their services. Consequently, the project never assumed the propaganda value in neutral countries which Casement and the Germans had envisaged.[23]

When Augustine Birrell heard of the Treaty from the Foreign Office, he commented to Mathew Nathan, his Under Secretary, that it was a tale of 'incredible folly' and queried flippantly whether the brigade were 'coming as open enemies . . . to seize our castles, or as *secret* agents of the Kaiser'. Even so, Robert Vansittart of the Foreign Office Prisoners-of-War Department subsequently admitted that Casement's project had set his department 'on edge', while the invasion scare was given sufficient credence for the Irish police, the military and the local population to be alerted on the west coast. The invasion threat had an inevitable American dimension, for, as Nathan reported to the General Officer Commanding in Ireland, General Friend, 'Rumours from Berlin of a plan for a descent on Ireland found an echo in the Irish and German communities of the USA.' However, such echoes invariably met with Foreign Office scepticism – as, for example, when the British Consul General in New York reported a rumour that a Clan na Gael contingent was being organised as a German legion by Hermann Ridder, a leading German-American politician. Eustace Percy's reaction was that, with elections imminent, Ridder was doubtless bargaining to deliver the German Democratic vote, which he controlled, and 'these negotiations probably take him and his henchmen into many Irish saloons where the talk is free and wild. But the "German Legion" is probably born of politics and whisky and will prove a phantom.'[24]

During the formative stages of the Irish Brigade scheme, Casement was distracted by a new development which seemed to him to have considerable anti-British potential. In America he had met a young Norwegian sailor, Adler Christensen, who became his servant and accompanied him to Berlin. While passing through Christiania, the Norwegian capital, Christensen contacted the British Legation and offered to sell information about Casement's plans. The British Minister at the Legation, Mansfeldt Findlay, consulted Arthur Nicolson at the Foreign Office and, after Christensen had revealed Casement's conception of both the Irish Brigade and a future German-assisted rebellion in Ireland, Nicolson sanctioned a promise to the young Norwegian of £5000 for information leading to Casement's capture. However, at this stage Christensen told his master that he had been offered money to 'knock him on the head'. Casement, sensing an opportunity to discredit British diplomatic methods, wrote an open letter to Edward Grey in February 1915, denouncing the attempted bribery, and sent copies to twelve diplomatic missions in Berlin and to the Holy See. To his intense chagrin, the disclosure met with indifference in Germany and the United States. Of its reception by the American press, John Devoy later recalled that Casement was 'grievously disappointed when the revelation of the plot was not featured in this country as a great sensation', while Casement himself wrote in his diary that the German authorities failed to appreciate 'the vast effect it would have on public opinion in Ireland and the USA'.[25]

Although Casement's letter has usually been written off as a propaganda failure, the accusations made a noticeable impression in parts of South America and neutral Europe. The British Ambassador in Berne, Evelyn Grant-Duff, suggested a public denial, because 'the Northern Swiss are so stupid and so prejudiced that any story to our discredit, however extravagant, is easily believed'. However, aware that the accusations contained an element of truth, the Foreign Office instructed Grant-Duff to take no action. Some Norwegian newspapers portrayed the episode as a dubious attempt by Mansfeldt Findlay to involve a young innocent in diplomatic intrigue, which provoked Findlay to ask for either an official statement by Edward Grey or, alternatively, Foreign Office permission to publish his own version. In the event, continuing Foreign Office belief in reticence paid dividends, for, owing to an effective muting of the country's press by the Norwegian Foreign Minister, the matter had, as Findlay admitted, 'practically died a natural death within a week'.[26]

The Findlay story was also circulated in South America, where the Germans were developing a propaganda network and where Casement's revelations of rubber-trade atrocities had made him well known. However, warnings to the Foreign Office from the British Minister in Rio, Arthur Peel, and his counterpart in Buenos Aires, Reginald Tower, went largely unheeded until the latter forwarded a pamphlet which reproduced the story in Spanish and which was being widely circulated in Argentina. Tower commented bluntly that, while lack of information prevented him from answering the charges, 'the pertinacity with which the German agency here harps on Findlay's conspiracy seems to me to require a contradiction on our part'. This led Hubert Montgomery in the News Department to question the official policy of reticence:

I am doubtful whether we should not have done well to issue an explanation of the Findlay–Casement affair when the Germans first began to make use of it, to the effect that Mr Findlay's offer of a reward was clearly for information which would lead to the perfectly legitimate arrest of a traitor.[27]

Although the Foreign Office tended to dismiss Casement's mission as galling but inconsequential, and his various pronouncements as 'so absurd that they are not likely to influence opinion in Ireland or elsewhere',[28] the propaganda repercussions of the Findlay affair eventually disturbed this complacency. Moreover, while Casement's extravagant schemes made little impact on Irish-Americans, they succeeded at least in raising a question mark in neutral areas against Britain's claim to be fighting for the rights of small nations.

IV

At the outbreak of the European War, President Wilson, concerned that the United States might be divided by conflicting ethnic loyalties, called for a strict neutrality in thought and deed. However, revolutionary Irish-Americans soon combined with German-American organisations to demand that the President's 'strict neutrality' should include an embargo on arms exports to all belligerents. Their contention was that, since the Allies controlled the seas and thereby monopolised the purchase of American war materials, a continuance of the existing 'neutrality' was in their favour. In January 1915, an Embargo Conference led to the establishment of the 'American Independence Union', prominently featuring Irish-Americans. This body, supported strongly by groups such as the Clan na Gael and Jeremiah O'Leary's American Truth Society (described by the *Morning Post*'s Washington correspondent as 'neither American nor truthful'[29]) exercised an increasing anti-British influence in Congress.

Many British observers were increasingly perturbed at the growing co-operation between German-Americans and Irish-Americans. Arthur Willert had spelt out this 'very notable' development to *The Times*, but was nettled when his warnings were not published. He therefore complained to his editor, Geoffrey Dawson, that he had 'not felt justified in following the subject up', but was doubtless mollified when his despatch appeared in the newspaper on the following day:

> For some weeks past Teutonic propagandists have been busy forming, to the accompaniment of vociferous meetings, joint German-American and Irish-American associations in various big cities. . . . The scheme is frowned upon by the more active and younger Irish-American element. But if the bark of the movement for the present is worse than the bite, it should not be ignored. It illustrates the determination of the German-Americans to use domestic politics in the interests of the Fatherland, and should anything happen before the end of the war to rekindle Home Rule animosities, it might become of the most serious importance.

Willert, a conscientious journalist, could have been forgiven for personal confusion at this juncture. Having been admonished by the proprietor of *The Times*, Lord Northcliffe, for his 'over optimism in regard to American sympathy', he was then taken to task by Dawson, who suggested that people in Britain were hearing too little of the 'enormously strong pro-British feeling' in the United States and too much of the German–Irish alliance, with its notorious 'love of twisting the lion's tail'.[30]

A few weeks later, Dawson's views were reinforced by Eustace Percy, who urged both Dawson and Willert to lay more stress in *The Times* on pro-Ally sentiment in the United States. Percy was doubtless influenced partly by his own pre-war diplomatic experience in the United States and partly by the reports of Spring-Rice. In fact, neither of these provided a reliable basis for judgement: the German–Irish alliance had closed ranks considerably since Percy left Washington in 1913, whilst the Ambassador's despatches, often contradictory from week to week, contained inconsistencies which could be interpreted so as to justify almost any viewpoint. For example, on 12 February he reported that 'nearly half the total Irish vote is solid with the Germans', and two weeks later that 'Most of the Irishmen, especially the more respectable ones, are inclined to follow Redmond'. However, despite his inability to quantify Irish opinion, Spring-Rice was convinced that 'Irish mastery of the English language, especially the terms of abuse' was invaluable to the Germans, and that the professional Irish politicians would follow the pull of the purse-strings and play a key supporting role in the embargo movement.

The Ambassador therefore anticipated considerable German–Irish pressure on Congress, and this concern must have increased when a Senate vote favouring embargo was 'unexpectedly strong', being narrowly defeated by a mere fifteen votes.[31]

Although the embargo movement caused some anxiety in the early months of 1915, Foreign Office officials generally believed that German–Irish pressure was not yet powerful enough to force serious changes in US policy. Many echoed Eustace Percy's view that Wilson had no wish to endanger the British war effort and that, in any case, American business requirements would deter him from sanctioning a complete embargo. George Russell Clerk, an Assistant Under Secretary, considered that the embargo threat was largely 'a good weapon for frightening us', but that the danger was 'not imminent until the big munition interests start to show alarm'.[32] The absence of departmental minutes at this time suggests that the Foreign Office saw little chance of the average Irishman in the United States becoming actively involved in this anti-British movement, but, equally, that there was little hope of overcoming the hostility of the extremist fringe. It was believed that only a major development in the Irish Question itself would produce a change in attitudes, and that this was unlikely since the problem had been shelved until the end of the war. However, this complacency was disturbed in May 1915 by the formation in Britain of the Coalition Government and by the Irish-American reaction which followed in its wake.

3
The Asquith Coalition; the Worsening Irish-American Situation (May 1915–April 1916)

I

In May 1915, disaffection in Britain with the Liberal Government's handling of the war effort forced Asquith to form a coalition with the Conservatives. This brought into the Government leading Unionists such as Bonar Law, Balfour, Curzon and Austen Chamberlain; but, for the Irish Nationalists and their American supporters, the most abhorrent appointment was that of Carson as Attorney-General. Most Irish-Americans could not understand how the man who had defied the parliamentary process by invoking open rebellion against Home Rule could now be promoted to a ministerial post. Carson's selection was clearly a major blow to the Redmondites in America, since it appeared to confirm the extremist claim that Home Rule was an empty promise.

Further controversy surrounded the choice as Irish Lord Chancellor of J. H. Campbell, who had been one of Carson's lieutenants during the pre-war Ulster crisis. Although Campbell was highly qualified for the post, Irish Nationalists argued that, in view of the promised enactment of Home Rule, Irish Government posts should not be included in the coalition changes. The issue became a trial of strength, with the Tories threatening early withdrawal from the coalition if Campbell was rejected, and the Nationalists vowing strong opposition should the appointment proceed.[1] In the search for cogent persuasion, the 'American argument' again featured. The Liberal *Daily Chronicle* warned of Irish-American alienation, while the *Manchester Guardian* reflected sombrely that the nomination would break the party truce, 'with consequences which can easily be imagined both in Ireland and in the United States'. In the opposition ranks, the *Belfast News Letter* carped that the Home Rule Party had intensified their 'American arguments' against Campbell's selection after the German sinking of the *Lusitania* had produced 'the startling but gratifying news of the possible intervention of the United States in the war'. At Westminster, Redmond and his colleagues were now reportedly spreading the view that, 'the sooner the parties can present a united front and bury their differences, the better will be the prospects of a complete understanding with America'.[2]

Nationalist concern over Campbell was shared by Grey's Private Secretary, Eric Drummond, who submitted a memorandum to Lord Crewe (acting for the absent Foreign Minister) advising, 'It is very important that when Irish questions are considered, due weight be given to their international aspect.' Drummond, a Liberal, argued that the Home Rule Act had mollified most Irish-Americans, but that the Campbell furore might 'tilt the balance' and cause a 'considerable landslide' against the Government. Unlike some of his Unionist-inclined colleagues at the Foreign Office, he believed that this danger should have a bearing on the appointment:

> It is, of course of the utmost importance in our relations with the United States that Irish opinion should be kept what is called by the Americans 'sweet'. If the Irish vote were allied to the German vote and used as a solid instrument against us the effect might be very serious, as the pressure that would be brought to bear on Congress and on the President, who is a close follower of public opinion, would make questions such as the Ship Purchase Bill and export of munitions of war doubtful. . . . Nothing would be more likely to make the Irish in the U.S. pro-German than to find that in a national Government called together for the prosecution of the war, the Nationalists were in opposition.[3]

Crewe circulated Drummond's memorandum to the new Coalition Cabinet, urging that to ignore it would be 'a grave error'. On the Cabinet's instruction, he cabled to Spring-Rice that ministers were 'much concerned' at the threat posed to American munitions exports by 'adding strong Irish opposition to the German and Pacifist elements which are bound to give trouble in Congress'. Spring-Rice replied that the pro-Ally sentiment of most Irish-Americans, resulting from the Home Rule Act, would be immediately disturbed by an 'open breach' on the Campbell issue. By way of illustration he added, 'I know that Cardinal Gibbons, whose prestige is great and who is one of our best friends, has difficulties owing to Redmond's not joining the Government when Carson did.' Moreover, he argued that any rupture would damage the confidence of ordinary Americans in the British war effort, since they believed that 'for a just cause we have been ready to sacrifice everything and lay aside all class, party and religious antagonisms'.[4]

Lord Eustace Percy, a Conservative of more than usual flexibility, considered it necessary to make at least one Unionist in the Cabinet appreciate the overseas ramifications of Campbell's appointment. He therefore wrote privately to Arthur Balfour, whom he probably believed to be more capable than most Tories of comprehending the wider problems of statesmanship involved. Percy contended that, although Irish-Americans had been 'the chief obstacle in the past to good Anglo-American relations', the passage of the Home Rule Act had reduced their hostility; as a result, 'the soberer and more respectable section of Irish-Americans either followed Redmond's lead and adopted a friendly attitude, or followed President Wilson's lead and maintained a strict neutrality'. It was therefore necessary to avoid reawakening old antagonisms:

> It is possible that the Irish-Americans are about equally divided – but while our enemies among them are irreconcilable, our friends among them are still on the fence. . . . I think the arrangement near the beginning of the war by which the entry into force of the Home Rule Act was postponed shook them a little. The Coalition Government will inevitably shake them much more. . . . If they are shaken further, I fear they will come off the fence. Then we shall have a combination of the Irish and German votes which will constitute a practically fatal threat to the Democratic Party at next year's election and will exert a correspondingly terrorising effect on the policy of the Democratic Administration in the present crisis. I do not, indeed, think that even this combination could prevent the United States going to war with Germany if President Wilson decided on that course; but I feel sure that it would largely prevent the belligerency of the United States being of even as much service to us as their present neutral attitude has been.

Percy, realising that any unsolicited intervention by a civil servant in party politics was a delicate matter, apologised for 'interfering in such a matter of policy'. His four-year absence in the United States during the pre-war Ulster crisis had left him 'totally out of touch with English politics', and Campbell was therefore 'only a name' to him. Since he had 'not the faintest idea' of the domestic implications of the appointment, he viewed the question in purely diplomatic terms:

> So far as a civil servant may confess any party politics, I am, of course, a Conservative. But I do most strongly believe that an appointment which appears to excite the hostility of Liberals here and Nationalists, and which appears to be regarded by them in the light of past Home Rule contests, will have an effect on Irish-American opinion so dangerous as to deserve most careful consideration.

Lest Balfour reply that a transatlantic understanding should not be forged on the basis of what Austen Chamberlain had once described as 'kowtowing' to the Americans, Percy concluded.

> To suggest that we must not settle domestic questions without reference to foreign opinion is always invidious, and I do not imply that such surrenders are either necessary or advisable in the establishment of permanent good relations with the United States. Those relations are, and will be increasingly, based on far surer and more dignified foundations. But as a question of momentary tactics at a moment of great strain and varied risks, I . . . advocate this measure of consideration [i.e. not appointing Campbell] for Irish-American susceptibilities.[5]

It is clear that, since the key to influencing Irish-American sentiment lay primarily in the domestic handling of Irish affairs, Foreign Office officials were in a difficult position whenever the Government's Irish policies created ill-feeling in the United States. As civil servants, should they remain aloof from what was, primarily, a domestic controversy, or should they intervene – as Percy did on this occasion – by dwelling on foreign-policy implications? Percy's own position was, of course, exceptional in many respects. Where Irish affairs were concerned, he was less rigid than many of his colleagues. Moreover, his four years of diplomatic duty in Washington had insulated him from the turbulent domestic atmosphere surrounding the Home Rule controversy, while experience of the Irish-American problem had convinced him that it was necessary to moderate some party scruples for the furtherance of Anglo-American goodwill. However, as the Irish Question came to figure more prominently in Foreign Office discussions, other officials stressed their view that the direction of domestic affairs was sacrosanct and should be free from foreign interference. Although such stands of principle were not confined to those with Unionist outlooks, it was generally this element which took the strongest line on Britain's sovereign right to determine her own internal affairs. Percy's decision to raise the Campbell question privately with Balfour may thus have been a prudent move to avoid antagonising the traditionalists, since there would probably have been some internal friction at the Foreign Office had he suggested an official approach.

Balfour's reply totally evaded American considerations. He stressed, instead, that he had not been involved in the appointment, but, in view of Asquith's earlier assurances that the appointment would be made, 'to revoke it in obedience to political pressure would shake the coalition to its foundations'.[6] Despite such views, the bitter attacks of the Home Rule Party and fear of American reactions had their effect, and Campbell, anxious not to embarrass the newly formed Coalition, withdrew. Almost a year elapsed before periodic Tory pressure to have the decision reversed was finally rewarded and, in April 1916, Campbell at last became Irish Lord Chancellor.

II

Although the end of the Campbell controversy prevented a major crisis, the inclusion of the Unionists in the Coalition Government gave considerable impetus to Irish-American Anglophobia. Sir Arthur Herbert, head of the British Relief Fund in New York, later reported that 'the action of the Government in regard to Campbell and Carson upset even the loyal Irish very much, because they said it was evident that they had nothing to hope for in regard to Home Rule'.[7] Indeed, the summer of 1915 was a time of 'alarm, confusion and divided counsels among the American people', with a growing campaign for an arms embargo in which 'German and Irish-American spokesmen grew frantic in their rage against the President's policy'.[8] Spring-Rice noted that this German–Irish pressure was 'greatly to be feared', while Arthur Willert, although confident that there was 'not the slightest chance' of the movement succeeding, believed it to be 'capable of becoming a very grave nuisance unless checked'. He was concerned that, apart from its effect on the Wilson Administration, the agitation might precipitate in Congress 'a quite unprecedented outbreak against Great Britain'.[9]

In view of this deteriorating atmosphere, the Foreign Office gave serious thought to a Home Rule mission to mollify disgruntled Irish-Americans. Strangely enough, the suggestion stemmed from the Unionist Robert Cecil, the new Parliamentary Under Secretary at the Foreign Office.[10] Eric Drummond considered it an 'excellent move', but Grey continued to oppose such a 'radical change of policy' and stressed the Government's determination to avoid 'any sort of interference with the natural course of public opinion in the United States'. Spring-Rice, while sharing Grey's misgivings, suggested that Redmond alone could 'rally the Irish' and silence rumours that Britain intended to default on its Home Rule commitment. The suggestion was welcomed by the News Department, where Geoffrey Butler, a specialist on American affairs, minuted approvingly, 'If not too theatrical a move, the dispatch of an R. C. like Redmond would strike a note that would find response from one end of the Union to the other.'[11]

However, the plan was rudely shattered when Redmond refused to make the trip, partly because of his increasing political vulnerability in the United States and partly because of continuing War Office refusal to allow separate Irish Nationalist regiments. At the News Department's prompting, Augustine Birrell appealed to Redmond to ease Spring-Rice's 'distress' at the state of Irish-American feeling, reminding him that the Ambassador had been 'a good friend more than once to the Cause'. Birrell urged that the 'F. O. would be grateful for a leg-up, whatever may be the shortcomings of the W. O.', but this appeal also failed, since 'the stupidity of the military authorities in regard to the Irish regiments had suddenly been demonstrated in a form which it was impossible to forgive'. In any case, by late September Spring-Rice accepted that in the worsening political climate 'the experiment would be dangerous', while the Embassy Counsellor, Colville Barclay, confirmed the extent of anti-British feeling: 'Mr Redmond and other Nationalist leaders could not be expected to come to this country at present, as they would certainly be exposed to insult by the pro-German minority.' Redmond clearly appreciated that his power base in America had been fatally undermined and that it was prudent to avoid giving further opportunity for public attacks on the Home Rule Party. For its part, the Foreign Office was now dubious as to the value of such schemes, a doubt which was soon strengthened in the disastrous wake of the Easter Rebellion in Ireland.[12]

The growing threat posed by the German–Irish combination was highlighted by Joyce Broderick of the British Consulate in New York – an Irish Roman Catholic with 'exceptional opportunities for gauging the state of Irish opinion in New York through his wide circle of acquaintance among Irish-Americans'.[13] Broderick reported that, since the outbreak of war, German propagandists had freely distributed subsidies which had 'prolonged the life or determined the attitude of all the Irish papers in the U.S.'.[14] The editor of the *Irish World*, for example, was alleged to be receiving subsidies to print and circulate 20,000 free copies in saloons and seaside resorts.[15] Another Irish-American to receive financial backing was James K. McGuire, former Mayor of Syracuse, who owned several pro-German newspapers and ran a small news service. Not surprisingly, McGuire's book *The King, the Kaiser and Irish Freedom* not only condemned Redmond's pro-Ally stance but also argued that a German victory would achieve more for Irish liberty than would parliamentary agitation at Westminster.[16] George Viereck, a member of the cabal which controlled German propaganda in the United States, later admitted that small Irish newspapers were a constant drain on German funds, but considered Irish propagandists well worth the investment, because,

> Unlike the Germans, they suffer no inferiority complex with regard to the English. In spite of their intense activities, the Irish escaped the obloquy heaped upon the pro-Germans in the United States. Those who kiss the Blarney Stone acquire the gift of disarming their foes with a smile.[17]

It was with a view to countering this overt German–Irish propaganda that Spring-Rice and his Embassy colleagues deliberated at some length over the establishment and covert encouragement of a pro-Ally Irish-American newspaper. Joyce Broderick believed that such a journal, if vigorously edited, would prove a 'useful corrective' to the *Gaelic American* and *Irish World*, since 'Irish Catholics do not naturally lean towards Germany'. The

Home Rule Party, he thought, could provide financial backing, and T. P. O'Connor's journalistic experience would prove invaluable. Colville Barclay, whilst agreeing that a moderate paper would 'exercise a very healthy influence', considered that it would have to avoid any suggestion of British Government assistance. Moreover, in contrast to Broderick, he urged that it should 'subsist solely on Irish-American support'. These reservations were shared by Shane Leslie, an unofficial liaison between the British Government and Irish-Americans. Indeed, when in November 1915 an Irish Nationalist MP arrived in America to look into the possibility of establishing a new paper, Leslie warned that any scheme inspired directly from Ireland would be attacked as proof that 'Redmond and his attitude towards the war are now practically without any journalistic support in this country'. It would, he argued, be 'followed from its cradle to its grave by the accompaniments of a first-class faction fight'. At the Foreign Office, Eustace Percy shared Leslie's concern that 'it ought not to bear the brand of Redmond at the start, but should represent a distinctly American point of view not necessarily characterised by open friendliness to this country'.[18]

In January 1916, just such a paper was launched by Irish-Americans under the name *Ireland*, with Shane Leslie as a sub-editor. According to Broderick, in its endeavour to appear truly American rather than a mere lackey of the Home Rule Party, it omitted any discussion of the pro-Ally stance of Redmondites in Ireland. Older Nationalists reportedly criticised the paper's 'lack of editorial vigour', and Patrick Egan, for example, dismissed it as a 'Kindergarten Magazine' and a 'humiliation' to loyal Home Rulers.[19] Perhaps because of this, the Foreign Office suspended any further attempts to encourage other Irish-American newspapers (since they would only compete for the same limited circulation) and concentrated instead on the religious aspect of the Irish Question.

Catholic hostility in America had become a serious matter for Spring-Rice, particularly in view of the tendency to replace moderate Irish-American clerics with 'bishops of a strongly political character connected with the German and German-Irish propaganda'. This had resulted in an increasing number of priests becoming actively involved in anti-British activities such as the embargo movement. The Ambassador was also concerned that clerics were assisting Hibernian extremists to obstruct the cause of Home Rule, which, if achieved, was 'thought to be fraught with disaster to the direct influence of the Catholic Church'. His report prompted Rowland Sperling of the Foreign Office American Department to minute that, if such 'remarkable views' were held by the Catholic Church in America, it was 'subordinating its religious convictions to political considerations'. These suspicions were borne out by the poet John Masefield, who, following a lecture tour in the United States, reported to Gilbert Parker at the British Government's propaganda office in Wellington House:

> There are a lot of damned disloyal Irish in this country who, I suppose, with the connivance of the baser kind of Roman Catholic priest, do a lot of harm among the Catholics here. They stand at the Church doors after mass and distribute devilish leaflets, all poisonously anti-English, among the faithful as they leave the church. . . . They are very clever and very bitter.[20]

Believing that Irish opinion in the United States was 'co-extensive with Catholic opinion', British propagandists explored many different avenues to further the 'education of the priesthood'.[21] In the early years of the war, they had placed great emphasis on the brutal German violation of Catholic Belgium's neutrality, and, when mission schemes were discussed in 1915, Spring-Rice even suggested a Belgian clerical visit to America. However, the Ambassador himself admitted that, 'although a certain amount of sympathy has been expressed by the Catholic clergy with the sufferings of Belgium, the general tendency is undoubtedly to belittle those sufferings and to justify the action of Germany'. J. D. Gregory, a Catholic with the British Mission to the Vatican, advised Edward Grey that, according to his information, the Catholic Church in America was merely a 'huge business concern' and that there was 'nothing to be gained by talking about the origins of the war or Belgium'. This view was thoroughly endorsed by Eustace Percy:

> I hope that in dealing not only with the American Catholics, but with the whole of America, we have long ago ceased to enlarge on the justice of our cause. Western American opinion regards that much as one would regard a middle-aged man boasting of what a good boy he was at school.[22]

Not surprisingly, the Foreign Office lost interest in the mission scheme and its caution was justified when Belgian priests went to America on a fund-raising mission of their own and received an extremely unfriendly reception from many Irish-American ecclesiastics.[23]

As an alternative means of combating Catholic enmity, Spring-Rice suggested an indirect approach to the Pope to advise him that clerical obstruction was hindering the Allies and might thereby damage Vatican relations with Britain. Thus, as Gregory explained in his memoirs, the British Mission at the Vatican became an additional diplomatic lever against Irish-American extremism: 'The Irish Question had become acute; Catholic opinion in America for or against war must crystallise before long. The Vatican became courted once more.'[24]

One of the most favoured means of influencing Irish-Americans was to publicise Irish heroism in the war. Most of the literature, which took the form of pamphlets and articles, was distributed by Gilbert Parker at Wellington House to libraries and personal contacts in the United States. As well as appealing to the racial sentiment of Irish-Americans, such material conveyed the impression that Ireland wholeheartedly supported the British war-effort. However, in its reluctance to glorify Irish Nationalism, the War Office deliberately restricted the flow of news regarding Irish valour, provoking Shane Leslie to complain to Spring-Rice with great feeling,

> In this war, the pride of race has been completely ignored. Thousands of Irishmen have perished and no more is heard of them, until a feeling has grown up that Irish soldiers are being thrown into a war which is primarily not theirs and get no credit for their achievements.

Leslie believed that the British authorities should publish full details whenever Irish troops performed 'conspicuous deeds', and that Spring-Rice's press contacts should ensure that the information received coverage in the American dailies. The Irish could not be moved by flattery, warned Leslie, but 'accounts of Irish prowess in the leading American papers would be above suspicion and without a chance of failure'.[25]

Spring-Rice passed this suggestion, together with his own endorsement, to the Foreign Office, where it prompted a variety of ideas. Geoffrey Butler urged pressure on the War Office for more information; Guy Locock, Cecil's Parliamentary Private Secretary, suggested that Wellington House should compile a collection of stories featuring Irish heroism; while Hubert Montgomery proposed that full details of all Irish Victoria Crosses be given to American newspaper correspondents and a series of articles on the Irish regiments be prepared for *The Times*. Meanwhile, Wellington House produced 2000 copies of S. Parnell Kerr's book *What the Irish Regiments Have Done*, and was planning to distribute 10,000 free copies of Michael MacDonagh's forthcoming work *The Irish at the Front*. However, the extreme reticence of the military authorities remained an obstacle and meant that MacDonagh had to rely on newspapers for his sources. News Department officials realised that the formation of the British Coalition Government had created an atmosphere in which propaganda, no matter how well devised, could have only a limited effect on Irish-Americans. 'I doubt', conceded Hubert Montgomery, 'whether we shall ever make much of this particular phase of the situation in America by any effort from here.'[26]

During the nine months preceding the Easter Rising of April 1916, the worsening Irish-American situation had compelled the Foreign Office to review its propaganda policy on Irish affairs, with the result that most of the schemes pursued in subsequent years were conceived during this period. The Foreign Office still viewed most of these projects as support for the Redmondites against the extremists, but there were signs that the enfeeblement of the Home Rule cause might compel the distribution of propaganda through other channels. Moreover, the Foreign Office was increasingly aware of the threat posed by the combination of Germans and Irish-American extremists. This applied especially to anti-British conspiracies, to which attention should now be turned before the Easter Rising – initially seen by the Foreign Office as only one of many such conspiracies – can be fully understood.

III

From the early months of the war, vigilant British agents helped the Foreign Office to compile dossiers on German plots originating in the United States and designed to restrict the British war effort. These conspiracies fell into three distinct categories: first, attempts to sabotage important Canadian communications; secondly, intrigues against those American munition factories and dockyards which were assisting the Allied cause; and, finally, the fostering of rebellion in two disaffected areas of the British Empire – India and Ireland. Although most of the Foreign Office information related to German–Indian conspiracies, Irish-Americans were often involved.

In early 1915, the New York Consul-General, Courtenay Bennet, warned the Foreign Office that St Patrick's Hall in the German–Irish quarter of Buffalo was a drill hall for an imminent raid over the Canadian border. He later discovered that arms for the raid had been shipped through the Krupps agent in America to a Dr McCarthy, an Irish dentist in New Hampshire who was believed to be in close touch with German societies in New York. The Boston Consul-General, Cornelius Leay, reported that McCarthy belonged to an Irish-American organisation, the John Boyle O'Reilly Club, which was 'thought to be ill-disposed to British interests'. However, no weapons were found and the Foreign Office was compelled to stifle its suspicions through lack of evidence. There was a more conclusive outcome in the following December, when the American authorities unearthed details of a plot against the strategically vital Welland Canal (an artery for the despatch of war supplies from Canada to Europe). Paul König, head of security on the Hamburg-Amerika Shipping Line, was accused of chief complicity, but Edmund Justice, an Irish-American watchman on the company's pier, was one of several others charged with preparing 'a military enterprise to be carried on from the United States against the Dominion of Canada' and with collecting military information which 'might be of value to the German Government'.[27]

A more complex story surrounded Bennet's discovery that, in sabotage attempts on three important bridges connecting America and Canada, the field agents had been Germans, while much of the organisation had been carried out by Irish-Americans – a reversal of the commonly held images of the two ethnic groups. Indeed, the dynamite had been obtained from Irish engineers in New York, believed to be Clan na Gael members, and stored in the offices of the Cantique Development Company. The company's manager, Anthony Brogan, formerly editor of an extremist newspaper, the New York *Irish-American*, was reported by Bennet to be 'strongly pro-German, a member of the Clan na Gael and . . . certain German societies', and to have gone to Germany to take up a commission in the German army. In fact, Bennet's account was incomplete and apparently inaccurate. John Devoy later claimed that Brogan was 'never a real Nationalist and sneered at the Clan na Gael at every opportunity'. He was perplexed that such a man had been invited to Germany and then, moreover, allowed to 'butt in' on Roger Casement's mission. However, both Casement and the Germans were impressed by the glib Brogan and considered him an asset in promoting recruitment for the 'Irish Brigade' – prompting Devoy to write indignantly in his memoirs that the Germans 'had no right . . . to inject any man not sanctioned by us into official Irish–German affairs'.[28]

While the embargo movement gathered momentum in the political arena, German–Irish groups simultaneously attempted to prevent the arms trade by sabotaging British shipping. In May 1915, Courtenay Bennet warned Spring-Rice that the manager and several other officials of the Cunard Company's American branch were pro-German. Moreover, the head of Cunard Dock's security police, an Irishman named Mallon, had openly denounced Irish recruits for the British Army as 'd...d fools to fight for any country that kept them down all their lives'. Mallon, a discharged New York policeman, was reportedly on 'very friendly terms' with men from the Vachris Detective Agency, which helped to guard the Hamburg-Amerika docks and which was 'sending men to Canada to blow up bridges'. Writing in the impassioned period following the sinking of the Cunard liner *Lusitania*, Bennet reported that, 'through the good offices of Mallon', Vachris staff had 'full access to every part of the Cunard Dock at all hours by day and night, as well as to the ships'. German agents might thus have been provided not only with the liner's sailing-time, but also with 'full particulars as to every piece of cargo and the hold in which it is stored' – thus pinpointing the most vulnerable target area for torpedo attack. Although subsequent evidence suggests that Mallon's collaboration was not a factor in the *Lusitania*'s fate, the Foreign Office was alarmed to find that the Cunard office had been 'closely connected' with German agencies and that inadequate precautions had been taken against the 'ubiquity of German spies in New York'.[29]

The third category of German plots in the United States – the promotion of sedition or rebellion in Ireland and India – had both propaganda and military objectives. By encouraging the liberation of 'oppressed nationalities' under British rule, the Germans hoped to destroy any image of imperial unity and make Britain's professed war aim of fighting for small nations appear hypocritical; while, militarily, the Germans believed that unrest at the heart of the

Empire would divert British efforts from the Western Front. In the year preceding the war, Indian revolutionaries in America had formed the 'Ghadr' organisation, later described by the Foreign Office as 'the most dangerous and active of the Indian organisations – ready and willing to help in supplying their brethren . . . with the means of starting a successful revolt'.[30] Although mainly seeking German support, Indian revolutionaries in the United States often found Irish-Americans more congenial allies, since both groups regarded themselves as victims of British colonial oppression, whereas the Germans were themselves tarred with the imperialist brush. Indeed, Irish-American extremists often provided articles for the German-backed *Ghadr* newspaper, encouraging Indians to strike against British domination, to which the newspaper reciprocated by featuring Irish revolutionary news and trumpeting that Ireland was in a state of rebellion.[31]

A captured Indian revolutionary, designated in official records as 'C', testified to the Foreign Office that one of the three leaders of Indian intrigue in the United States was George Freeman, a 'disaffected' Irish-American extremist who worked for both the *Gaelic American* and *Free Hindustan* newspapers and who was 'the intermediary between the Indians and the Germans . . . and also between the Irish and the Germans'. 'C' revealed that Freeman, who was in 'intimate touch' with Indian leaders in the United States and whose activities were financed by the Germans, was also playing an important part in encouraging Irish emigration to the United States: 'When Irish[men] are going to America and have no money, they wire to Freeman, and he meets the boat and claims them. I heard the Germans pay Freeman well for Irishmen landing in America who are of military age and who will not join the army.' This may not have come as a complete revelation to the Foreign Office, for Courtenay Bennet had already reported the arrival in America of at least 1500 young Irishmen, whose passages 'were provided through some agency which is working on behalf of Germany' and who were attempting to 'avoid being enlisted in our army'. Despite the dissenting voice of Matthew Nathan, the Under Secretary at Dublin Castle, that it was 'improbable that German money is being spent in getting young men out of Ireland', corroborative evidence from the Irish peer Lord Dunraven, from W. F. Bullock, New York correspondent of *The Times*, and from William Ridgeway of the New York *Tribune* all appeared to confirm Germany's provision of the emigrants' passage money. Moreover, it seems probable – although the Foreign Office did not seem to realise it – that the 'agency' described by Bennet was, in fact, the one operated by Freeman.[32]

In addition to his Irish activities, Freeman was also involved in the organised reception of Indian revolutionaries arriving in the United States. The offices of the *Gaelic American* were used as a 'safe house', while Freeman and other staff acted as intermediaries between new arrivals and their contacts in America. For example, in April 1915 a new arrival, Jodh Singh, called on the German Consul in New York to obtain the address of the Indian revolutionary leader H. L. Gupta, but was advised that it was safer to use the *Gaelic American* offices as a contact point. The newspaper arranged a meeting with Gupta and helped to procure a false passport which Singh required for a gun-running mission. In fact, Singh testified after his capture that *Gaelic American* staff were 'taking as much interest in the movement for liberating India from British rule as other societies expressly formed for the furtherance of Indian seditious movements'.[33]

The United States was the most widely used base for supplying arms and ammunition to the Indian rebels, and Irish-Americans played a part in this activity. In December 1914, von Bernstorff telegraphed the German Foreign Office that 11,000 rifles and 500 revolvers had been 'purchased for India', adding ambiguously, 'Devoy does not think it possible to ship them to Ireland.' It has been suggested that this might have been an attempt to 'dodge the British blockade' by sending arms to Ireland via India.[34] However, the arms were probably for Indian use, since the Clan had traditionally conspired with groups as diverse as the Zulus and the Boers.[35] Sending arms to promote rebellion in India would therefore have been a logical extension of this policy. In early 1916, Foreign Office reports from New York and the Pacific coast indicated continuing activity among Indians and Irish-Americans, 'directed towards the shipment of arms to India'. This raises a conflict of evidence, for, in his account of the subsequent German gun-running mission to Ireland at Easter 1916, the expedition leader, Captain Karl Spindler, expounded a commonly held view:

> The Irish in America were naturally quite prepared to offer every possible assistance to their compatriots in the homeland . . . [but] the strict control carried out in those days by the American authorities made it practically impossible to smuggle any

worthwhile quantity of arms and ammunition out through American ports. What other course, therefore, was left open in these circumstances except that Ireland should seek aid from Germany.[36]

It is difficult to reconcile Spindler's claims with Foreign Office reports on Irish-American participation in Indian gun-running and on the laxity of security in American ports. The only explanation seems to be that surveillance over eastern ports, used for arms shipments to Ireland, was more severe than that over western ports, from which expeditions to India would leave. This would explain why gun-running to India continued while Devoy and his colleagues could not send similar consignments for the imminent rising in Ireland.

In the first twelve months of the war the Foreign Office was reluctant to make premature representations to the US Government regarding anti-British conspiracies on American soil, fearing that this would only worsen Anglo-American relations. Even before the war, Spring-Rice had advised that the hostility of the powerful 'hyphenate' vote – particularly the Irish and German elements – would thwart any hope of persuading the State Department to take action against agitators; and as late as September 1915 Colville Barclay still adhered to this belief:

> On the Pacific coast the Germans and Irish together exercise a strong control over local politics and this control is exercised to our disadvantage. As a general rule the action of the local authorities has a strong anti-British bias. . . . Under these circumstances it would be very difficult for the United States Government to take any action, except on a clear case of breach of the law which would admit of no doubt.[37]

Not surprisingly, the Foreign Office had generally preferred to catalogue the evidence of conspiracies with a view to 'counter-claiming' any American complaints over the British naval blockade. However, as anti-British plots in the United States multiplied, pressure from the India Office, in particular, at last induced the Foreign Office to make representations to the State Department. These still made little mention of Irish-American participation, since it was known that the Wilson Administration would be wary of alienating the largely Democratic Irish vote. From late 1915, the

American Government released revelations of plots to its mouthpiece, the New York *World*, and simultaneously began to strengthen its federal laws against 'unneutral acts'. Charles Tansill, a bitterly Anglophobe historian, alleged that, although the revelations were largely 'duds', nevertheless 'the impression was created in the American public mind that Germany was plotting against America'. Spring-Rice's report to Grey predictably welcomed the Administration's tougher line: 'The odious policy of treachery, disloyalty, outrage and crime which is being pursued before the American people and on American soil by the agents of a foreign government . . . is more and more working its effect upon public sentiment.'[38]

It was in this atmosphere of anti-hyphenism that the Easter Rising occurred, and initial Foreign Office reaction to this event was therefore shaped by its preoccupation with American-based plots. The growth of these plots, together with the decline of the Redmondite cause in the United States, presented a two-pronged threat for the Foreign Office: clandestine and conspiratorial on the one hand, overt and political on the other. The events of Easter 1916 brought home forcibly the gravity of the clandestine threat and, even more seriously, escalated Irish-American political agitation.

4
The Easter Rising and its Aftermath (April–November 1916)

I

From February to April 1916, plans had taken shape between the Germans, the rebel leaders in Dublin and their Clan na Gael confederates in America for a gun-running mission to Ireland to coincide with a general insurrection of the Irish Volunteers. It was only when these plans had been all but finalised that Casement – still in Germany but by-passed by both the German Government and the Dublin leaders – discovered what was afoot and persuaded the Germans to transport him by submarine to Ireland in time for the outbreak. Casement was duly set ashore in Tralee Bay on the Irish west coast just before dawn on Good Friday, 21 April. Quite by accident, his small landing-craft was soon discovered and early that afternoon he was captured in the ruins of nearby McKenna's Fort. Casement had intended to urge that the German aid was inadequate, but even after the German arms ship had been intercepted by a British patrol vessel – also on 21 April – and had scuttled itself, the rebel leaders went ahead with their plans for insurrection. The Rising began on Easter Monday, 24 April, but, owing to a confusion in the Volunteers' mobilisation orders, it was confined to only a few areas – notably Dublin, where the General Post Office was occupied as rebel headquarters for five days. By 29 April the Dublin Volunteers had surrendered, and all sign of conflict elsewhere was soon quelled.[1]

Initial Foreign Office interest in the Rising was the consequence of an event in New York a few days earlier. On 18 April, American Secret Service agents entered the Wall Street office of the German Commercial Attaché, Wolf von Igel, and seized papers revealing German subversion and espionage in the United States. Among the papers were details of the planned gun-running to Ireland, which led John Devoy to allege that the subsequent interception of the arms ship was 'the direct result of information treacherously given by a member of the Washington Administration on the orders of President Wilson'. In his memoirs, Devoy further claimed that 'copies of the papers' were passed on by the Attorney-General, Thomas Gregory, via the New York *World*, whose editor, Frank Irving Cobb, was 'probably the most malignant enemy of the Irish cause on the American press'.[2]

Although Devoy's claims have been accepted by many historians,[3] evidence from the Foreign Office archives shows that the British Government was not given *copies* of the documents, and received only one indirect warning, communicated to Spring-Rice by an American journalist and cabled to London on 22 April:

> I hear from a sure source that among papers seized by authorities in New York are indications of plan for gun-running in Ireland to begin not before April 23rd. Detachments of men are subsequently to be landed whilst German fleet and Zeppelins make demonstrations to engage the attention of our fleet.[4]

Spring-Rice clearly did not realise that this warning had been deliberately leaked by the Administration. 'I have no knowledge of the contents of these documents', he wrote to Grey, 'and no intimation as to the evidence contained in them has been made to me by the State Department.' Rowland Sperling, the Foreign Office expert on American-based conspiracies, later minuted in confirmation, 'As far as I know, we can truthfully relieve the State Department of their embarrassment that the U.S.G. ever gave any information about the intended rising.' It would be difficult to reconcile these statements with Spring-Rice's gun-running warning unless both he and his colleagues in London were unaware that the disclosure had been contrived by the United States authorities.[5]

The Wilson Administration, concerned by Devoy's accusations, publicly stated that the few documents relating to the Irish rebellion were not 'sufficiently specific to have enabled the American officials to tell the British anything tangible'. Moreover, the State Department deliberately clouded the issue by fostering the illusion already existing in the public mind that the gun-running expedition and Roger Casement's separate journey by submarine were one and the same. Consequently, although Devoy's original accusation related purely to leakages regarding the gun-running, the State Department stressed irrelevantly that there was no information in the papers which 'could have aided the British Government in locating or capturing the Casement expedition'. In the following year the Wilson Administration reinforced its line of defence with a statement which traced the progress of the seized papers until they arrived at the State Department late on 21 April. In conclusion, the statement triumphantly pointed out that, by this time, 'Casement had spent several hours in an Irish prison'. This must have exasperated John Devoy, who knew that Casement's activities were peripheral to both the gun-running expedition and the Rising. Spring-Rice was one of many misled by such irrelevancies, as he showed when reporting accusations that 'news had been given to this Embassy by officials of the United States Government, in consequence of which Casement had been arrested'. Although Foreign Office records bear out the State Department's assertion that no information was leaked regarding Casement's movements, the emphasis on this line of defence was a deliberate and largely successful red herring.[6]

The State Department could have likewise emphasised that the seized papers also arrived too late to facilitate the capture of the arms ship (which had already occurred earlier in the same day). The warning which was leaked to Spring-Rice from the von Igel papers was based on a last-minute message sent by the rebel leaders to Berlin (via von Bernstorff), requesting that the gun-running be delayed several days until 23 April, and this was the date relayed to London in the Ambassador's telegram. It was merely a twist of fate that the rebels' message arrived in Berlin too late to delay the departure of the arms ship, which, consequently, was intercepted off the Irish coast on the earlier date of 21 April. The United States Government was, of course, unaware that the rebels' request had arrived in Berlin too late, and, believing therefore that the sailing-date would be set back, it leaked the warning in the expectancy that this would help to thwart both the gun-running and the rebellion. In the event, both Casement and the arms ship were captured on 21 April, the day before Spring-Rice sent the warning cable and two days before it arrived at the Foreign Office. Moreover, the import of the warning was little appreciated on arrival, as Lord Crewe (deputising for Grey) exhibited when he minuted vaguely on 23 April, 'Was there not a report in the press quite lately of the landing of some mysterious arms on the West Coast?'[7]

The only warnings received by Dublin Castle in sufficient time to have prevented either Casement's landing or the gun-running came, not from America, but from Admiralty Intelligence code-interceptions and from British spies in Europe. In March 1916, Admiralty warnings concerning the planned gun-running were transmitted to the GOC in Ireland, General Friend, and to the Naval Commander at Queenstown, Sir Lewis Bayly (who immediately ordered that the Irish coast be patrolled). On 16 April, a specific warning that two submarines and an arms ship had left Germany for Ireland was received by Bayly and quickly transmitted to General Friend and to Matthew Nathan at Dublin Castle.[8] In view of the inadequate military precautions taken, it is questionable how seriously the warnings were heeded, but it is indisputable that such timely warnings as were received were not supplied by the United States Government from the von Igel papers.

II

It was amidst the suspicion and rumours created by the von Igel raid that news of the Irish rebellion and the abortive gun-running first reached America. It is not surprising, therefore, that most Americans – who had accepted that Ireland would be the 'one bright spot' during the war – now concluded that the rebellion had been conceived and organised by Germany. This belief was strengthened, first, by the rebels' 'Proclamation of the Provisional Government of the Irish Republic', which asserted that Ireland was supported by her 'gallant allies in Europe', and, secondly, by the role of Casement, whose dramatic submarine journey to Ireland led many observers to regard him, wrongly, as the key figure in the rebellion. The New York *World* condemned the Rising as a 'German conspiracy', adding a few days later, 'German money financed it, and a German ship carried Sir Roger Casement to the shores of Ireland to lead the uprising. "Der Tag" had dawned again, and Germany waited patiently over its beer for the downfall of the British Empire.' The *New York Times* censured the 'cruel heartlessness of Ireland's "gallant allies in Europe" who encouraged these Irish dreamers to acts which have brought them to their death', whilst, at a Redmondite meeting in New York, Irish-Americans deplored an insurrection motivated 'either from blind hatred of the English people or, worse, with German gold in their pockets'. This widespread condemnation prompted Spring-Rice to comment with evident approval to Grey, 'The attitude of public opinion as to the Irish rebellion is on the whole satisfactory. The press seems to be agreed that the movement is suicidal and in the interests of Germany alone.'[9]

In truth, it was the Irish leaders who had asked for German aid as part of their overall plan. At his court martial, the rebel leader, Padraic Pearse, emphasised, 'I asked for and accepted German aid in the shape of arms and an expeditionary force . . . but I should have been glad of any Ally's aid.'[10] Nevertheless, the British Government made every effort to impress upon neutrals – especially Americans – the German origin of the conspiracy and the gravity of the rebels' treachery. On 24 April the Irish Viceroy, Lord Wimborne, issued a proclamation denouncing the 'attempt, instigated and designed by the foreign enemies of our King and country to incite rebellion in Ireland, and thus endanger the safety of the UK'.[11] Horace Plunkett, an Irish moderate with strong American links, was also active. He first telegraphed Arthur Balfour, First Lord of the Admiralty, that it was 'important to let the American people know the German origin of the trouble', and then sought the help of General Sir John Maxwell (newly appointed as Commander-in-Chief in Ireland) in collecting 'all the available evidence of German initiative and direction of the insurrection'. Plunkett considered that this would probably destroy the German-Irish alliance in America, as 'the Irish would be furious at having been duped into a mad revolt by promises of naval and military assistance'.[12] Plunkett also secured the aid of his friend Karl Walter, who had a close knowledge of the newspaper world on both sides of the Atlantic. At Walter's prompting, the Foreign Office News Department appealed to the Irish Office in London for any information that would indicate 'German intrigue' behind the rebellion, since there was 'an attempt in the United States to make it out as a labour movement resulting from bad social conditions due to English oppression'. Such information was vital, the letter concluded, since Ireland 'does loom rather large just now in Anglo-American affairs'.[13]

The Foreign Office line was also expounded in America by British publicists. Shane Leslie, who was working closely with the British Embassy, said publicly of the rebellion that 'the real and moving cause was German conspiracy. The blood of the slain lies on Germany. The Irish people are not responsible.' Pursuing this chain of thought, he later wrote to Redmond that the policy of his newspaper, *Ireland*, had been 'to turn the popular odium from the Irish Party to the Germans' and that, if there was 'any evidence of a callous German barter, the Irish Party should publish it. It would help to swing the sympathy here'.[14] In fact, the Foreign Office had already given wide publicity to Redmond's vehement denunciation of the Rising, that 'Germany plotted it, Germany organised it, Germany paid for it, while her Clan na Gael allies remained in the safe remoteness of American cities.' According to the Wellington House American Press Résumé of 25 May, the statement was 'most conspicuously reproduced in almost all the American papers', while *The Times* referred to its 'excellent reception' and added that it was 'precisely what was wanted to give things the right perspective'.[15] Indeed, the rebellion would undoubtedly have been dismissed by most Americans as yet another 'German plot' had not the British military authorities executed most of the rebel leaders in the ensuing weeks. This produced such an emotive reaction against the British Government that the 'German plot' argument was forgotten amidst what Shane Leslie described as the 'great lyrical tide of hysteria' sweeping Irish-America.[16]

III

In addition to the outcry over the German role in the Rising, controversy also centred round the part played by certain Irish-Americans. The New York *Herald* alleged that pro-German Irishmen in the United States had furnished arms and were 'in no small measure responsible for the blood that has been shed in Ireland'. It denounced the Clan na Gaelers for keeping alive 'the fires of bitter hate against the English', and warned that 'these are no friends of the United States when they are aiders on American soil of a scheme to turn England, Ireland and Wales over to German domination'. The Wellington House American Press Résumé, usually circulated to the Cabinet, cited a particularly scathing attack by the Dallas *Morning News*: 'A few German-Americans have long been attacking Great Britain and its allies from the soil and under the flag of the United States, and now it looks as if some Irish-Americans have been guilty of emulating their disloyal conduct.'[17]

Further information came from the Wellington House American informants – notably H. J. Whigham, staunchly pro-Ally editor of the Republican magazine *Metropolitan*. Whigham's opinions were highly valued both by Gilbert Parker, head of the Wellington House American section, and by the Foreign Office. Parker believed him to be 'exceptionally reliable in giving us the impressions of American opinion', while Eric Drummond saw him as representative of 'well-informed circles' in the United States. During the rebellion Whigham pointed an accusing finger at Devoy, Justice Daniel Cohalan and other Irish-American extremists who had openly denounced the Allies and had been 'accepting large sums of money from the Germans'. Not surprisingly, Walter Long, President of the Local Government Board, demanded a Cabinet inquiry into the relationship between the German–Irish alliance in the United States and the rebels in Ireland, while General Maxwell was already quite positive that the rebellion was a German–Clan na Gael conspiracy.[18]

Although Spring-Rice, in his official despatches, was reticent as to how far the Rising originated in America, he was less circumspect in private. He suggested to fellow Irishman Horace Plunkett that both Devoy and his German allies 'probably did know a great deal', and reflected, 'It seems strange looked at from here why the government was not better prepared. On the other hand, it must look strange from over there why we were not better informed here.' The Ambassador was, in fact, well aware of his own restricted sources of information, as he frankly acknowledged to Grey:

> I have, of course, always assumed that H.M.G. have their own special means of obtaining information regarding ramifications and secret activities of hostile Irish societies in U.S. Obviously, Embassy is not in a position to keep in touch with such activity or to obtain inside knowledge of criminal plotting. Most we can do is to keep you informed of all public agitations and of such inner activity as they chance to come to our knowledge.

Eustace Percy later confirmed Spring-Rice's assumptions when he wrote that Britain had 'a brilliant counter-espionage service, for which our diplomatic representatives could not, in the nature of things, accept responsibility'.[19] Thus, during the period of American neutrality, Spring-Rice was forced to glean information from his own contacts, since the Wilson Administration was not, as many Irish and German extremists alleged, co-operating in exposing American-based plots. This was especially true in the election year of 1916, when the President dared not risk accusations of pro-British leanings. Furthermore, there was a marked reluctance to divulge information which might justify British complaints of violated neutrality.

It was on the legal implications of American involvement that Spring-Rice concentrated in his reports to Grey. He pointed out that, if this could be proved, 'the United States, under accepted principles of international law, would be forced to take action to punish such an open breach of neutrality'. However, the Ambassador admitted that, aside from vague rumours, the only certain facts were that American money had been sent for Irish revolutionary purposes and that evidence in the von Igel papers was, according to the State Department, 'not such as to justify an enquiry still less a prosecution'. Rowland Sperling, ever impatient with the attitude of the United States Government, pointed out that well-documented evidence on Indian conspiracies in America had already been passed to the State Department without result, and it was therefore 'doubtful whether the U.S.G. will be much troubled by the thought that the Irish plot was encouraged from America'. Edward Grey shared Sperling's pessimism and closed the discussion by minuting, 'Better for us to leave it alone unless we get some indication that the U.S. Government wish us to do something.'[20]

The 'indication' sought by Grey was unlikely to materialise. When, in early June, Spring-Rice discovered that fund-raising was continuing in America for 'stirring up further troubles in Ireland', Frank Polk, Counsellor of the State Department, was quick to assure the Ambassador that there was no further sign of plotting in the United States. This irritated Rowland Sperling, who expostulated,

> There may be a technical distinction between 'plotting' and 'raising funds' but the practical result is the same. That is to say, it makes very little difference whether the funds raised are remitted to the revolutionaries direct, or are converted into arms and ammunition or passage money for agents. The U.S.G., needless to say, takes a different view where their own interests are concerned.

Herbert Malkin, a Foreign Office legal adviser, doubted whether the 'mere raising of funds' breached American neutrality laws, and added that it would be 'necessary to demonstrate that something more was on foot than the mere collection of money and general agitation in favour of the independence of Ireland'. However, despite a concerted effort by Sperling, Eustace Percy and other specialists in American affairs to collate all the information on American-based plots, concrete evidence of Irish involvement remained elusive.[21]

Clearly, Foreign Office officials first saw the Rising as a mere extension of the pattern of American-based plots with which they had long been confronted. Indeed, it was only after the fierce American reaction to the subsequent execution of the rebel leaders that the Foreign Office began to consider seriously the effect of the Rising on Anglo-American relations as a whole.

IV

Between 3 and 12 May, fourteen of the leading rebels were court-martialled and shot by the military authorities in Ireland. Unfortunately for Britain, American public acceptance of the German origins of the Rising had produced an unwelcome side-effect. Believing that the Germans had instigated the rebellion, most Americans had reached the conclusion that the Irish rebels were merely the victims of German duplicity; consequently, even before the first execution, a clemency campaign was launched in the press and at Irish-American meetings throughout the country. The New York *World*, for example, argued on 2 May that 'the British Government can afford to deal leniently with the misguided authors of this farce tragedy'. Two weeks later, Spring-Rice reported severe criticism of the first executions and transmitted a warning from Cardinal Gibbons that clemency would avoid the 'danger of manufacturing martyrs for American use', and that 'severity, however much it might legally be justified, would be politically inexpedient'.[22]

When John Redmond received a telegram from the United Irish League in New York, that Irish-Americans were 'revolted by this sign of reversion to savage repression', he forwarded it to Asquith with the ominous comment, 'if more executions take place in Ireland, the position will become impossible for any constitutional party or leader'. Asquith admitted that he had been shocked to hear of the first executions, but reassured Redmond that in future these would only occur 'in very special cases'. Redmond's deputy, John Dillon, never as restrained as his party-leader, complained bitterly in the House of Commons that his party, having laboured to prevent a German–Irish alliance in America, was 'entitled to be consulted before the bloody course of executions was entered upon'.[23] Editorials in the Liberal press underlined the danger of American revulsion, but similar warnings from Arthur Willert to *The Times* were suppressed by his editor, Geoffrey Dawson. Not for the first time, Dawson disagreed with Willert's view of the Irish problem and telegraphed him to 'go slow' in reporting American reactions, since his messages, if published, might 'seriously prejudice Anglo-American relations'. He suggested, instead, that the execution of a few rebel leaders, 'whereof all the best Irish opinion approves', be contrasted with the 'appalling deathroll' of British soldiers and civilians. Willert must have wondered how his telegrams could 'seriously prejudice' Anglo-American relations, which were already deteriorating as a result of the continuing executions. Discreetly, he replied that there may have been considerations, of which he knew nothing, that would make his own reports inadvisable, and that, as he did not wish to misrepresent feeling in America by adopting Dawson's line, he proposed to 'leave the thing alone' until the situation clarified.[24]

Meanwhile, Spring-Rice urged that, from the American point of view, it was advisable to treat the rebels as innocent victims of a German plot. While careful not to intrude in 'matters of internal policy in which, no doubt, other considerations prevail', he suggested that continuing the executions would cement the German–Irish alliance and prevent the adoption in America of 'any measure favourable to British interests'. It is questionable how far Spring-Rice's warning influenced Foreign Office thinking, since there was a growing tendency to discount his more sombre communications. A recent sympathetic biography has shown that, as a result of failing health and the strain of war, the Ambassador was by now showing signs of emotional and mental instability, which caused him to lose much influence with President Wilson and his advisers.[25] Lord Hardinge, who succeeded Nicolson as Permanent Under Secretary in June 1916, voiced a common view that 'we are always hearing of the rising tide of unpopularity in which Great Britain finds herself in the U.S. I wonder whether this is so, or whether the idea is not inspired by Sir Cecil Spring-Rice's inborn pessimism.' This was also the view of Cabinet ministers such as Lord Curzon, the Lord Privy Seal, who described the Ambassador as 'by nature an alarmist', and Robert Cecil, who considered that it was 'not much use asking him questions'. Spring-Rice himself, sensitive to any hint of criticism, complained to his wife in June 1916 that, after dictating a large quantity of despatches, it suddenly occurred to him that 'no one would read a word of what I wrote except Percy who would sniff'.[26]

The Irish historian Owen Dudley Edwards has argued that the Ambassador's warnings regarding the executions were particularly suspect since 'his Irish antecedents brought to him rather different attitudes to the Rising than were held by British officials at large'. However, in other respects Spring-Rice's Irish sympathies were an advantage to him, since he was spared much of the Anglophobia roused by the executions. In mid June he wrote to his wife that the Irish-American extremists were 'out for the destruction of England' but 'don't seem to object to me personally, I suppose owing to my antecedents', while a 'well informed' contact of Arthur Willert reported 'a strong feeling among the Irish that S.R. will go out of his way to aid the Irish cause. He is the right man for the crisis.' Despite his personal leanings, however, Spring-Rice was a 'loyal public servant' who at all times implemented his Government's policies faithfully. It is therefore not surprising to find, as recently as 1979, Colville Barclay's widow defending the Ambassador as 'a very loyal and correct diplomat who would be *most* unlikely to adopt a partisan attitude in spite of being Irish'. Notwithstanding these endorsements of diplomatic rectitude, Owen Dudley Edwards has claimed that Lloyd George's decision in late 1917 to appoint a new Ambassador was partly owing to Spring-Rice's 'regard for Ireland'.[27]

By the summer of 1916, most of Spring-Rice's warnings on Irish matters were scarcely heeded and there was, therefore, a tendency to underestimate the growing Irish-American hostility towards the executions. Thus, on 10 May, despite several anxious telegrams from Spring-Rice, Eustace Percy (just back from a visit to the United States) suggested with misguided optimism that the collapse of the rebellion afforded 'an opportunity which we might take advantage of. The Clan na Gael meeting of April 30th . . . is a measure of the ridicule to which that organisation has now laid itself open.' Foreign Office confidence arose partly from the fact that, despite strong pressure from Irish Nationalists for American intervention, the Wilson Administration took the orthodox stand that, 'as to the treatment of Irishmen, as they are not citizens of the United States, this Government has no right to speak'. However, when a Senate resolution demanded 'the safeguarding and protection' of American citizens in Ireland, Wilson's new Secretary of State, Robert Lansing, took the more active stance that the Administration would 'intervene diplomatically in cases where its citizens suffer . . . a failure or denial of justice'. Thus, the only instances where American pressure contributed to a reprieve concerned two men with claims to American citizenship – Eamon de Valera and Jeremiah Lynch.[28]

De Valera, who was born in Brooklyn of a Spanish-born father and an Irish-born mother but who, in fact, never formally acquired American citizenship, commanded a battalion in the Rising and was duly condemned to death by court martial. One explanation of his reprieve came from General Hutchison of the War Office, who related to Shane Leslie that 'anxious telegrams from America' forced Asquith to intercede and that Hutchison himself took these telegrams to Dublin. The American Consul in Dublin, Edward L. Adams, also claimed to have saved de Valera on a plea of American citizenship, while, on the other hand, Denis Gwynn contended that the reprieve was attributable solely to the 'personal intervention of John Redmond'. In all probability, de Valera's reprieve on 10 May arose from the combined weight of these appeals, reinforced by a Cabinet decision five days earlier that only 'ring leaders and proved murderers' should be executed (after which only those rebels who had signed the Proclamation of the Provisional Government were put to death).[29]

The other reprieve stemming from transatlantic pressure was that of Jeremiah Lynch, a naturalised American citizen who had returned to Ireland to join the Irish Republican Brotherhood and had been sentenced to death for his part in the rebellion. In response to senatorial appeals, President Wilson cabled Ambassador Walter Hines Page in London to request a suspension of Lynch's sentence pending State Department investigation.[30] When the appeal was relayed to General Maxwell in Dublin, he complained of being 'bombarded' by telegrams on the subject, but assured the War Office that, despite clear evidence of Lynch's participation in the rebellion, his death sentence had been commuted to ten years of penal servitude. There was no mention of American factors in the announcement of reprieve which Miles Lampson of the Foreign Office News Department issued to the American newspapers, but the latter nevertheless loudly proclaimed that Wilson's intervention had saved Lynch's life.[31]

Consul Adams again supplied a personal account to the State Department, describing how he had verified Lynch's American citizenship to the court martial and had then been led away without being told the court's verdict. There, through a waiting-room window, he was horrified to see Lynch in the courtyard below, 'placed against the high stone wall, the soldiers forming a hollow square about him'. At this point Adams was sent on his way, and only later did he learn that Lynch had been reprieved. It seems, therefore, that the macabre courtyard incident had been either a mistake or an attempt to frighten Lynch.[32]

Thereafter, Grey asked Asquith to ensure that the Dublin military authorities should consult London before imposing the death sentence on any American citizen and should supply full information to enable the Foreign Office to give 'early replies to enquiries from the United States Government'. Dublin HQ replied that the only American court-martialled was Lynch and that further trial of American citizens was unlikely. Strangely, no mention was made either of the disputed citizenship of de Valera or of Thomas Clarke, who had become an American citizen many years earlier but was executed as one of the seven signatories of the Proclamation of the Provisional Government.[33]

V

It was to be expected that Irish-American extremists would be enraged by the executions, but many moderates, although less vociferous, also reacted bitterly. This was only appreciated at the Foreign Office towards the end of May, when comprehensive reports were received at Wellington House from Gilbert Parker's American correspondents. One such informant, Kenneth Durant, observed 'an estrangement' of many Irish-Americans who had previously been 'staunchly pro-English'. H. J. Whigham was even more daunting:

> I am convinced from talking with a number of the best Irishmen in New York that Great Britain has finally alienated all Irish-American sympathy in the country. Before the Irish revolt it would probably have been true to say that 25% of the Irish were actively pro-German and 75% were more or less pro-Ally. . . . One hundred per cent of the Irish are now actually anti-British,

although a number of them will not become actively pro-German. . . . There was a chance that this war might lead in the end to a rapprochement between the United States and Great Britain. All ideas of that kind may now be abandoned. The Irish will see to it that there will be nothing of the kind at all events for fifty years to come.

Whigham concluded that all thinking Americans regarded the Irish executions as a 'far greater blunder' even than the German shooting of Nurse Edith Cavell, whose fate (for assisting Allied soldiers to escape from Belgium) had been exploited by British propagandists in America.[34]

Such reactions were not confined to Irish-Americans. Whigham emphasised that disgust and indignation were felt 'in all sections of the community', while Durant noted that a 'considerable shocking of sentiment and sympathy' was widespread. German activists in the United States were quick to appreciate this development. Hugo Munsterberg, a Harvard professor, informed German Chancellor von Bethman Hollweg in Berlin that the executions had 'undoubtedly aided the German cause. Circles which, a few weeks ago, were enthusiastically pro-British, are now against England.' Another activist, Dr Alexander Fuehr, considered that England's 'incredible folly' would prove to be of crucial diplomatic importance:

> The Irish rebellion has a direct historical parallel in the American revolution; the Irish declaration of independence therefore met with much sympathy from the Americans of old revolutionary stock; the brutal English treatment of the 'traitors' let loose not merely the fury of the Irish-Americans but also a good deal of honest indignation in British–American circles, which had hitherto firmly supported England in the war. Thus, in a few weeks, the situation has completely changed here, and we may hope that the U.S. may now be definitely counted out, i.e., their entry into the war is no longer to be feared. This . . . has altered the whole war situation in our favour.[35]

Unofficial warning of German exploitation was received at the Foreign Office from the American Secretary of State, Robert Lansing, and was reinforced by Guy Gaunt, the British Naval Attaché, who reported, 'The Irish situation has completely upset things here, and the Germans are working it for all they are worth.'

Indeed, the German–Irish alliance in America gained a new lease of life after the executions. Whigham predicted that Congressional attitudes towards the British blockade would be 'greatly influenced' by Irish-American feeling, while Spring-Rice feared that the situation was 'extremely convenient to the German managers, as just before the Presidential nomination, they are at once put into possession of the Irish organisations, the Irish newspaper writers, and the Irish politicians'. Thus, a strong German–Irish understanding had developed, devoted to 'the destruction of pro-British sentiment' in the United States.[36]

Despite these warnings, officials in London were either unable or unwilling to recognise the worsening situation. The one exception was the Director of Wellington House, Charles Masterman, a 'convinced Home Ruler' who considered that, 'in the deferring of Home Rule, the Irish had been unfairly treated'. According to his wife, the Rising and its aftermath distressed him, since he was 'emotionally on the side of the Sinn Feiners' and not unsympathetic to their action. Moreover, the rebellion was 'a serious complication' to Wellington House work in America, since 'several Irishmen who had been helping propaganda cabled that it was useless for them to go on'. However, other Wellington House officials seemed impervious to this 'serious complication' – as was illustrated by Gilbert Parker's assistant, Ronald Roxburgh, who merely reflected, 'No doubt the German-American and Irish-American press will be furious; but the bulk of this is consistently and implacably hostile.' Parker himself replied to Whigham's letter of 5 May with a combination of optimism and traditional principles:

> I think that when the storm has subsided and the facts become better known, the 75% of the Irish who were pro-Ally in the United States will come back again. If it is not so, and we are to suffer, well then we must endure it with sadness and deep regret. But there are times when strength and decision are better than any paltering with principles in order to placate an enemy that still remains an enemy when all placating is finished and over.[37]

The use of the term 'enemy' to describe those who had now defected from the pro-Ally camp is a serious indictment of official attitudes towards the Irish-American community. Significantly, Parker had been Unionist MP for Gravesend since 1900, and in an electoral address of November 1910 he asserted that it was 'a national duty to keep the Union intact, and to protect the interests of the minority in Ireland', while ensuring that the political parties should 'never be subject to outside influence or alien power'. In an election speech of the same week, Parker reinforced his objection to Irish-American interference: 'We want to settle our own differences by our own forces inside the kingdom. . . . Hands off. Take back your gold and leave us to work out our own salvation.' Although this was partly election polemic, Parker's firm adherence to these traditional Unionist principles was reflected, six years later, in his uncompromising reply to Whigham:

> There are things even more dear to England than the friendship of the American-Irish, there are things more dear to England even than the friendship of the United States: there is self-respect, and local honour and local justice, to be considered. . . . I am certain that the promoters and convenors of this atrocious conspiracy got not only what they deserved but what was inevitable in the circumstances.[38]

Foreign Office officials, also, were sensitive to any implied criticism of the executions. Geoffrey Butler, a Cambridge don and future Conservative MP for the University, considered it 'impertinence' for Whigham to compare the Irish executions with Edith Cavell's 'murder', while Edward Grey instructed that Whigham should be told 'how many people, including soldiers, were shot by the Irish revolutionaries' and that it was 'impossible for any Government to let so many people be shot and execute nobody'. When Spring-Rice warned that the increasingly hostile Irish-American vote could be a dangerous, anti-British factor in the forthcoming Presidential election, Rowland Sperling commented tartly that Britain 'could expect nothing but hostility from the Irish vote in any case', but added in unwitting contradiction that there was 'evidence of an undercurrent of better feeling among moderate Irish circles in Eastern States'. Arthur Nicolson, also displaying questionable optimism, minuted that, 'when sound American opinion knows all the facts, a different view [of the executions] will be taken', and tersely added the traditional Unionist viewpoint already expounded so emphatically by Parker: 'I hope we shall be allowed to deal with our own internal troubles in our own way.' Two days later, Nicolson again typified Foreign Office sensitivity when he responded sharply to a telegram from Spring-Rice which described the shooting of the rebels as 'executions in hot blood':

> I do not understand what Sir C. Spring-Rice means by 'executions in hot blood' – all those condemned presumably had a fair trial. We need not, in my opinion, steer our course with reference to elections in a foreign country but act simply according to the dictates of justice.[39]

Despite an 'unshakeable belief in the logic and inevitability' of Irish Home Rule, Lord Crewe, the acting Foreign Secretary, had already stressed in the House of Lords that the rebellion was a 'purely domestic matter', and he agreed with Nicolson that the phrase 'executions in hot blood' was 'improper and should not have been used'. Lord Hardinge, who had recently chaired the Royal Commission which investigated the rebellion, deprecated the growing American sympathy for the rebel leaders and considered their execution to be 'thoroughly justified' in view of the 'most brutal and cold-blooded murders' which they had committed. Hubert Montgomery was equally outspoken. Writing privately to his father the Ulster Unionist Hugh Montgomery, he underlined his dislike of Irish Nationalism by referring acidly to the rebels who were shot 'for stabbing us in the back and for being responsible for the murder of a lot of decent people'.[40]

In order to justify such attitudes, many officials continued to voice an optimism regarding American reaction which was unrealistic in view of the pessimistic reports being received from various correspondents. As the comments of Nicolson and Parker suggest, this optimism was partly based on the anticipated publication of the 'facts', which, in their eyes, failed to materialise through excessive War Office caution. However, even without these 'facts', most Foreign Office officials would have been unwilling to alter their stance, which was deeply rooted in the principle of national sovereignty. Grey's ministry was dominated by men of Conservative – and in many cases Unionist – persuasion who strongly resented foreign intrusion into British domestic politics and who, following the Rising, believed that justice should take an independent course unfettered by external pressure. Moreover, the reactions of Grey and Crewe show that such principles were, to some degree, shared by many Liberals.

Many Foreign Office officials were especially reluctant to

recommend sacrifices merely to placate American opinion, being either hostile or condescending towards the United States. In this respect, Grey was an exception. His memoirs clearly indicate his guiding principle that a breach with the United States would have been the 'one mistake in diplomacy that, if it had been made, would have been fatal to the cause of the Allies'.[41] With the exception of some of its younger officials, the Foreign Office did not share Grey's enthusiasm for close relations with the United States. One historian has argued that this was one of the few policy areas where there was a clear divergence of opinion between senior and junior officials. Many senior officials, he contends, 'had not yet learned to take America altogether seriously', an attitude typified by Hardinge, who saw the country as 'a ramshackle state like Austria–Hungary rather than a true great power',[42] and by Nicolson, who regarded its citizens as 'boorish and uninteresting'.[43] Even Lord Crewe, Grey's frequent deputy, displayed 'an attitude of amused tolerance for the Americans', while Eyre Crowe, an Assistant Under Secretary, warned that the concessions on the blockade would expose Britain to 'all the corrupt and absolutely immoral pressure of the President, the State Department and the whole electioneering apparatus which stands in the place of government in America'.[44] Thus, it was unfortunate for Anglo-American relations that the various warnings to the Foreign Office on Irish-American activities encountered not only a widespread bias for the Unionist cause and against Irish Nationalism, but also strong resentment at America's self-appointed role as a moral crusader in world affairs.

VI

Four factors were advanced by Wellington House correspondents to explain the fierce American reaction against the shooting of the rebels. First, there was what Kenneth Durant described as an 'inherited American feeling for any rebel against the British crown'. This anti-British revolutionary tradition was not immediately stirred by the Rising, which appeared an 'insane and pernicious collusion with Germany', but 'the executions seemed to explain the revolution and sympathy was awakened (such is the effect of martyrdom)'. Secondly, as several commentators pointed out, executions by court martial were abhorrent to the 'humanitarian streak' in the American character and were seen as a vestige of a bloody and barbarous past. Critics such as John D. Moore of the extremist organisation 'Friends of Irish Freedom' exploited this trait by stressing that 'these executions – they can properly be called murders – prove that England today is the same cruel England that first covered its Irish victims with pitch before burning them'. Whigham informed Parker that the 'cold-blooded' shooting of the rebels after surrender was regarded by Americans as 'against the laws of humanity. They think that it is just as bad to shoot the Irish rebels as it would have been to shoot General Lee after his surrender.' Moreover, as Kenneth Durant explained, there seemed a 'deeper damnation' in killing two of the rebel leaders, Pearse and MacDonagh, whose poetry was popular with many Americans. This prompted an indignant comment from Ronald Roxburgh:

> There is a tendency to dwell upon the literary prominence of the chief rebels, and no American newspaper seems to have realised that any of the rebels committed murder, or indeed brought about the death of a large number of loyal subjects. They are rather considered as 'patriots' who held riotous meetings on street corners.[45]

American criticisms prompted Rowland Sperling to suggest a search for historical precedents of similar executions in United States history. However, when he suggested a possible precedent in the Philippines, Lord Crewe quashed the idea with his insistence that 'there can be no question of arguing with the US over the Philippines or any other precedents. It is a purely domestic question.' In late July, the editor of the Unionist *Spectator*, St Loe Strachey, asked Hubert Montgomery whether any courts martial and executions had followed the Irish draft riots during the American Civil War. If so, 'it would be rather interesting to rub the fact into those foolish Americans who are now trying to lecture us as to the way in which we put down our Irish rebellion'. Montgomery replied that the Foreign Office could not involve itself officially, but it would be 'excellent' if Strachey could 'go into the matter a little more and draw a comparison in the Spectator'. Montgomery, however, suspected that after the riots 'the participants were on the whole gently treated', and Geoffrey Butler's research verified that 'the parallel to the Irish rebellion is not as close as one might wish'. Spring-Rice's sole contribution was that, although no executions followed the draft riots, 'the action of General Kilpatrick in suppressing the revolt gave rise to the remark that he was most appropriately named'.[46]

The third factor affecting American opinion was the British Government's contrasting treatment of the rebel leaders on the one hand and Carson and the pre-war Ulster Covenanters on the other. Whigham noted that Americans regarded Carson as being 'every bit as guilty' as the rebels, adding that his appointment had been 'seriously criticised in this country and did real harm to the Allied cause. That appointment is now bearing fruit. It is impossible for people who are not Irish to overlook the glaring discrepancy in the treatment of the two cases.' Indeed, even the former President and pro-Ally Theodore Roosevelt wrote to an English correspondent,

> Two years ago Carson and the Ulstermen were openly talking of armed resistance to the Imperial Government, and some extremists among them were not obscurely hinting that they would under certain circumstances not look askance at a possible understanding with the Emperor of Germany. Under these circumstances I wish your people had not shot the leaders of the Irish rebels after they surrendered.[47]

The Foreign Office and Wellington House prudently avoided this delicate issue, so that the only efforts to defend the Ulster Unionist position came from Unionists themselves. St Loe Strachey's *Spectator*, widely read by the American intelligentsia (including President Wilson[48]), sought to justify Carson's past actions by citing parallels from American history:

> Sir Edward Carson did not rebel. How can a man who urges the right of those he represents to retain their status, and not be cast out of their community in which they were born, be called a rebel? Suppose the Southern States, instead of seceding, had refused to be driven out of the Union, would Mr Lincoln have denounced them as rebels?[49]

However, Ulstermen still refused to make serious efforts to explain their case to Americans, whose opinions they considered irrelevant to any discussion of the Irish Question. Indeed, almost two years later, Horace Plunkett argued that 'the Ulster case has never been explained in America and . . . in the view of the American democracy the Irish Question has only one side'.[50]

The fourth and final factor which aggravated the effect of the executions was the growing American criticism of the British Government's general conduct of the war. Whigham warned that 'the growing feeling that Great Britain was suffering failure after failure was not improved at all by the outcome of the Irish revolt', while Durant reported that the executions had produced a 'weakening of confidence in the efficiency, the common sense, and imagination of the British Government'. In bringing Durant's view to the Cabinet's attention, the American Press Résumé underlined the nadir to which the British cause had fallen by reporting that 'a reading of the American press supports his view that British prestige in the United States has never during the war stood lower than today'.[51]

VII

The British Government naturally hoped to convince Americans of the justice of its handling of the rebellion. To this end, the two main objects were, first, to censor unfavourable news from Dublin, and, secondly, to propagate the Government's own version of events. H. C. Peterson has termed these 'the Siamese twins of public opinion',[52] but, as the Irish example was to illustrate, they were not always compatible and, on occasions, could be counter-productive. Indeed, while the Foreign Office continually pressed for more details of the Rising, rigid War Office censorship not only prevented the rebels from broadcasting their own interpretation of the Dublin troubles but also stifled much potential Government propaganda.

In House of Commons question time, Augustine Birrell admitted that the Government had been 'very anxious . . . that news should not reach neutral countries, and particularly our friends in America, which would be calculated to give them an entirely false impression as to the importance of what has taken place'. However, Ronald McNeill, an Ulster Unionist MP, retorted that a mere 'riot' did not warrant military censorship and that, as a result, foreign nations would inevitably gain 'a very exaggerated sense of the seriousness of the situation'. This was echoed by the *Belfast News Letter*, which argued in a caustic editorial that the best way to counter exaggerated reports of the rebellion was to 'tell the truth, and tell it promptly', and by the *Daily Mail*, whose proprietor, Lord Northcliffe, held that secrecy and censorship might deliver a death blow to the British war effort. Northcliffe's other leading newspaper, *The Times*, published several Washington despatches from Arthur Willert who, in focusing attention on the 'tongue-tied imbecility' of the authorities, asserted,

> So far as the United States are concerned the British Censor is perhaps the greatest factor in deciding how serious the reverberations of the Irish uprising are going to be. If he . . . persists in his present course of allowing only the most meagre and tantalizing items to filter over the cable the American public will be inclined to draw sombre conclusions, and the German–Irish party will be able to make free use of its most valuable asset – a picturesque and ingenious imagination, unfettered by any regard whatever for the truth.[53]

Before the executions, therefore, censorship was deemed to be giving Americans an *inflated* impression of the gravity of the rebellion, leading them to draw 'sombre conclusions'. After the executions, however, criticism underwent a marked change and it was increasingly argued that the censorship was, in fact, *belittling* the Rising in American eyes, so making the executions appear unnecessarily brutal. Indeed, a *Times* editorial now argued that, with American opinion based on 'half-reported facts', there was clearly no conception of 'how serious the outbreak was or how much cold-blooded murder was committed by the rebels'. This shift in criticism extended to the House of Lords, where Lord Midleton, leader of the Southern Irish Unionists, argued that 'the Government have made the greatest possible blunder by doing everything in their power to belittle the Rising . . . to the level of a street riot', thereby producing 'a false impression on neutral nations and in America'. Thus, after complaints that censorship had given a mere riot the appearance of a serious outbreak, it was now argued, rather illogically and often by the same critics, that censorship was making a serious outbreak appear a mere riot.[54]

Although most Foreign Office officials opposed the introduction of American opinion into discussion of Irish affairs, they nevertheless endeavoured to justify the Government's handling of the rebellion in American eyes. The first step in such a task was to arrange special reporting facilities for American newspapermen to see the havoc created in Dublin. On the day following the outbreak of the rebellion, Geoffrey Dawson called at the Foreign Office and asked Lord Newton, head of the News Department, to seek permission for the press to go to Dublin 'so that the news should be known in America'. When Kitchener at the War Office would not give an immediate decision, Newton characteristically by-passed him and organised the departure next day of the first Dublin-bound reporters. It was then left to Lord Crewe (in Grey's absence) to seek Kitchener's belated support:

> I understand that there is a project of sending some American journalists to Ireland at once. . . . It is important to get a true picture of the situation to America as soon as possible. There will be a network of German lies about it, and the hostile Irish in the U.S. will play up to them. No contradiction of ours will have effect, but the evidence of some Americans will: so I hope you will encourage in any way you can.[55]

It was the policy, both in Britain and on the Western Front, for American newspapermen to receive flattering attention in order to encourage the propagation of the British point of view. Frederick Palmer, a leading American war correspondent, claimed that the more important visitors from his country were 'courted assiduously' and 'chaperoned by most attentive and diplomatic reserve officers who had notes in hand from the Foreign Office about the standing and character of each visitor. . . . The guests were shown what was good for them to see.' However, after the first party of American journalists arrived in Dublin, their official 'chaperon', Captain Ralph Butler, informed the Foreign Office that problems were arising from the absence of promised reporting facilities, which might deprive the journalists of a 'scoop'. By 30 April, with the Rising quashed, more journalists were permitted to cross to Dublin and move freely within the city, but 'chaperoning' the new arrivals proved so difficult that Captain Butler reported 'we do not know where they are or what they are doing'. This disorganisation created an abrasive atmosphere at press conferences, where the visiting journalists 'heckled poor Birrell and the Lord Lieutenant with alarming acrimony'.[56]

Ironically, when the journalists voiced resentment at the lack of passes to Dublin, it was a War Office official, Colonel Warburton Davies, who wrote brusquely to Hubert Montgomery: 'There appears to be a good deal of trouble as a result of the American correspondents' trip to Dublin. We propose to put it down to the

Foreign Office.' In reply, Montgomery highlighted the divergence between the Foreign Office desire for greater facilities and the War Office distrust of free reporting on delicate military matters:

> The Government attach great importance to American opinion being kept sound on this matter, and the best and only way of doing so was clearly to let America have, at the earliest possible moment from correspondents of American papers, a proper version of the facts.[57]

This policy divergence was underlined by another News Department official, Miles Lampson, who complained to Montgomery of his fruitless efforts to obtain a permit for the correspondent of the staunchly pro-Ally *New York Times*: 'Frankly, I think the attitude of the War Office is deplorable; one cannot blame any particular person, or at least not Colonel Davies, for no doubt he has got others above him who are obdurate.' According to Lampson, an American Embassy official had 'expressed amazement that such an obvious move from the publicity point of view should have encountered opposition from any quarter whatsoever'.[58] Clearly, the selection of correspondents for Dublin was not the most judicious. Even allowing for the enforced restrictions, the exclusion of major newspapers such as the *New York Times* from the first party appears to have been a serious error of judgement. However, in the final analysis, friction with the correspondents arose because the War Office aim of curtailing damaging news from Ireland and the Foreign Office policy of spreading the Government's view of events proved to be incompatible.

VIII

In the face of cautious War Office censorship, Government spokesmen were forced to improvise with the meagre facts at their disposal. Their attempts to justify the handling of the rebellion fell into two categories: the first stressed rebel barbarity, while the second emphasised the leniency with which the rebellion was quashed. Gilbert Parker typified the first approach when he drew H. J. Whigham's attention to 'the murdering of innocent people, civilians and soldiers . . . in a country where more has been done for the welfare of the people during the last twenty years than in

England itself'. The second approach was exemplified by Lord Crewe, who assured his fellow peers that there was no country in the world 'where a rising of such a character would have been put down with so little bloodshed and with so rare a recourse to the capital penalty'. When Arnold Bennett, the author, wrote an article for the *New York Times*, the choice of tactic became an issue of taste. In order to 'ensure his approaching the subject from the proper angle', Bennett was supplied with guidance notes by Raymond Needham, a Recruiting Department official, whom the Foreign Office had chosen to present the British view of the rebellion in the American press. Needham's notes echoed Gilbert Parker's sentiments by denouncing the 'hideous' and 'horrifying' conduct of the rebels, but Bennett ignored such colourful polemic and emulated Crewe's restraint, claiming that 'an assaulted government has rarely shown greater magnanimity in a more dangerous crisis'.[59]

To most Government officials it seemed imperative that a public revelation of the casualties and destruction suffered during the rebellion was essential to transatlantic propaganda. An obvious source for this information was General Maxwell, the Commander-in-Chief in Ireland, but publication of his official despatches was repeatedly blocked by the War Office. As an alternative, Edward Grey recommended to Asquith that, as Americans appeared to view the Rising as a 'toy affair of misguided but comparatively harmless people', General Maxwell should produce an account of the 'violent character' of the insurrection and the need for its quick suppression. Maxwell duly prepared a statement for the American press, condemning rebel atrocities with their 'foreign incitement', and defending the courts martial as 'absolutely fair'. On hearing of the proposed statement, Spring-Rice hastily telegraphed that the General's part in the death sentences had created 'great prejudice' against him and the statement would therefore only 'meet with derision'. Moreover, as the Irish Question had 'fallen into the background', such propaganda might merely revive controversy. The Foreign Office News Department reluctantly accepted the Ambassador's advice and suppressed the statement, but remained convinced that Maxwell's despatches should be published immediately since, in Geoffrey Butler's words, further delay could mean that Britain had 'again missed the hour of interest'.[60]

For the News Department, this period was a catalogue of frustration in their efforts to present the full facts for American consumption. Four weeks after the suppression of Maxwell's intended press statement, Hubert Montgomery prepared a statement of his own for publication, decrying rebel brutality and deploring American criticism of the executions. In an accompanying memorandum, he vented his frustration at excessive War Office caution:

> It is not astonishing that people in America have taken, and are still taking, this misguided view of the executions of the rebel leaders. The crimes and cold-blooded murders which they perpetrated have never been officially published to the world. Even those facts which I have got together are . . . based on information collected from private persons. They are all absolutely authenticated and we have sent them to America by various channels, but even these few among the many similar cases have never been officially published. . . . Neither we nor the public have been given any full report at all of the trial of the rebel leaders. I have pleaded several times for the publication of Sir J. Maxwell's despatches and anything else that was available. I think that even now these might help to get the thing seen in proper perspective in America – but it is very late.

Montgomery's departmental head, Lord Newton, agreed that it was impossible to counteract Anglophobia when the facts were 'persistently suppressed', while Lord Hardinge lamented that 'all moderate and sane people in the United States would have adopted quite a different attitude' if they had been made aware of the atrocities which he had catalogued as chairman of the commission investigating the rebellion. Ironically, by the time the Maxwell despatches were released, in mid July, Montgomery opposed overseas distribution because they had been 'issued so very late in the day that their circulation will only keep alive memories of the rebellion which are otherwise disappearing'.[61]

Miles Lampson, however, remained less optimistic that memories of the rebellion were 'disappearing'. In late August he persuaded his chief, Lord Newton, to seek the release of the courts-martial findings, this being 'the obvious thing to have done at the time and no thinking American . . . can imagine why we do not do so'. Although Newton gained Edward Grey's support, such little progress was made that Lampson, chafing under the bit of official caution, took matters into his own hands. He privately requested St

Loe Strachey, editor of the *Spectator*, to publish details of rebel 'atrocities' as a 'jog to those in authority here'. Lampson acknowledged that he had 'no business whatsoever to have mentioned the thing to you as, in a sense, I am acting behind the backs of my superiors'; but he justified this breach of Civil Service ethics with the conviction that 'it is to the public good that we should get something more done on this extremely important question'. It was, he complained, 'heart-breaking' to see opportunities slipping away, especially when the right material existed and yet 'for some mysterious reason it is not considered desirable to use it'. Strachey, requiring little further persuasion, protested vehemently to Lord Desart, the Irish Censor, at the 'appalling folly of letting the legend of British oppression, and the cruel putting down of amiable rebellion, grow up', and announced that he would resume his attack on the Government's publicity policy.[62]

News Department persistence eventually paid off when a Foreign Office nominee – John Buchan the author – was allowed to select matter for publication from the courts-martial records. However, the War Office still harboured strong reservations, and the War Minister, Lloyd George, was advised by his Parliamentary Under Secretary, Lord Derby, that the revelations would 'give cause for a most awful row as the evidence at some of the courts martial is very thin'. The warning had its effect, for, after the formation of the Lloyd George Coalition Government in December 1916, the new War Cabinet forbade the disclosure of the records as being 'contrary to the public interest'. This saga of continued delay is illustrative of the military caution in propaganda matters which caused such exasperation at the Foreign Office and which frustrated many News Department schemes to justify British policy.[63]

Although most Foreign Office officials agreed on the need to defend Government handling of the rebellion, opinions frequently conflicted when schemes were mooted for mollifying Irish-Americans. Eustace Percy, for example, argued that with the suspended Home Rule Act 'now a dead issue' as potential propaganda, any future mission to America would have to go on a promise of the Act's immediate implementation. Such advice indicates that, although Percy subsequently entered Parliament as a Coalition Unionist, he had little close attachment to the Union principle. Hubert Montgomery, an inveterate opponent of Home Rule, quashed the mission concept: 'I don't think that any Nationalist member would take on the job of making pro-British propaganda – public or private – in America at this time.' In the end, all mission schemes were postponed until after the November Presidential election, so as to avoid any appearance of interfering in American politics during this sensitive period.[64]

Similar divisions occurred when *Ireland*, the Redmondite journal in America, was criticised by Birrell as a 'spiritless, unreal concern', requiring new force in its 'faltering accents'. Lampson suggested consulting T. P. O'Connor on the establishment of a new paper, but, typically, Montgomery saw no point in consulting Nationalist MPs and minuted rather sourly, 'I don't see why a further Irish paper in the USA should be any better success than "Ireland".' The scheme was finally dropped on Spring-Rice's advice that 'no Irish newspaper which did not voice opinions strongly hostile to the British Government could long survive in the U.S. under present conditions'. These abortive propaganda schemes were significant in marking the end of any lingering proposals for Foreign Office co-operation with the Irish Nationalists.[65]

Noticeably, the most active proponents of schemes to win over Irish-Americans were Eustace Percy, who 'loved America'[66] and constantly sought closer relations with her, and Miles Lampson, whose son, Lord Killearn, recently recalled that, with an American grandfather and American mother-in-law, Lampson 'could not but be favourably inclined' towards the United States. Throughout Lampson's diplomatic career, his relations with American counterparts were, according to Killearn, always 'most cordial', and, 'after the Americans had taken our place as a major force in the Western World, I often heard him say that we should welcome with open arms both their interest and investment'. Lord Killearn also stresses of his father that, as a 'good civil servant', he could 'never have taken sides' on the Irish Question.[67] This is, indeed, more true of Lampson than of many of his Unionist-minded colleagues, who did not always abide by this fundamental ethic of their profession.

It is significant that, whereas Lampson and Percy were still willing to work with the Redmondites, the traditionalists at the Foreign Office remained aloof. Rowland Sperling, for example, wrote of 'the futility of any attempt to conciliate the Irish' and considered that, 'as the Irish are bound to be anti-British in any case, it is just as well that they should blow off steam now'.[68] This was typical of Sperling's disparaging attitude towards Irish-Americans and his complete indifference to the problems posed by their Anglophobia. (Appropriately, he took the *Morning Post*, the extreme right-wing newspaper[69] which strongly defended the Union against American interference.) A similar disdain was exhibited by the Assistant Under Secretary, Lord Newton, whose early career as a Unionist MP during the tumultuous days of Gladstone's Home Rule campaigns had convinced him that the Home Rule Party was 'a blackmailing body, animated by a common desire to extract as much as possible from the Government', and that the Irish Nationalist MPs were 'ill-educated and ill-mannered men whose main object was to impede legislation and flout authority'. Doubtless, such early impressions coloured Newton's attitude towards the Irish-Americans and, after the Rebellion, strengthened his conviction that 'any attempt to conciliate these people would only expose us to justifiable contempt'.[70]

Although officials such as Sperling, Newton and Montgomery considered Spring-Rice's reports of American opinion to be irrelevant to any discussion of the Irish Question, they nevertheless sought to reinforce their own prejudices by selective use of extracts from his varying recommendations. Thus, although the Ambassador frequently supported schemes to mollify Irish-Americans, hard-line officials could also point to his pessimistic comments that such efforts would be 'doomed to failure', since 'the Irish would not listen because they are Irish and the Americans will not listen because they are busy. The Irish events, from the American point of view, are a back number and the dead are dead.'[71] Under the combined weight of Spring-Rice's vacillation and Tory traditionalist disdain, the Foreign Office paid diminishing attention to justifying the executions. Indeed, as the Presidential election drew nearer, officials deemed it prudent to avoid the subject of the rebellion so as to deny Irish-American extremists further ammunition for propaganda. Nevertheless, by severely damaging British standing in America, the executions marked a turning-point in the Irish Question, foreshadowing the growth of anti-British extremism among Irishmen on both sides of the Atlantic.

5
Sir Roger Casement's Trial and Execution (April–September 1916)

I

The Irish rebel who attracted most controversy was Sir Roger Casement, whose mission to Germany and subsequent journey to Ireland by submarine set him apart from the other rebels. When Casement was captured, it was wrongly assumed in both Britain and the United States that he was the leader of the rebellion. The Irish and German extremists in America hailed him as a second George Washington who, if executed, would be a martyr to the Irish cause, and they contrasted his probable fate with the immunity enjoyed by Edward Carson during his pre-war activities. However, extremists apart, most Americans and almost all the leading newspapers condemned Casement's treason, but advocated that, for reasons of expediency, the death sentence should be commuted to life imprisonment on grounds of insanity. As early as 26 April, Spring-Rice urged Grey that executing Casement 'would make his name a centre of agitation', and later warned that 'the great bulk of American public opinion, while it might excuse executions in hot blood, would greatly regret an execution some time after the event'; consequently 'the Germans here look forward with great interest to his execution of which they will take full advantage'.[1]

Moderate Irish-Americans were especially anxious that Casement should be spared, so as to deny further propagandist ammunition to the extreme faction. During a short visit to Washington in April 1916, Eustace Percy was repeatedly pressed on this point by influential Irish-Americans such as John Quinn, the eminent lawyer, and Bourke Cochrane, the orator, and subsequently embodied their views in a memorandum for the Cabinet. Spring-Rice transmitted similar messages from Redmondite politicians and from moderate Catholic Church leaders such as Cardinal Gibbons, who counselled against 'manufacturing martyrs' by any intemperate punishment. Indeed, King George V's Private Secretary, Lord Stanfordham, pressed Asquith to hold Casement's trial as soon as possible, since 'already Cardinal Gibbon[s] in New York is talking of leniency'.[2]

Foreign Office officials and diplomats found the American appeals unpalatable, for Casement was regarded as more treacherous than the other executed rebels, while his previous consular career made his actions appear even more heinous. On receipt of Gibbons's warning, one official, Lancelot Oliphant, minuted caustically that 'it would require a vast amount of manufacturing to turn Casement into a martyr'. The private reaction of Lord Bertie, British Ambassador to France, probably reflected feeling towards Casement in most diplomatic circles:

> He is much more guilty than many of those who have been shot as rebels in the fighting or have been executed as signatories of the Proclamation of the Irish Republic. I would hang him and chance public opinion in the States. The German–Americans are, of course, against us, also the Irish sympathisers in America of the Sinn Feiners, but the Americans other than these two classes would, if they were in our shoes, most decidedly hang, shoot or lynch Casement, and it would be an act of weakness on our part to let him off and would be so regarded in America.[3]

The Casement trial, as with the courts martial, was viewed as a domestic matter, in which the Foreign Office role was merely to present the true facts to an uninformed American public. Rowland Sperling recommended that pains be taken to stress that 'Casement will receive a fair trial before a jury with every opportunity for his defence and that, if he is not executed, this is about the only country in the world in which such leniency would be shown'. Arthur Nicolson considered that such assurance 'ought to be quite sufficient for the Americans or anyone else', while even Miles Lampson, normally more flexible, was equally adamant: 'I do not feel that the course of justice should be influenced by whatever the Americans may think . . . and feeling in this country also has to be considered.' On Eric Drummond's suggestion, Geoffrey Butler 'rubbed in' to American correspondents the complete impartiality of

Casement's trial for high treason and found them 'very sensible' on the matter.⁴

Another significant indication of Foreign Office attitudes followed the receipt of a telegram from Guy Gaunt, the Naval Attaché in Washington, which ran counter to the overwhelming mass of appeals for clemency. Gaunt contended that many Americans would condemn a reprieve and that some of them, unaware that Casement was now penniless, believed that his special treatment (i.e. a civil trial instead of a court martial) showed British justice to be 'one law for the rich and one for the poor'. In what appears to be a calculated manipulation of the available evidence, Drummond picked out Gaunt's telegram, with its contrary assessment, and persuaded Grey to place it before the Cabinet as an illustration of 'this point of view which seems now to obtain in the U.S.'. Ironically, Gaunt later admitted receiving many threatening letters at this time, one of which warned that, 'if one hair of the noble Casement's head is harmed, your life will be forfeit. You and other vile slaves of the English King must be exterminated.'⁵

A more balanced appraisal of American thought was provided by Spring-Rice, who warned that, if Casement were spared, the Irish extremists would 'accuse the British Government of sparing him because he is a Protestant and a British official', whereas, if he were executed, he would 'become a martyr and be exploited accordingly'; on balance, the majority of Americans thought it 'wiser in his case not to proceed to extremes'. Such advice made little impression on Foreign Office officials such as Walter Langley, Assistant Under Secretary, who asserted that 'nothing can now be allowed to affect the course of Casement's trial'. Possibly sensing that clemency appeals would meet with a cool reception, Spring-Rice had already turned to Arthur Willert for support; but the journalist, who was experiencing a similar lack of sympathy from his editor, Geoffrey Dawson, had been instructed to curb his reporting on the reprieve clamour and had prudently decided to leave matters alone until Casement's trial took place.⁶

Although the Foreign Office sought to avoid involvement in the Casement question, it was drawn into the case because of efforts by Michael Doyle, an Irish-American lawyer, to help Casement's defence. Doyle, who professed to exercise a moderating influence over many Irish-Americans, claimed the friendship of Woodrow Wilson and declared his intention of persuading the President to intercede. Spring-Rice, however, reported Doyle's reputation as 'a self-advertiser', while the Home Office feared that he would try to ingratiate himself with Irish-Americans by criticising the conduct of the trial and by initiating a reprieve campaign in the American press. This apprehension would have been even greater had it been known that he had been given $5000 by the Clan na Gael for Casement's defence.[7]

On arrival in England, Doyle immediately confirmed official fears by making severe accusations regarding Casement's prison conditions. Fortunately for the Government, Guy Gaunt was soon able to congratulate Geoffrey Butler on the British version being fed to the American press, showing that, in reality, 'Casement is comfortably housed and drinking port, instead of the fearful picture of the desperately ill martyr slipping on the blood of previous occupants.' However, Doyle's accusations reinforced the Home Office resolve to apply the law prohibiting foreign lawyers from representing clients in British courts, and to insist that Doyle should only see Casement at Brixton Prison in the presence of warders. Doyle then obtained an interview with Edward Grey, at which he hinted that, if given full facilities to assist Casement, he 'might exercise an influence in the U.S. favourable to the action of the British Government'. Grey endorsed the sentiments of his subordinates by replying firmly that Casement would receive a 'perfectly fair trial' and that 'it would be immensely resented if it were supposed that we were influenced here by public opinion outside'. Despite this outward firmness, Grey advised Herbert Samuel, the Home Secretary, to adopt a more conciliatory attitude towards Doyle's request, since, if it were claimed in America that Casement had not been allowed full facilities for preparing his defence, the effect would be 'very undesirable'. The warning proved effective, for Doyle was allowed to accompany Casement's solicitor on his next prison visit.[8]

On 26 June at the Old Bailey, Casement was tried for high treason, the chief prosecutor being F. E. Smith, the Attorney General, who had gained notoriety for his prominence in the pre-war Ulster agitation. Despite strenuous efforts by friends and sympathisers, Casement was found guilty and sentenced to death – a verdict which received mixed American reaction. Wellington House reported that the judgment had given 'much food for moralising to American journalists but less to the detriment of Great Britain than the anticipatory comment on the case might have suggested'. The sentence caused little regret among Foreign Office officials, the only note of compunction being sounded many years later in the memoirs of J. D. Gregory of the Political Intelligence Department: 'Though I did not for a moment question the justice of the sentence, I was much troubled at being concerned in the matter, as Roger Casement had at one time been a personal friend of mine.' More typical of the time was Lord Hardinge's remark to Spring-Rice that the verdict would produce a 'storm amongst the Irish in America' and that Casement would be 'held up as martyr and patriot – neither of which he is, but a very commonplace and thoroughly immoral man'.[9]

II

Behind Hardinge's statement lies an unsavoury and discreditable episode in Foreign Office history. It began when the British authorities discovered amongst Casement's possessions several diaries which, they claimed, showed very clearly that he was a practising homosexual. In order to discourage a reprieve movement, extracts from these diaries were circulated to influential figures in both England and America. However, it has never been firmly established which Government ministry initiated the smear campaign. Henry Nevinson, a Casement sympathiser and radical journalist with the *Nation*, later recalled that, in early June 1916, London editors were informed of a Casement diary which revealed his 'perversion' and 'unnatural vice'. The diary, he added, was 'exhibited in the Home Office to many curious inquirers, and care was taken that gossip about it should be widely spread among leaders of society – not a difficult matter'. Moreover, in his authoritative biography of Casement, Brian Inglis alleges that there is 'now little doubt' that the Home Office was behind the campaign and that its legal adviser, Ernley Blackwell, was the chief architect. However, it has not previously been made clear that the Foreign Office was equally involved in the character assassination almost from its inception; indeed, whilst disclaiming any duty to intercede over the clemency appeals, most Foreign Office officials considered it expedient to inform Americans of Casement's 'perversion'. As early as 13 May, Eric Drummond had contended that it would be almost impossible to reprieve Casement and that consequently it was most important that he should 'emerge from the trial thoroughly discredited from the moral side'. Believing that the influence on Irish Catholics would be considerable, Drummond hoped that, at the trial, there would be 'no danger of the evidence proving his addictions being ruled as inadmissible'. In the event, F. E. Smith's suggestion that the diaries be used to support a plea of insanity was rejected by Casement's counsel and, at the trial in June, Smith merely hinted at the existence of the diaries.[10]

Spring-Rice, while still pressing for a reprieve to satisfy American opinion, was also willing to use the diaries to curb sympathy for Casement. As early as mid May, he urged that 'if Casement can be shown to be abnormal in every way – and the impression amongst people who knew him here is that he is so – his influence here would be destroyed'. In fact, the Ambassador offered to show transcripts of the diaries to both Shane Leslie and John Quinn, but Leslie refused even to look at the extracts, while Quinn was so incensed by this scandal-mongering that he threatened to denounce the diaries as forgeries.[11]

After sentence of death had been passed, the campaign against Casement was intensified. F. E. Smith has often been painted as the leading figure in the campaign, but this is doubtful in view of his letter of 29 June to Edward Grey:

> I am told that the Foreign Office is photographing or proposing to photograph portions of Casement's diary with a view to showing them to various persons, so as to influence opinion.
>
> It is, I think, a rather ghoulish proposal and, without expressing a final opinion upon it, I should be glad if you would see me before sanctioning it.

On the same day that Grey received Smith's letter, the News Department drafted a telegram to Guy Gaunt in Washington, informing him that he would soon receive extracts from the diary, which was 'a daily record of amazing unnatural vice' and 'quite unpublishable'. The draft suggested that, meanwhile, Gaunt could hint to newspaper editors and other influential persons of facts which threw 'appalling light on Casement's past life' and which, when disclosed, would 'make it quite impossible for any self-respecting person to champion his cause'. Grey immediately vetoed the telegram and replied to Smith,

> I had not heard of the proposal to photograph and show parts of

Casement's diary nor do I approve of it. I will see that it is not proceeded with so far as the Foreign Office is concerned without the authority of the Cabinet, to whom I think such proceeding would not be agreeable.[12]

Some historians have cited this letter as proof that the Foreign Office could not have been involved in the smear campaign.[13] However, it is clear from the Foreign Office records that this is not so and that Grey's veto was ignored. Indeed, on the following day Newton revived the issue by minuting to Hardinge that the Foreign Office would have to face 'a huge pro-Casement propaganda' in America and that 'unless we are prepared to make use of the materials in our possession it will be almost impossible to combat it successfully'. Hardinge agreed that 'an effort should be made to place Casement and the Irish rebellion in their proper perspective in the US', but, on referring the matter to Grey, again met with the Foreign Secretary's insistence that it was a question for the Cabinet to decide. Frustrated a second time, Newton complained to Spring-Rice,

> I foresee that we are going to have a hard time over Casement. I have not been permitted to do what I should have liked, but I really think that steps ought to be taken to show what sort of man he is. Probably there are a lot of people who look upon him as a lofty-minded patriot whilst in reality he is the lowest of the low. I have seen his diary, and the details are so revolting that it would be impossible to publish them. Surely his admirers, especially Catholics, might be given the hint that he is anything but a worthy object of sympathy.[14]

There is no record to indicate that the Cabinet reached a decision regarding the use of the diaries; indeed, following the Cabinet meeting on 5 July, Asquith merely reported to the King that one of the diaries was to be submitted for psychological analysis. However, although Grey's veto had temporarily blocked Foreign Office exploitation of the diaries, other Government departments were not so restricted, and both the Home Office and Captain Reginald Hall of Admiralty Intelligence continued to show extracts to influential Americans such as Ben Allen of the Associated Press Agency, and Walter Hines Page, the American Ambassador in London. In early July, Page advised Lansing that American intervention would produce a 'very disagreeable impression' in Britain, and added,

> Not only does Casement, a British subject, stand convicted of treason but I am privately informed that much information about him of an unspeakably filthy character was withheld from publicity. . . . If all the facts about Casement ever become public it will be well that our Government had nothing to do with him or his case.[15]

Meanwhile, the Foreign Office continued to be inundated with petitions for reprieve, especially after Casement's appeal was turned down on 18 July. The English academic Gilbert Murray, who was touring America on a fact-finding mission for the Foreign Office, telegraphed that execution would 'produce a most unfortunate effect on public feeling in America', while John Quinn warned Grey that the death penalty would merely play into the hands of the Irish irreconcilables. Commuting this to life imprisonment, urged Quinn, would convince 'thoughtful and sympathetic Americans' that the execution of the Easter rebels 'was brought about in a moment of panic and . . . that her dealing with Casement represented the real Great Britain'. A more unexpected plea came from the Negro Fellowship League of America, which based its plea on Casement's humanitarian acts on behalf of the exploited negroes of the African Congo. The Foreign Office, however, took the view that such appeals were not its concern and merely passed them to the Home Office.[16]

The growing tide of appeals was not, of course, addressed only to the Foreign Office. Reprieve lobbyists from the Irish Parliamentary Party wrote to Asquith citing American feeling as a prime argument against making Casement a martyr, and both Lloyd George and Herbert Samuel were pressed by the eminent Liberal peer Lord Bryce to deny the Irish-Americans another opportunity to vilify the Government. Arthur Willert later reflected that the appeals had given the British Government 'an opportunity of Lincolnian clemency which would have been applauded by all Americans and would have disarmed the extremists'. Unfortunately for Casement, most of the appeals were directed at Liberal ministers, whereas the main opposition to reprieve lay within Tory ranks. Lord Curzon, for example, confidently predicted that Casement's execution would produce no serious effects in the United States, while Walter Long, the President of the Local Government Board, left a note in his private papers of his strong conviction that Casement should be executed because (in Long's mistaken view) he was the rebels' ringleader. F. E. Smith, the Attorney General and chief prosecutor at Casement's trial, subsequently claimed in an interview to have taken an even sterner line by threatening to resign from the Government if the sentence was not carried out.[17]

Cabinet views were divided across party barriers, as Asquith illustrated in his report of the Cabinet meeting on 5 July. Edward Grey, a Liberal, and Lord Lansdowne, a Unionist, were among several ministers who considered it better that Casement be 'kept in confinement as a criminal lunatic' rather than 'executed without any smirch on his character, and then canonised as a martyr both in Ireland and America'. Asquith himself clearly inclined towards this view, for he added sombrely, 'Others took the contrary view.'[18] But these were largely disagreements as to expediency. The Cabinet as a whole clearly believed that Casement deserved execution on purely legal grounds (even the most insistent reprieve campaigners admitted this), but many ministers held such a course to be inadvisable in view of probable American reaction.

During July, the opposition to reprieve was strengthened when two senior Home Office officials, Ernley Blackwell and Sir Edward Troup, wrote powerful memoranda which were circulated to the Cabinet by Herbert Samuel. Troup cited Spring-Rice's despatches as evidence that Americans were taking 'little interest' in Casement's fate, having recognised that he was 'guilty of crimes which any country would punish with death'. Troup admitted that the Irish-Americans would use an execution to the 'utmost of their power for propaganda purposes', but he considered that they had no special regard for Casement and that, if his sentence was commuted, they would be 'equally ready to use this as a means of attacking the British Government'. Blackwell, who, according to Brian Inglis, had 'a malignant hatred' of Casement and 'set himself to prevent ministers from weakening in their resolve that there should not be a reprieve', argued that, if Casement had reached Dublin and been shot with the other rebels, no one in Britain or in America would have disputed that his fate was 'as richly deserved as that of any of the other leaders'. Blackwell urged that Casement should first be executed and, if necessary, morally discredited afterwards. However, contrary to Inglis's claim that the Home Office was chiefly responsible for the smear campaign, Blackwell's memorandum clearly indicates that much of the responsibility lay with the Foreign Office:

> The Foreign Office from the start appear to have taken the view that in order not to alienate more Irish-American sentiment, we could not safely hang Casement unless we first published the fact of his private character as disclosed in his diaries. There are obviously grave objections to any sort of official or even inspired publication of such facts while the man is waiting trial or appeal, or even awaiting execution. Perhaps I do not fully appreciate the danger which the Foreign Office sees ahead in America if the law is allowed to take its full course in this country, but the attitude adopted is rather a humiliating one.
>
> I see not the slightest objection to hanging Casement, and afterwards giving as much publicity to the contents of his diary as decency permits, so that at any rate the public in America and elsewhere may know what sort of man they are inclined to make a martyr of.[19]

As Blackwell observed, the Foreign Office believed it necessary to mount a full-scale smear campaign in America in order to prepare public opinion for Casement's execution. In his memoirs, Lord Newton, who considered Casement's morals to be 'on a par with treachery', related how, following Cabinet dissension over the use of the diaries in America, he had personally taken the initiative:

> The papers were in the custody of my Department, and, when the time came for the despatch of the diplomatic bag, without waiting for further instructions from the Government I took the responsibility of sending the necessary documents to America.[20]

However, Newton's account is not completely accurate. In fact, following a request from Spring-Rice in late July that a copy of the diary be sent for confidential circulation, Newton, with Hardinge's consent, forwarded a typed copy, but stipulated that no use be made of it until authorised. A week later, photographs of specimen pages of the diary – supplied by Blackwell – were sent to the Ambassador for 'dispelling any doubts which may exist as to its authenticity'. On 29 July, with Casement's execution less than a week away, Newton and Montgomery sought Robert Cecil's approval for immediate use of the material by Spring-Rice. 'The

Prime Minister spoke to me on the subject', wrote Cecil in reply, 'and wished, as I understood, that such action should be taken. It certainly seems desirable.' Meanwhile, Grey, who had never lifted his veto on the use of the diaries, was now absent with severe eye-strain. Newton therefore decided that Cecil's authority was sufficient to by-pass the Foreign Secretary and instructed Spring-Rice to use the copies at his discretion. Thus, although Newton claimed credit for sanctioning transmission of the diary material, this was clearly dependent on the approval of Cecil.[21]

Such an episode clearly demonstrates that Grey's continued absences from the Foreign Office were weakening his authority over certain areas of decision-making, and that, in matters such as Casement's fate, many senior officials at the Foreign Office were willing to circumvent Grey's more conciliatory policy. Moreover, it is clear from Cecil's authorising minute that Asquith was deeply involved in the decision to ignore Grey's wishes, and this is borne out by a conversation between the Prime Minister and Walter Page, the American Ambassador. According to Page, Asquith referred to his anxiety about the many American telegrams for clemency, but explained that he was not prepared to intervene in view of Casement's treason and the depravity revealed in the diaries.[22] According to an American Embassy official, the Prime Minister even offered to show the diary to Page, and, when the Ambassador explained that he already had photographs of certain pages, Asquith replied, 'Excellent and you need not be particular about keeping it to yourself.'[23]

The pressure for reprieve would have been immeasurably strengthened had President Wilson intervened officially on Casement's behalf, but in late July he emphasised to his secretary, Joseph Tumulty, 'It would be inexcusable for me to touch this. It would involve serious international embarrassment.' Many historians, entirely ignoring the delicate state of Anglo-American relations at this time, have censured Wilson severely for his inaction, but the President had consistently taken the view that he had no grounds for involving his office in British domestic affairs. Nevertheless, Spring-Rice remained apprehensive that the President, despite his refusal to intercede, would be alienated by an execution. On the day before the hanging, the Ambassador cabled that, because of the Irish influence in the Democrat Party, executing Casement would make Wilson hostile 'by force of circumstances', whereas clemency would constitute a personal favour. The telegram actually arrived at the Foreign Office after Casement had been executed, but, even had it arrived in time, it would have made little impression on British officialdom. In fact, Rowland Sperling commented that it was 'grotesque' to suppose that the Government would be influenced by the considerations outlined in the telegram, but that Spring-Rice was 'only doing his duty in reporting the American point of view'.[24]

Spring-Rice's anxiety was doubtless increased by pressure emanating from the American Congress. Although the latter had shown little interest in Ireland for many years and Home Rule resolutions had attracted scant support, the executions galvanised renewed concern. This culminated on 31 July in a Senate resolution which expressed the hope that the British Government would 'exercise clemency in the treatment of Irish political prisoners', and which the President was requested to transmit to Britain. As a *Times* correspondent observed, 'the resolution does not mention Casement, but the debate showed that he was chiefly concerned'. Spring-Rice immediately telegraphed a paraphrase of the resolution, together with a personal appeal from the influential Republican Senator Henry Cabot Lodge, and, when the Cabinet discussed Casement's fate for the last time on 2 August, these and other 'urgent appeals from authoritative and friendly quarters in the United States' were weighed in the balance against the demands for the death penalty.[25] However, there was 'never any real prospect' of ministers granting a reprieve, especially since the 'Black Diaries' left them 'secure in the knowledge that Casement's reputation could later be destroyed'.[26] Thus, after an hour and a half's discussion, the hard-line members of the Cabinet, fortified by the cogent memoranda of Blackwell and Troup, carried the day and Casement died on the scaffold early next morning.

Herbert Samuel, usually considered a humanitarian Home Secretary, perhaps typified the mood of many ministers when, immediately after the crucial Cabinet meeting, he confided to his wife that he had been suffering 'a time of some anxiety on account of the Casement case'. Samuel admitted that there had been 'much doubting in the Cabinet – among a few', but he himself considered that, as Casement was 'certainly not insane', there were no grounds for a reprieve. The execution, he anticipated, would create a 'somewhat artificial show' in America, but there were even more compelling factors in the opposite direction:

His reprieve would let loose a tornado of condemnation, would be bitterly resented by the great mass of the people of Great Britain and by the whole of the Army, and would profoundly and permanently shake public confidence in the sincerity and the courage of the Government. In the end, the Cabinet unanimously came to this conclusion. There are moments when a Home Secretary's Post is far from agreeable. Had Casement not been a man of atrocious moral character, the situation would have been more difficult.[27]

At the Foreign Office, Lord Hardinge, having observed the Cabinet's agonising, gave his own appraisal of the outcome to Valentine Chirol:

It has been a very difficult case for the Government to decide, as tremendous pressure has been put upon the Government by the President, by Springy, and all sorts of independent people in the United States, in favour of a reprieve, but the Government decided against it. . . . There is no doubt that he is a horrible man and deserves everything, while really a foreign country has no right to interfere in a purely internal matter of this kind. Still we must foresee great bitterness of feeling in America, followed by every sort of outrage and hostility on the part of the [U.S.] Government which will be encouraged by impending elections.[28]

The Cabinet's decision was undoubtedly eased by the fact that the Senate resolution had still not been transmitted *officially* when Casement died at the scaffold. The resolution had arrived at the White House on 31 July, but, inexplicably, only reached the American Embassy in London on 2 August. By this time, Ambassador Page had left on a visit to the United States, and the Chargé d'Affaires merely handed over the resolution at a routine interview with Grey on the following day.[29] This was embarrassing to the Wilson Administration, as many Irish-Americans insisted that the delay in transmission had cost Casement his life. However, in an official defence of the Administration, Frank Polk, State Department Counsellor, confirmed that, on the day before the execution, Spring-Rice had shown him a Foreign Office telegram which stated that, despite the Senate resolution, the Cabinet could not grant clemency.[30] Rowland Sperling considered that the furore over the resolution was part of the vote-catching struggle in the

Presidential election campaign and minuted complacently, 'I do not think we need pay any attention to this purely domestic controversy.' Even the unofficial reply which Grey tardily sent to Wilson's confidant and adviser, Colonel House, on 28 August, chose to interpret the resolution literally by justifying the punishments of 'Irish political prisoners' in general, but making no specific mention of Casement. The Foreign Secretary tetchily concluded with a coda more reminiscent of his Unionist colleagues: 'We are not favourably impressed by the action of the Senate in having passed a resolution about the Irish prisoners though they have taken no notice of outrages in Belgium and massacres of Armenians.'[31]

Following the execution Spring-Rice prudently ceased his jeremiads and reported that the execution had been 'taken very quietly by the mass of Americans', although German and Irish agitators were exploiting it underground 'for all it is worth'. In an obvious attempt to placate any ruffled feelings at the Foreign Office, he endorsed the Government's action by adding, 'On a review of the facts I cannot see that the Government could have done otherwise than . . . let justice take its course, especially after the less guilty people had suffered the extreme penalty.' During a War Committee meeting two days after the execution, a relieved Edwin Montagu, the Minister of Munitions, congratulated Lord Curzon on the accuracy of his forecasts that Americans would take the execution quietly, since, 'in a matter of this kind, I should have thought effects apprehended by some of us would be immediate'. At the Foreign Office, Lord Hardinge expressed satisfaction that Spring-Rice's 'gloomy predictions have so far been falsified', while Rowland Sperling commented stonily that 'it would have made no difference to the action of the Irish-Americans if Casement had been spared'.[32]

The low-key reaction in America was, of course, partly owing to the revelations concerning the 'Black Diaries'. In the days before the hanging, Spring-Rice and Gaunt had warned influential public figures that Casement's moral character rendered action in his defence unwise. It was not until 4 August that Grey, returning from sick leave, heard of the renewed campaign and quickly telegraphed to Spring-Rice,

> I think it much better that you should make no use whatever of Casement's diary. Page has, I believe, taken photographic copy with him supplied by Home Office and it is obviously advisable

that information with regard to it should come from him and not from British Embassy. In fact, I had given instruction that F.O. was not to make use of the diary.[33]

It is strange that matters could have proceeded thus far in direct contravention of Grey's wishes, but, apart from his prolonged absence through fatigue, he was fully occupied with the whole range of foreign affairs and had not followed Irish matters closely during the preceding months.[34] Coincidentally, as Grey's rebuke was on its way to Spring-Rice, the Ambassador was reporting with some satisfaction that Congressional agitation had been 'rather checked by the dread that some publication will be made exposing the private character of Casement'. A few days later, he added that members of the Roman Catholic hierarchy had been alerted against any public attempt to 'ascribe to Casement the character of a Christian martyr, whose life should be held up as a model to the faithful'. When friends of Casement in America argued that he had shown no signs of homosexuality and that the diary was a forgery, Spring-Rice was sufficiently worried to inquire whether the original could be authenticated. Geoffrey Butler's reaction was extremely positive. Citing Basil Thomson, the Metropolitan Police chief, for corroboration, Butler minuted, 'There can be no doubt . . . of the genuine nature of the diary.' Soon afterwards the Ambassador appears to have received the photographs of specimen pages, for he reported their 'discreet use' in warning dignitaries against 'praising as a hero and a Christian one who was neither'. He emphasised that, although the material had 'only been used by request and only in the strictest confidence', it had had 'an immediate effect'.[35]

Spring-Rice's role in the campaign was later criticised in verse by W. B. Yeats, to which Alfred Noyes responded that Spring-Rice must have believed the revelations to be bona fide since 'he was a chivalrous as well as an upright man and would never have lent himself to an abominable slander'. Ironically, the Ambassador initially intended the revelations not as justification for Casement's execution, but rather as grounds for reprieve and detention as a criminal lunatic. 'Publication of Casement's diary', he had cabled on 2 August, 'will only be looked upon as an act of revenge and would only be effective if his life is spared.'[36] Nevertheless, Spring-Rice's key role in the character assassination played a large part in quashing any chance of a reprieve and served to blacken Casement's image after his death.

In their defamatory activities, Spring-Rice and Guy Gaunt enlisted the aid of certain American newspapermen – thereby avoiding much of the scepticism and anti-British hostility which would have resulted if British officials had been solely responsible for the task. The President of the Associated Press, for example, acquainted many editors with the facts,[37] while Frederick Dixon, who was visiting London when the execution occurred, silenced many critics with an article cabled to his own newspaper, the Boston *Christian Science Monitor*:

> Roger Casement's champions are in danger of finding their cause a tolerably unsavoury one and their hero a member of a fraternity the world does not usually delight to honour. It is necessary to say this because the silence of the British Government has been taken advantage of in certain disreputable political quarters. . . . The fact is that Roger Casement is what is known as a degenerate. . . . The culprit has provided such evidence with an almost inhuman wealth of detail in his diary which fell into the hands of the police. The ghastly revelations of this diary can scarcely be exaggerated, and it is certain that the friends of the unhappy man had better not try the Government too far.

Dixon subsequently assured Robert Cecil that his article had 'shut up' the Casement agitation in Boston: 'Miles of protests, resolutions and editorials were in print for a grand scream and chorus of execration, but they disappeared in a night. They were simply afraid to go on after what we said lest we should say more.'[38]

Spring-Rice clearly believed the diary revelations to have been effective. This opinion was shared by Stephen Gaselee, a News Department official, who later recorded that 'the disclosures had the effect of completely alienating US sympathy from Sir Roger Casement', and also by Lord Newton, who subsequently recollected that, after Spring-Rice's use of the diary material, 'nothing more was heard of the pro-Casement agitation'. A less reassured note was sounded by Robert Vansittart (working in the Foreign Office Prisoners Department at this time), whose memoirs recalled American ill-feeling after Casement's death and admitted that the Irish-Americans had 'made an idol of such clay'.[39]

Quantification of contemporary reaction to Casement's death is almost impossible, since this was inevitably intertwined with emotions aroused by the other rebel executions. It is, moreover, difficult to distinguish between American attitudes towards Casement's morals and the response to the British Government's campaign to exploit them. The muted reaction to Casement's death does not, therefore, preclude bitterness against use of the diaries, while, conversely, such bitterness does not prove that the campaign failed in its aims.

It has often been argued that the statesmanlike solution to the Casement question would have been to reprieve him in the interests of improved Anglo-American relations. However, this ignores what many in the British Government considered to be a point of principle: namely, that external pressure should not fetter the application of justice within the United Kingdom. Criticism of the Cabinet appears to be more justified in its passive sanctioning of the smear campaign. Convinced as it was that Casement should hang, it felt justified in safeguarding war supplies by using any means to stifle criticism in America. Moreover, although Brian Inglis has attributed the major responsibility for the campaign to the Home Office, it is clear that the Foreign Office was equally involved. Men of integrity such as Spring-Rice, Hardinge and Cecil were so appalled at what they deemed to be Casement's moral shortcomings that they felt justified in displaying his true character to influential Americans. Even allowing for wartime pressures, this active participation was one of the more discreditable chapters in Foreign Office history.

6
The Home Rule Negotiations; the American Presidential Election (May–November 1916)

I

After the executions of the rebel leaders, Irish-American disillusionment with the Home Rule cause intensified. In mid May, Michael Ryan, President of the United Irish League in America, cabled to Redmond that the promise of Home Rule was widely considered a 'mockery', while Shane Leslie warned the Irish leader: 'Until you are in charge of a provisional Government, Irish-America will prove intractable to all except German agents.'[1] P. T. Barry, a leading Irish moderate in Chicago, stressed that, although the shootings were 'stupefying', they would be forgotten in time if the British Government could 'permanently settle the relations of England and Ireland' on Home Rule lines. These depressing tidings nevertheless provided useful levers in the campaign for a new settlement. Redmond cited Leslie's warnings when lobbying ministers, and John Dillon told C. P. Scott, editor of the *Manchester Guardian*, that he would press for the quick establishment of a Home Rule parliament while the British Government was still uneasy about American repercussions.[2]

Spring-Rice's personal belief in both the expediency and justice of immediate Home Rule made him very sensitive to the growing Irish-American anxiety. On 16 June he wrote to Grey that 'one of the commonest accusations against England is that Home Rule is always promised and never granted. To take it from the shelf and serve it on the table would no doubt have a considerable effect here.'[3] This and similar advice from other quarters in America impressed many members of the Cabinet, and it was partly for this reason that Asquith persuaded Lloyd George (then Minister of Munitions) to mediate in the search for a settlement. Grey, although 'traditionally the coolest towards Home Rule of the senior ministers',[4] firmly supported the new initiative at Cabinet meetings,[5] but many of his Foreign Office colleagues were sceptical. Although, officially, they treated Home Rule as a domestic question beyond their purview, several of them displayed a marked distaste for Irish Nationalism and privately criticised fresh proposals as a concession to treason. Hubert Montgomery, with his strong family attachment to the Ulster Unionist cause, wrote scathingly to his father that the idea of 'pushing through a lasting settlement' immediately after the rebellion was 'insane' and would enable the 'shot rebels to be held up as martyrs and heroes'. Lord Hardinge, whose chairmanship of the commission investigating the rebellion had convinced him of the Cabinet's folly in leaving Irish administration increasingly in Nationalist hands, complained that, under the Birrell régime, 'there was no government of Ireland at all'. However, Hardinge by no means confined his criticisms to the Liberals and dismissed the Unionists in the Coalition as having 'neither influence nor vigour'. During the pre-war Irish crisis, Hardinge had favoured Home Rule with Ulster exclusion as the only means of avoiding domestic strife. With the lessons learned from the Easter Rebellion, however, he questioned why, as Maxwell was 'ruling the country very well under modified martial law', Asquith had not left matters alone:

> There can be no doubt whatever that Ireland is in a very disturbed state, and to give Home Rule to the Nationalist provinces at this moment is simply to put a premium on rebellion. It would have been far better if the question had been postponed till the end of the war, and if Ireland had been governed firmly in the meantime. My conviction is that Ireland responds to firm government better than almost any other country.[6]

In the difficult task of finding a settlement, Lloyd George, who always made a point of cultivating good relations with the press, enjoyed the solid backing of all the Liberal newspapers. The *Manchester Guardian*, whose editor, C. P. Scott, was a strong Home Ruler, contended that a settlement would 'remove perhaps the chief obstacle to active friendship between this country and the United States', while the *Daily Chronicle* questioned the effect in America of another Home Rule failure during the 'critical months of Presidential electioneering'. On the Tory side, J. L. Garvin at the *Observer* continued to stress the American aspect of the unsolved Irish Question, while the *Daily Express* withdrew its former opposition and now argued that, in view of feeling in America and the Dominions, Irish self-government was an 'Imperial necessity'. Perhaps Lloyd George's most influential press ally was Lord Northcliffe, who, by secret negotiations and through his influential newspaper *The Times*, worked assiduously for a settlement. However, although the editor of *The Times*, Geoffrey Dawson, was now reluctantly advocating a settlement as necessary for the successful prosecution of the war, the newspaper's editorials studiously avoided any discussion of the American dimension – a void filled by Arthur Willert's despatches.[7]

Even with strong newspaper support, Lloyd George's search for a settlement demanded all his political guile, including some dubious negotiating stratagems. His approach was to see the principal factions separately and to cajole them into agreement by giving misleading assurances as to what others had conceded. The immediate difficulty was the dour resistance of the Ulster Unionists to any dismemberment of the Union and, in particular, to Ulster's inclusion in Home Rule. Lloyd George therefore reverted to the scheme of Home Rule for twenty-six counties, with the six north-eastern counties excluded – although aware that this would arouse Nationalist hostility. In an interview with Carson and the Irish Nationalist MP William O'Brien, Lloyd George sought to overcome their respective objections by urging, 'In six months the war will be lost . . . the Irish-American vote will go over to the German side. They will break our blockade and force an ignominious peace on us, unless something is done even provisionally to satisfy America.'[8] This argument failed to convince O'Brien, but secured the support of Carson, who on 6 June successfully urged these considerations at a meeting of the Ulster Unionist Council.[9] The Ulster leader subsequently claimed to have supported the proposals purely because of Lloyd George's representations as to 'the urgency of the matter for the prosecution of the war and the encouragement of America to join the Allies'.[10]

Despite the Council's agreement, the Lloyd George scheme still had many opponents throughout the six counties. Adam Duffin, subsequently a member of the Northern Ireland Senate, condemned the idea of using an unsuccessful rebellion as the occasion for a settlement to 'placate American sentiment, as represented by our ass of an Ambassador'. The implacable Hugh Montgomery complained bitterly to his son Hubert that Grey was mistaken in his use of the 'American argument' and that no amount of American pressure could justify 'the encouragement of Rebellion' by granting Home Rule. Hubert Montgomery, far from supporting the arguments of his ministerial chief, Grey, shared his father's views and had already advised him to seek out those who had been pressured by Lloyd George and warn them of 'the disastrous effect at home and abroad of what would really be a concession to the shades of the shot Sinn Feiners'.[11]

By late June, Hugh Montgomery concluded that the negotiations were merely a temporary sop to American opinion rather than a serious initiative. He suggested to his son that the object of the proposals was to buttress the Home Rulers in Ireland and America, 'so as to persuade our Allies and neutral nations that we are a United Kingdom for the purposes of the war'. Accordingly he completely reversed his previous attitude:

> The best thing to do now, I suppose, is to conduct the negotiations so as to produce the maximum of eye wash with the minimum of mischief and danger. . . . There is no reason why the negotiation should not be protracted till after the presidential election or the conclusion of peace.[12]

This cynical *volte-face* is one of the first examples of an inveterate opponent of Home Rule favouring a protraction of Irish negotiations merely to keep America passive. Although this was a new development, it later became commonplace during the Irish Convention of 1917–18. Moreover, these exchanges between father and son again demonstrate Hubert Montgomery's close attachment to the Ulster Unionist cause, which possibly accounts for his coolness towards Foreign Office schemes for placating Irish-Americans. They also show that, although most senior civil servants would claim to remain above party politics, many become actively involved in emotive domestic issues.

In addition to provoking individual Ulster critics, the 'American argument' also roused the ire of the *Belfast News Letter*. In a forthright editorial entitled 'President Wilson and Blackmail', the newspaper stressed the futility of sacrificing British interests in order to retain United States goodwill:

We are told again and again that the immediate establishment of Home Rule has become a diplomatic necessity. The Government is afraid that the influence of the Irish-American vote will be strong enough to compel President Wilson to adopt a hostile attitude during the war, and the object of the Lloyd George negotiations is to appease the Fenians of the United States rather than to effect a real settlement in Ireland. . . . But the fear of the Irish-American vote is groundless, for President Wilson will not alter his policy because of it. If it were otherwise, however, it would be the duty of the Government to make it clear that it will not tolerate foreign influence in the internal affairs of the United Kingdom.

In contrast to the outspoken *News Letter*, its rival, the Belfast *Northern Whig*, voiced no criticism of the American argument, probably because Lloyd George had privately written to its editor, R. J. Lynn, 'We cannot afford a hostile America at a time when victory is still in the mist.'[13]

Ironically, although Lloyd George had won grudging acquiescence from the Ulster Unionist leaders, he still had to contend with strong resistance among Nationalists. Sinn Feiners inevitably rejected Home Rule as being a denial of full independence, whilst a small group of Home Rulers, calling itself the 'All for Ireland League', stubbornly opposed any partition scheme. This group, with its power base in south-west Ireland, included the MPs William O'Brien and Tim Healy, and was supported by Ireland's most widely read newspaper, the *Irish Independent*. O'Brien was highly critical of the Government's sudden anxiety to satisfy America, and, at a public meeting in his political stronghold of Cork, he accused the Government of forcing partition on Ireland, 'not through any interest in Home Rule, but in the insane hope that it would strengthen England's electioneering interests in America and win back Irish-American sympathies estranged by the shootings'.[14]

While many Nationalists resented partition because it would thwart their vision of a united Ireland, the Southern Irish Unionists were hostile for totally opposite reasons. Determined to remain part of the Union, they totally rejected the American argument and felt betrayed by Ulster's submission. The Southern Unionist leader, Lord Midleton, subsequently recalled that both Lloyd George and Northcliffe had attempted to convince him that disaffection over

Ireland would be a dominant issue at the American Presidential election in the autumn and might strengthen the embargo movement. Northcliffe, exhibiting newspaper cuttings 'of the most menacing character', which indicated that the munitions question was 'blowing up to fever heat', stressed the increasing difficulty of supplying arms to Russia and asked, 'Are you going to antagonise America and hamstring Russia at such a moment? Why, you may be the cause of the whole war being lost.' Midleton, concerned that Home Rule would bring fresh anarchy to an already strife-torn Ireland, queried whether the American danger was not exaggerated. 'What the Southern Unionists were asked to do', he reflected, 'was to surrender all that was most dear to them on the off-chance that it might put America into a better humour.'[15]

In order to underline their enmity for Home Rule, the Southern Unionists mounted a campaign of public appeals and deputations to ministers. They stressed that partition would be 'regarded by Irish-American opinion with even greater contempt than in Ireland', and declared that the 'policy of endeavouring to placate American opinion, real or exaggerated', was 'unworthy of the British Empire and foredoomed to failure'. Indeed, Midleton considered that the principal historical significance of the Lloyd George scheme was that it marked 'the first occasion when Irish policy was shaped to meet American opinion'.[16]

Although the American argument had become a controversy in the Home Rule negotiations, it would be wrong to infer that it was merely a party political shuttlecock. Midleton readily conceded that both Lloyd George and Northcliffe were genuine in their fear of American repercussions, while Grey's sincerity was never questioned by his Cabinet colleagues. Moreover, with American pressure growing, Tory ministers became increasingly divided over Home Rule, as Roy Jenkins has indicated:

> The division in the Unionist Party was a strange one. The 'new men' who had made the running over Ulster in 1913 and 1914 – Bonar Law, Smith and Carson – were all moderates on this occasion. So was Balfour, whom Asquith had described at the time of the Buckingham Palace Conference as 'a real wrecker on the Irish issue'. It was the old Tories who made the trouble, men who had never cared much for the Orange cause, but who were wedded to Imperial supremacy throughout Ireland.[17]

Indeed, by early June it was apparent that the Southern Unionists were, as Lloyd George complained, 'moving Heaven and the other place to thwart settlement',[18] and directing their strongest entreaties towards the 'old Tories' within the Cabinet – Walter Long, Lord Lansdowne and Robert Cecil.

Perhaps the key figure in this group was Long, one of the few remaining landed gentry in the Cabinet and a minister 'whose influence with the Conservative back benches allowed him great weight in Irish policy'.[19] Moreover, he had strong ties with Southern Ireland and, within the Cabinet, shared with Balfour the distinction of having once been Chief Secretary for Ireland. Responding vigorously to Southern Unionist pressure, Long deluged Cabinet colleagues with protestations against the new scheme. Lloyd George, he alleged, had not been empowered to reach a settlement without reference to the Cabinet; but the principal target for his ire was the American argument, which Lloyd George had used with such telling effect on the Ulster Unionists but which Long regarded as entirely bogus. He first encountered the argument at a Cabinet Committee meeting on 1 June, when Lloyd George emphasised the need for a settlement to ensure continued munitions supplies from America. Long protested that several ministers, including Robert Cecil, held an opposing view, and he warned that such a reason, even if real, could never be given publicly. Asquith, in reply, assured him that only domestic reasons would be given.[20] As a counterweight to Lloyd George's use of Spring-Rice despatches, Long relied on the flimsy authority of Sydney Brooks, a *Daily Mail* correspondent in America, who had 'an extraordinary power of worming himself into the confidence of politicians . . . in the United States'. In early June Brooks informed Long that there was 'not the smallest chance' of an arms embargo, because attempts at such legislation were merely 'anglings for the German vote by timid Congressmen anxious for their seats' and because Americans were too self-interested to give up such a lucrative trade.[21]

When Long used Brooks's assurances to support his own view that Americans would 'never sacrifice their pockets to their politics', Lloyd George was so upset that he came near to resigning. He complained to John Dillon that Long's manoeuvres were 'treacherous' and later wrote that the Tory minister's letter typified 'the bitter partisan hostility . . . from extremists who would rather see no settlement at all than one which did not fully conform with their ideas'. Long vented this 'partisan hostility' in numerous Cabinet memoranda, complaining that Ulster Unionists had been duped by assurances that the Cabinet 'unanimously' supported the Lloyd George scheme 'on account of the American complications and in order to bring the war to a successful issue'. The American consideration, he contended, had 'never been submitted to the Cabinet or discussed by them' and he totally rejected any scheme to 'govern Ireland in accordance with the dictates of U.S.A. citizens'.[22]

Long's most detailed analysis of the American argument – indeed, the most comprehensive exposition of the diehard stance – is contained in a thirteen-page memorandum which was never circulated to his colleagues and has remained buried in his private papers. Long argued that potential crises with the United States were often exaggerated through misjudgement of the American character. This, he believed, was immature and easily distracted by transient controversies, which 'held the field for a time and then passed out of the public mind to give place to other matters'. Following this pattern, Ireland now occupied 'very little space' in American opinion, which, being 'wholly indifferent to the war, would be equally indifferent to the smaller question of Home Rule for Ireland'. However, it was in a handwritten postscript that he touched on the most delicate aspect of the American argument and one which, despite his strong feelings on the subject, he seems to have refrained from raising in Cabinet – namely, the principle of national sovereignty:

> Is the Empire to decide vital questions of principle merely in an endeavour to secure the benevolence of another power, or rather to avert unfriendly feelings among a section of their population? It is not on these lines that the Empire has been run in the past and for myself I strongly deplore the introduction of such an argument into the controversy.[23]

Long clearly not only regarded Lloyd George's predictions as ill-founded, but also his negotiating methods as unethical, even dishonest. The Home Rule crisis revealed the Tory minister in his most querulous but also most determined mood, and there is no doubt that his abhorrence of the Lloyd George scheme and its apparent deference to American opinion was genuinely heartfelt.

One of Long's closest Cabinet allies, Lord Lansdowne, was a former Tory Foreign Secretary and a great landowner in County

Kerry. His biographer, Lord Newton, considered that Lansdowne's experience of imperial and foreign affairs gave him a less insular view of the Irish Question and that this 'distinguished him from the majority of Irish Unionists, for whom the Home Rule issue was a narrowly domestic affair'. However, Lansdowne was no more favourable than Long towards framing domestic policy to placate America, and warned, 'I am afraid we shall disgust our friends without conciliating our enemies if, in consequence of the rebellion, we make a surrender which would not have been tolerated before the rebellion took place.' A few weeks later, Lansdowne showed his distrust of Lloyd George's tactics when he wrote to Long, 'I think as you do that we are being bluffed by the alleged American peril – as to not discussing or referring to it, Lloyd George cannot make his case without doing so, and it is being freely discussed at the moment.' In preparation for an important Cabinet discussion, Lansdowne produced a memorandum urging that the Irish Question be left until after the war and then considered in conjunction with the much larger problem of 'refashioning the fabric of the Empire'. Convinced that law and order would soon collapse under a Home Rule government and that partition would merely embitter Ireland, he queried whether the American difficulty was 'quite so formidable as we sometimes suppose'. He admitted that Grey's concern over American repercussions 'could not fail to produce an effect on our minds', but he noted that in an American Press Résumé American reactions were dismissed as 'merely momentary', with 'an element of impressionism and of the storm of the passing hour'.[24]

Robert Cecil, the third member of the diehard faction, was perhaps the most difficult of the Tory ministers to mollify during the Home Rule discussions. His Foreign Office experience had made him sceptical of the American argument, as he indicated to St Loe Strachey: 'Nine-tenths of what the Americans say is directed solely to the internal situation there, and may usually be disregarded as far as international relations are concerned.' Nevertheless, in a Cabinet memorandum on the Home Rule question he cautioned,

> I do not doubt that if we tried to set up again Castle Government and to govern Ireland on the old coercionist lines, we should have to face a considerable outcry in the United States which in certain circumstances might become formidable. If, however, Home Rule were in principle conceded I should not be afraid of Irish-American protests against deferring the grant of executive powers

till after we had disposed of our foreign enemies. Such a course would be in itself so reasonable that I do not believe that the general body of American opinion would disapprove it.[25]

Many Ulster Unionists were aggrieved to hear from Long and others that they had been misled by Lloyd George's overtures and that many Tories in the Cabinet supported neither his Home Rule proposals nor his views of the American threat. In the three Ulster counties which were to come under Home Rule government, there was a particular sense of betrayal. One County Cavan delegate to the Ulster Unionist Council, Travers Blackley, demanded reconsideration of the proposals, since he doubted whether his delegation would have given their consent without the alleged American munitions threat. Similarly, a visiting Southern Unionist J. Mackay Wilson found that many Donegal Unionists criticised their leaders for being 'completely hoodwinked by all the talk of the American bogey'. Carson's closest supporters reacted angrily to Long's implied criticism of their leader. Alexander McDowell, a Belfast solicitor, sternly advised Long that, as Carson had acquiesced to help the war effort in general, 'all this talk of America should be dropped'. Lady Carson privately accused the Cabinet, especially Long, of 'playing a low game, except Ll. G[eorge]', adding, 'I think the real truth is that a good many of them would have liked to have thrown over Edward and have failed.' Indeed, it is a tribute to the loyalty which Carson commanded that he retained the support of the great majority of Ulster Unionists even after securing their agreement to an unpopular scheme on controversial grounds.[26]

Many Unionists would have been swayed by the fact that the proposals were supported not only by Carson, but also by Balfour, Bonar Law and Austen Chamberlain. In the rift that was developing among Cabinet Tories, Balfour, as both a former Prime Minister and previous Irish Chief Secretary, was a key figure. He was, moreover, a 'consistent pro-American, . . . one of the few in the Coalition',[27] and the memorandum which he prepared for the Cabinet meeting of 27 June urged that the implementation of Home Rule was necessary to maintain American goodwill. However, the American argument was, for him, just one of many factors favouring a settlement. For example, he considered that after the war Unionists would be unable to obtain better terms than six-county exclusion, whilst, in any case, he now regarded Home Rule as a lesser evil than any arrangement demanded by Sinn Fein. 'It is better', he concluded, 'that pro-German Irish Republicans should be put down (or kept down) by pro-Ally Irish Home Rulers than by Castle Government.' At the Cabinet meeting itself, he reiterated these views in what Asquith judged to be 'the most effective pronouncement in this prolonged conclave'.[28]

Bonar Law also supported the Lloyd George proposals at the Cabinet meeting, but there is no record of his referring to the American dimension until a crucial Carlton Club meeting of the Unionist Party on 7 July:

> I should certainly be the last to say that we here in the United Kingdom should allow our policy to be dictated to us by America . . . [but] if this war goes on till the end of next year, we shall still be dependent, especially for the provisioning of the Russian Army, on the United States. I do not say anything we do would prevent us getting this, but it is a danger and one of the considerations which no sensible man would leave out of account.[29]

While Bonar Law was cautious in his use of this emotive argument – possibly because Long, Lansdowne and Cecil had already done much to discredit it – Austen Chamberlain was surprisingly assertive. In 1910 Chamberlain had severely castigated J. L. Garvin for suggesting 'kowtowing' to the Americans over Home Rule, while at the outbreak of war he berated Winston Churchill on similar grounds. However, in the tense situation following the Rising, he feared that withdrawal now from the Lloyd George scheme would be dangerous and therefore tempered his intransigence. He warned his Carlton Club audience that, although Lloyd George exaggerated the American danger for tactical reasons, there were more subtle complications arising from American displeasure:

> The danger is this, that with the Presidential election coming on, you will have both the American parties vying with one another to secure the Irish vote, and at every turn of diplomacy and at every turn of your financial progress the good will of America will be wanted. . . . You who are urging that we should buy more and more munitions from America if we cannot make them for ourselves must appreciate that that policy is not consistent with needlessly taking steps which antagonise American political

feeling and force the Government of America to be an unfriendly neutral.[30]

It was still difficult for a Tory minister to espouse the American argument, about which most Tories remained extremely sceptical. Aware of this, Bonar Law, whose 'refusal to swim with the main current of Conservative thought' was leaving him in a 'dangerously isolated position', adjourned the meeting without putting the proposals to a vote. Soon afterwards, Lord Lansdowne quashed any remaining chance of a settlement by declaring in the Lords that partition would be 'permanent and enduring', thus provoking Redmond to announce that all hope of a settlement was irretrievably lost and a continuance of negotiations pointless.[31] Contemporary American opinion was almost unanimous in its criticism of the breakdown. H. J. Whigham, for example, informed Gilbert Parker that 'a most unfortunate impression' had been created, while Colonel House attributed the failure to Tory obstructionism and warned President Wilson that 'the Conservative or reactionary forces in England are getting a firm grip on the Cabinet and Asquith is not strong enough to withstand them'. In Britain, accusations of ill faith were freely voiced on all sides. St Loe Strachey's *Spectator* alleged that Nationalist complaints of Government perfidy were 'only dust thrown in the eyes of the British public and possible American sympathisers'. William O'Brien, on the other hand, claimed that it was Lloyd George who had been guilty of deception by seeking to 'keep America in play by exhibiting before her eyes the spectacle of a great Home Rule settlement . . . until the American elections were over'.[32]

The American argument had thus developed into a controversial issue among – and even within – the different parties on whom it was urged. At the Foreign Office, Grey's views were at odds with those of senior colleagues such as Montgomery, Hardinge and Cecil. Disagreement was also apparent within the Conservative Party, but it was most evident in the serious rift which occurred in the Cabinet and which, at one point, almost caused the break-up of the Asquith Coalition. Moreover, it is arguable that, with the collapse of the negotiations, the ever-dwindling reservoir of Irish-American goodwill was breached beyond repair.

II

Whatever the opinions of Foreign Office officials on the Home Rule issue, it was largely beyond their brief to offer advice on what was seen as purely a domestic question. However, their opinion of Irish matters again became relevant when an Irish relief fund was established in New York to alleviate suffering caused by the Rising. Assurances from the organisers that the collections were for genuine relief purposes, and not for the purchase of arms, induced eminent Irish-Americans such as Cardinals Gibbons and Farley to join extremists on the fund's committee. As a result, well-attended meetings throughout the United States duly yielded hundreds of thousands of dollars. Spring-Rice recommended a show of Foreign Office sympathy towards the distribution of the Fund, since this would prevent it from becoming a focal point for further anti-British agitation. Almost inevitably, Rowland Sperling counselled against any British involvement and voiced suspicions of the organisers' motives:

> It is hard to see how such a fund could fail to be an encouragement to revolutionary principles. It is also probable that much of the money collected will be lost in transmission and our enemies in the U.S. would welcome any chance of saying that it had been diverted by H.M.G.[33]

Sperling's departmental head, Sir Maurice de Bunsen, despite his private leaning towards the Conservative Party,[34] was always more conciliatory on Irish-American issues. While agreeing that the Government should avoid involvement, he suggested that distribution should be facilitated or 'at least no obstacle placed in the way'. However, Lord Newton, the News Department head, shared Sperling's view and considered that any further attempts to accommodate Irish-American activists would merely expose the Government to contempt.[35]

Official doubts increased when the Relief Fund Committee selected four Irish-American activists as distributing agents. Although the Foreign Office was assured that the purpose of the mission was purely philanthropic, the first two delegates, John D. Murphy and John Gill, were kept under surveillance on arrival in Ireland at the end of July. The two remaining delegates, who were due to arrive a week later, posed even greater problems. Little was known initially of Thomas H. Kelly, the fund treasurer, but his travelling-partner, Joseph Smith, editor of several Boston newspapers, was reported to be violently anti-British and possibly a German agent. Nevertheless, although fearing misuse of the funds for political purposes, Spring-Rice counselled that it would be diplomatically expedient to allow Smith and Kelly to land unimpeded and then keep watch on them during their stay. Lord Hardinge accepted that it would be 'impolitic' to prevent their landing, but minuted sceptically that 'the bitterly hostile attitude of Irishmen in America and the suspicion surrounding J. W. Smith preclude the possibility of regarding these persons as messengers of peace'. Such a possibility became even more remote when, a few days later, the British Consul in New York reported to Grey that Kelly also had become 'a violent opponent of anything British' after being 'greatly disturbed' by the rebel executions in Dublin.[36]

By this time Foreign Office opinions had become purely academic, for, on Maxwell's advice, the Home Secretary had barred both agents from entering Ireland – Smith because 'there was good reason for believing that he was engaged in business hostile to this country' and Kelly because his close association with Smith tarred him with the same brush. Dissatisfied with this explanation, the Nationalist MP Alfred Byrne complained, 'Why do the British Government stop American citizens doing what the British Government should do – compensate the victims of rebellion in Ireland?' In the event, the Government's decision was amply justified when Military Intelligence confirmed that the true objective of both men had been to discover whether Ireland was ready for another rising.[37]

Despite some ruffled American feelings at the exclusions, culminating in a Congressional resolution calling for the suspension of diplomatic relations over the alleged insult, British official attitudes towards relief collections hardened considerably by mid September. A report from Commander Harrell of the Dublin Metropolitan Police held that Smith and Kelly were illustrative of 'doubtful agents' using ostensibly charitable movements as 'a cloak for other work'. In laying this report before the Cabinet, H. E. Duke, who had replaced Birrell as Chief Secretary, attributed much of the unrest in Ireland to the 'incitement and pecuniary aid of revolutionary Irish-American organisations'. This and other reports underlined the need for closer surveillance of American visitors, 'especially those connected with Relief Funds'. Such caution was reinforced when the Foreign Office received disquieting information that Gill, one of the first two relief-fund distributors, had delivered violently anti-British speeches on his return to America and had predicted another rising in Ireland. This led Basil Thomson, Metropolitan Police Chief, to advise that no more fund distributors be allowed into Ireland, but Maurice de Bunsen continued to show exceptional concern for American opinion and minuted, 'I doubt if such absolute exclusion would be politic, even though they make disagreeable speeches on their return to the U.S.'[38]

Although the Rising itself caused distress in Dublin, the major factor boosting relief collections in America was the widespread belief that the insurrection had been caused primarily by bad social conditions. This idea was fostered by Home Rulers such as Tim Healy and by separatists such as Eoin MacNeill (titular head of the Irish Volunteers) in order to stigmatise the economic condition of Ireland under the Union. Even Asquith, Birrell and Wimborne, the Lord Lieutenant, conceded that there was some truth in the allegations – Wimborne asserting that urban slums had created the 'labour dissatisfaction which was, and is, to a great extent responsible for the Sinn Fein animus'.[39]

Ironically, while many Liberals admitted that there was some truth in the distress allegations, Foreign Office and Wellington House officials turned to propaganda to demonstrate that Ireland had, in fact, prospered under the Union. The News Department asked the Irish Office for facts to disprove that economic factors caused the rebellion, while Gilbert Parker was at pains to stress to his American correspondents that Ireland was 'a country where more has been done for the welfare of the people during the last twenty years than in England itself'. Spring-Rice, although a Home Ruler in sympathy, suggested that the Government should publish the benefits obtained in Ireland under the Union – the increased wealth per capita, the industries set up and supported by the Government, and the benign operation of the Irish land laws.[40]

By September, the News Department was keen that something more constructive should be done to discourage the rumours of Irish distress, for, as Geoffrey Butler noted, 'Every report that we get from the United States points to Ireland as the chief cause of friction between the two countries.' However, the previous policy of sending chaperoned American newspaper correspondents to Ireland was now deemed inadvisable. There was, as Butler remarked, always the possibility that such methods 'would be resented by the American press as an official attempt to use them' and that, with the Irish situation deteriorating, a roving reporter 'would take up a good many things we would rather not have known'. Consideration was given, instead, to the idea of an interview with a leading Irish public figure. Hubert Montgomery asked Dublin Castle to suggest a suitable person, and at the same time made a similar request to his father, to whom he complained of the 'rubbish being talked in America now about distress in Ireland. . . . My impression is that the farmers are having the time of their lives and there is no distress in any quarter.' Although unable to help, his father echoed the common Foreign Office view that Ireland was 'never so well off' and that the relief funds were probably 'a subterfuge for collecting money for some form of rebellion'. The correspondence with Dublin Castle was more fruitful and resulted in the Lord Mayor giving an interview to the Associated Press, in which he asserted that Dublin, far from suffering distress, was more prosperous than it had been a year earlier. It is noteworthy that, from the time of Montgomery's request to Dublin Castle, the interview took almost six weeks to materialise, and, at a time when the Irish situation was extremely volatile, such delays robbed propaganda schemes of their full value.[41]

As a complement to its publicity on Irish prosperity, the Foreign Office sought to stifle further talk of suffering. Thus, when an Englishwoman, Lady Kingston, planned an Irish relief tour to America, Butler and Montgomery dismissed it as unnecessary since, in their view, no distress existed, while Lord Newton minuted haughtily that 'the idea of cadging in America . . . seems very undignified, to say the least'. The News Department observed tetchily to Gilbert Parker that 'begging in America for Ireland only confirms Americans of a certain type in their belief that Ireland is a suffering martyr past the help of England. It tends to lower our prestige.' Parker, who fully shared these views, had, in fact, already vetoed the mission before receiving the Foreign Office recommendation.[42]

Campaigns for Irish relief presented awkward problems for the Foreign Office. If allowed, they encouraged the American belief in Irish deprivation, while the fund distributors who visited Ireland posed a security threat; if forbidden, they furnished fresh ammunition to anti-British propagandists. However, those Foreign

Office officials who asserted that a co-operative attitude would merely incur Irish-American contempt were more concerned with the principle of domestic sovereignty than with improving Anglo-American relations.

III

The principal danger envisaged in the American argument was the threat of repercussions during the Presidential election campaign. One of the most popular vote-catching stances of American politicians was 'twisting the lion's tail' and the Irish troubles provided ideal fodder for practising this traditional stratagem. Sensing this, Spring-Rice warned in May that 'the German–Irish alliance will direct its energies to forcing both candidates to adopt an anti-British attitude during the term of the election'.[43] The Irish cause was expected to receive greater prominence from the Democrats, for whom Irish-Americans traditionally voted. However, shortly before the Democrat Convention in June, Wilson launched his Americanism campaign against 'hyphenate' or disloyal citizens, as a result of which Irish-independence resolutions received short shrift.[44] Some British diplomats tended to overestimate the significance of these developments. Joyce Broderick in Washington concluded that the Irish-American lobby was 'no longer a compelling consideration for aspiring politicians', while Eustace Percy at the Foreign Office forecast,

> The Irish vote in the U.S., though it may often avail to defeat individual measures friendly to England, . . . will never again be strong enough to modify the general trend of U.S. policy. What we have to reckon with is the American vote, not the Irish vote or the German vote.[45]

Although little effort was made to introduce the Irish Question into the Republican Convention, the party's campaign of 'honest neutrality' appealed to many Anglophobes as being preferable to Wilson's aggressive 'Americanism'. Indeed, it was partly to attract the 'hyphenate' vote that Charles Evan Hughes, a Supreme Court judge and former Governor of New York State, was chosen as Republican candidate in preference to the anti-hyphenate Theodore Roosevelt. However, although Hughes courted the German–Irish vote whenever possible, he was not pro-German and was at pains to deprecate the use of American soil 'for alien intrigues, for conspiracies and the fomenting of disorders in the interests of any foreign nation'.[46]

The principal targets for Irish-American vituperation were the British blacklist and blockade (which affected American trade with Europe), while their main objective was a retaliatory embargo on American war supplies to Britain. Following a Convention attended by leading activists, the American Embargo Conference resolved to support whichever Presidential candidate would pledge the stronger anti-British measures.[47] To this end, Jeremiah O'Leary led a delegation in October 1916 to ascertain Hughes's attitude towards alleged British violation of American rights, including the 'unwarranted and inhuman interference' with relief funds for Ireland.[48] O'Leary also telegraphed Woodrow Wilson, attacking him for surrendering American rights to British pressure and threatening him with the loss of many German–Irish votes. In a tactical masterstroke which 'struck like a thunderbolt over the country' and which, according to Colonel House, was the turning-point in the campaign, Wilson replied, 'I would feel deeply mortified to have you or anybody like you to vote for me. Since you have access to many disloyal Americans and I have not, I will ask you to convey this message to them.' The *New York Times* praised the President's 'stirring and emphatic telegram' as being 'in striking contrast to the secrecy of the negotiations in the interests of Mr Hughes candidacy'.[49]

The Foreign Office still believed that embargo legislation was unlikely to materialise. An official in the American Department, Lord Colum Crichton Stuart, considered that, although both candidates would woo the hyphenates, the new President would 'show his independence when he need no longer fear their displeasure. On the whole, that independence should be favourable to us.' Lord Hardinge, who regarded Spring-Rice's warnings on the embargo as 'somewhat extravagant and unduly pessimistic', wrote soothingly to the Ambassador,

> I can well imagine how irritated you must be at the attempts at tail-twistings that are now being practised in the United States, presumably chiefly as an electioneering move. Here we are quite calm, and recognise how little they count. We are confident that the Americans are making too much out of the war and do not

wish anything to stop the supply of munitions, etc, and that they go no further than big words and strong notes.

The Ambassador, for his part, had been encouraged by what he perceived as the inherent frailty of the German–Irish alliance. 'When brought into close contact with the German,' he explained, 'the Irishman is rather apt to find him an aggravated form of Englishman. There is wanting the element of personal sympathy. . . . As is often said here, beer and whisky do not mix well.' Moreover, the Irish were well aware that co-operation with Germans might call into question their loyalty to America and so damage their political influence. They would, concluded Spring-Rice, combine 'only so far as their common cooperation is based upon hatred of England'.[50]

In addition to the embargo campaign, Irish-Americans participated in the growing peace movement in the hope that either the United States (as possible mediator) or Germany might embrace the cause of Irish independence at a future peace conference. 'Ireland is now one of the belligerents', claimed the *Gaelic American*. 'She has title to recognition as one of the small nationalities and sealed the claim with her blood.'[51] Irish hopes that American pressure would advance this claim rose when, on 27 May, President Wilson made the first of his speeches enunciating the right of every people 'to choose the sovereignty under which they shall live' and of small nations 'to enjoy the same respect for their sovereignty that great and powerful nations expect and insist on'.[52] This concept of 'self-determination' was part of Wilson's attempt to establish himself as the figurehead of international liberalism and the obvious candidate for the role of peace mediator.[53] In addition to idealistic considerations, Wilson was also aware that the speech would attract support from German and Irish voters. 'The Irish vote', wrote Spring-Rice, 'is at present directed to the humiliation of England and, as it is supposed that England does not desire peace under present conditions, the Irish vote is necessarily in favour of mediation.' The Ambassador warned that the Allies should view American mediation with suspicion since it might embrace Irish independence.[54] In fact, Wilson never expressed more than 'keen interest' and 'sympathy' over Ireland,[55] and, as the head of a neutral power, it would have been difficult for him to guarantee Ireland a voice at any peace conference.

The Foreign Office favoured a policy of reticence in most spheres of Anglo-American relations, for it was anxious not to antagonise the Wilson Administration during the pre-election period. Indeed, Spring-Rice advised that, 'with the Irish in a particularly pugnacious mood and both sides hungering for the German vote', it was essential to 'lie as quiet as possible and occupy as little attention as we can'. Such prudence did not, however, tally with the more vigorous ideas of Lloyd George, who by now was Secretary of State for War. On 28 September he took matters into his own hands and, in an interview with an American reporter, gave a blunt warning to both President Wilson and the American people that England would consider any American peace move as unwarranted interference and would continue fighting until a 'knockout' was achieved. Although the interview was well received by many officials, notably Hardinge, it ran contrary to Grey's penchant for restraint and was made without consulting him. Accordingly, on the following day the Foreign Secretary wrote to Lloyd George, complaining that the interview would probably draw Wilson closer to the Germans and induce him to yield to anti-British pressure in Congress. Until the Allies were sure of victory, 'the door should be kept open for Wilson's mediation. It is now closed forever so far as we are concerned.' In his reply, Lloyd George cited Spring-Rice's predictions of an imminent peace move and continued,

> If the hands of Wilson had been forced – and there is every indication that the Germans and Irish could do so – then we should be in a very tight place. Any cessation of hostilities now would be a disaster; and although we could always refuse or put up impossible terms, it is much better that we should not be placed in that predicament. You could not have warned off the United States without doing it formally. I could commit a serviceable indiscretion; you could not. It would ruin you: I am inoculated.

Two weeks later, the Cabinet, at Grey's insistence, agreed that no more interviews should be given to the American press until after the election, and Grey himself instructed the Foreign Office, 'We must adhere to a policy of reserve till the Presidential election is over.'[56]

Lloyd George's reply to Grey clearly indicated his belief that Wilson's peace feelers were prompted by the knowledge that many vital German–Irish votes were still uncommitted. The newspaper, the *Irish World*, claimed that, if Wilson offended Irish susceptibilities, he would 'not be able to carry a single state outside the Solid South'. Although this was an exaggeration, it is clear that, if Irish-Americans had rejected Wilson's policies, his electoral prospects would have been seriously jeopardised. However, extremist calls to vote Republican fell largely on deaf ears, for, as Joyce Broderick reported, 'the great mass of Irish voters declined to accept guidance in domestic politics from the extremists, either because they mistrusted their prophecies or – what is much more likely – because loyalty to the Democrat Party gave them a fairer prospect of personal profit'. This has been confirmed by subsequent studies of election returns, which show that Irish-Americans voted strongly for Wilson on domestic issues alone and had little regard for foreign affairs.[57]

Perhaps the most powerful factor in Wilson's favour was his policy of non-involvement in the European war, a policy popularised by the slogan 'He kept us out of the war.'[58] This won votes from all sections of society and it was therefore ironic that within five months of re-election he was to take his country into war against the Central Powers. However, throughout the winter of 1916–17 Wilson was, in fact, primarily concerned with the British blockade and blacklist and was still anxious to avoid American involvement in the war.[59] Thus, despite Foreign Office confidence that the most serious dangers would subside after the election, diplomatic tension persisted, with Irish-Americans continuing to play a key role in fomenting friction. Spring-Rice and his Embassy colleagues tried to impress upon a largely unheeding Foreign Office that, although the Irish-Americans had not followed the extremists' lead during the election, they would still be influenced on purely Irish matters by organisations such as the Friends of Irish Freedom.[60] As the Foreign Office was soon to discover, Irish-Americans remained a potent force and had yet to exert their maximum impact on Anglo-American relations.

7
Lloyd George Takes the Helm (December 1916– April 1917)

I

December 1916 was a watershed for the Irish Question as a problem in Anglo-American relations. The American Presidential election was over, leaving the re-elected Wilson Administration free to pursue its foreign policy without electioneering constraints. In England, dissatisfaction with the conduct of the war had contributed to the fall of Asquith's Coalition Government and its replacement by a new régime under Lloyd George, with Arthur Balfour as Foreign Secretary. The change of government led Irish Nationalists to hope that Lloyd George would again attempt to reach an Irish settlement, as he had done earlier that year. Moreover, commentators such as J. L. Garvin of the *Observer* believed that American opinion would accelerate such an initiative:

> In the United States Irish feeling since the Sinn Fein troubles and the fiasco of the subsequent attempt at settlement has poured a good deal of cold water into the wine of pro-Ally sentiment . . . we shall never again have good relations between the two great Powers of the English-speaking world, the Empire and the Republic, until we make a more respectable hand at our Irish affair, which we have bungled again by faults on all sides.

Spring-Rice similarly warned that, with Irish pressure renewing the threat in Congress of a retaliatory embargo, only a Home Rule settlement would offer the prospect of a permanent rapprochement with the United States. However, such advice once again elicited little response at the Foreign Office. Encouraged by the failure of the German–Irish vote to influence the American elections, Rowland

Sperling had already deduced, 'The morals for us are that we need not take German propaganda in the U.S. too seriously, that peace is the first object of the U.S. and prosperity the second.'[1]

A few days after taking office, Lloyd George asked his highly respected Cabinet Secretary, Maurice Hankey, to compile a memorandum embodying his views on the principal aims of war strategy. The memorandum, which was circulated to all members of the newly created War Cabinet, included a plea for 'an entirely conciliatory policy towards Ireland'. Like Lloyd George, Hankey viewed an Irish settlement not from a domestic angle, but as 'one of the greatest services that could be rendered to the cause of the Allies'. It would release British troops tied down in Ireland, stimulate Irish recruiting, and improve relations with the United States, 'where the whole financial situation would probably be most favourably influenced, and the insidious propaganda of the enemy countered'. This, he considered, was particularly important 'owing to the power which our dependence on America for supplies places in the hands of President Wilson'. Lloyd George strongly endorsed these views, but, as he informed Redmond on the following day, he was not yet ready to risk the possible consequences of a new Home Rule initiative.[2]

Meanwhile, the growing tide of Irish-American propaganda was becoming increasingly concerned with Ireland's claim for representation as a 'small nation' at any future peace conference. To the chagrin of the Friends of Irish Freedom, the peace move which Germany made on 12 December totally ignored the subject of Ireland. George Viereck, the German-American propagandist, tried vainly to repair the damage by asserting that the German declaration issued at Roger Casement's behest in November 1914 amply demonstrated Germany's good faith: 'Germany stands on record as the foremost champion of Irish independence. No further declaration of the Imperial Government is needed.'[3]

On 18 December, Wilson made his own, independent offer of mediation. This produced a mixed response in British circles. Spring-Rice, apprehensive that rejection of Wilson's offer would spark a violent agitation among the 'fanatically hostile' Irish-Americans, warned the new Foreign Secretary, Balfour, that the Administration was under pressure to 'put an end to the war before the war comes over to this side of the Atlantic'. By contrast, Eyre Crowe at the Foreign Office was anxious to have Wilson excluded from any mediation. As an unyielding critic of American politics,

Crowe believed that there would be three unpalatable German demands which would 'enlist Wilson's most determined support' – freedom of the seas, international arbitration of disputes, and Irish independence – and that their inevitable rejection would be used to blame Britain for continuing the war. In the spirit of Lloyd George's 'knockout blow', Crowe stressed that it was 'desirable to say very clearly that we cannot allow the intervention of anybody until we have mastered and overthrown our enemies'. However, Robert Cecil, concerned that such bluntness would disgruntle the radicals in Entente countries and 'offend Wilson and a good part of neutral opinion', saw little chance of American mediation leading to demands for Irish independence or the other ills which Crowe foresaw.[4]

The Cabinet was nevertheless concerned that continuing unrest in Ireland might prejudice any future mediators to Britain's detriment. Consequently, in order to 'foster the impression in the U.S., as well as at home, that the new Government was approaching the Irish Question in a generous but not too timorous spirit', the War Cabinet decided to release most of the Irish political prisoners who had been detained without trial since the Easter Rising. This gesture followed months of persistent campaigning by the Home Rule Party, during which Redmond had warned the Prime Minister that the plight of the prisoners would have a disastrous effect on American opinion. This was the first clear example of concern about the peace settlement influencing the Government's Irish policy, although, during the previous summer's Home Rule negotiations, the Redmondite T. P. Gill had alleged that they were designed to 'save England (after the Dublin executions) from appearing in an International Congress as an oppressor of small nations'.[5]

To atone for the alleged 'desertion of Ireland', the German Government issued a press communiqué a month later, pointedly contrasting the British Government's moralistic statements on the rights of 'small nations' with her harsh treatment of Ireland. The Foreign Office reply, issued to Reuters and Associated Press as 'coming from a well-informed source', refuted this criticism and stressed that Ireland's contribution to the war effort showed her to be 'united with the rest of the Empire in repelling German aggression'. The *Belfast News Letter*, assertive as ever, claimed that England had 'nothing to fear from the fullest examination of Ireland' and totally rejected comparisons with repressed nationalities within the Central Powers: 'It is absurd to talk of the oppression of the Irish people as if they were the Poles of Prussia, the Slavs of Austria, or the Christian subjects of the Sultan.' However, the vehemence of such retorts suggests that the Germans had touched on a tender nerve concerning the possible repercussions of the Irish impasse on a post-war resettlement of Europe.[6]

A further opportunity for Germany to capitalise on Britain's Achilles heel arose when Wilson made his 'Peace without Victory' speech in January 1917. The President's pronouncement in favour of self-government for small nationalities was instantly supported by the German Ambassador in Washington, von Bernstorff, who, with shrewd opportunism, proclaimed, 'Germany would be sincerely glad if, in recognition of this principle, countries like Ireland and India, which do not enjoy the benefits of political independence, should now obtain their freedom.'[7] Germany thereby paid lip service to the cause of Irish independence, but the manner in which this was tardily offered suggests that, as in 1914, Germany was merely using Ireland as a pawn in the propaganda struggle.

In addition to its belated propaganda in favour of Irish independence, the German Government persisted with its covert aid to anti-British conspiracies in America. Although the United States Administration took tentative steps after the presidential election to prosecute German agents – causing Rowland Sperling to comment grudgingly that it was 'being kicked into action at last' – the process was slow and there was a marked reluctance to prosecute Irish agitators. Consequently, rumours of continuing seditious activity convinced Spring-Rice that 'the forefront of the German agitation against the Allies will be directed against Ireland and our policy there'. His fears took on firmer substance when, on protesting to the State Department about a San Francisco fund 'to help arm the Irish Volunteers for revolt', he was assured by Robert Lansing that there was no evidence of a military enterprise on United States soil and, therefore, no violation of American criminal law. In the Foreign Office American Department, Lord Colum Crichton Stuart condemned this as an 'unwillingness on the part of the U.S. Government to act, as well as a lamentable omission from U.S. law', but controlled his impatience sufficiently to recommend,

> I should think it would be better to remain content with what the U.S. Government are doing against the Indians and Germans, and not to worry them over the Irish question. Even if they went

to war and helped the Allies they would in other ways be strongly averse to arousing strong feeling amongst the Irish.[8]

It is ironic that, while Irish-American extremists assailed Wilson for his subservience to British interests, British officials viewed his Administration's tolerance of Irish intrigue as negligent. In the event, Crichton Stuart's conclusion was proved wrong, for a few months later, after America had entered the war, the United States Government launched a strong campaign against the Irish extremists. In the winter of 1916–17, however, such a development was not foreseen and Sinn Fein agitators took advantage of their comparative immunity to descend upon the United States in greater numbers than ever before. Perhaps the most successful, and certainly the most notorious, was Hannah Sheehy Skeffington, wife of an Irish pacifist whose brutal murder during the Easter Rising aroused indignation in the United States. In December 1916, Mrs Skeffington defied attempts to keep her in Ireland by escaping to America. Once there, she drew large crowds with her bitter denunciation of British brutality in Ireland and her fervent reiteration of Ireland's right to a place at the post-war peace conference. 'When the day of settlement comes', she declared in New York, 'and the claims of other suppressed nations are considered, the voice of Ireland will not be stifled.'[9] This self-styled 'big offensive for Ireland's rights as a small nation' extended beyond Congressmen and party leaders to a private interview with President Wilson in January 1917,[10] eventually provoking Rowland Sperling to a melancholy reflection on the whole mismanaged affair: 'We could hardly have done worse than decide to keep her in Ireland and then let her escape.'[11]

In their widely publicised lecture tours, Mrs Skeffington and other Sinn Feiners stimulated American sympathy for what they depicted as a depressed Ireland, moving even the moderate Cardinal Farley to deplore Ireland's 'unspeakable want and distress'. This sympathy found expression in numerous Irish relief committees, whose motives were often as much political and anti-British as philanthropic. Indeed, the Chicago committee on which Farley sat issued an appeal which Rowland Sperling criticised as 'most offensive', and which led Crichton Stuart to regret 'the impression which must be made on unbiased American minds by such declarations'. Acerbic relief appeals thus supplemented the barrage of anti-British attacks being mounted by such organisations as the Boston Friends of Irish Freedom (FOIF), whose penchant for dramatic embroidery led them to ask President Wilson to protest against the confiscation of Irish staple foods and 'the wholesale deportation of Irish men and women' to work without wages in English munition factories. In order to rebut these charges, Hubert Montgomery arranged that the Dublin correspondent of the Associated Press should write an article based on information from H. E. Duke, the Chief Secretary.[12]

Although the Associated Press correspondent proved reliable, the News Department was not always so fortunate in its choice of visiting newsmen to Ireland. During the same winter, Montgomery induced Dublin Castle to chaperon three American journalists of repute: Robert Mountsier of the New York Adams Newspaper Service; Arthur Gleason of the New York *Tribune*; and Norman Hapgood, a noted magazine writer. Since all three were viewed as pro-Ally, Montgomery assumed that their reaction to the Irish situation would prove favourable. In the event, the News Department was soon alarmed to find Mountsier and Gleason in communication with extremists and matters worsened when Gleason's first article was rejected as too outspoken. The correspondent, showing little appreciation of Foreign Office sensitivity, reproached Geoffrey Butler that to ignore the 'present-day Irish aspiration for colonial self-government' would not help him to 'interpret England sympathetically in American terms'.[13] Montgomery knew beforehand that the third journalist, Hapgood, also held 'advanced' views on Irish independence, and was concerned that the American probably had 'introductions in a good many undesirable quarters'. He therefore urged Dublin Castle to take 'special pains' to put the visitor 'into touch with some steadying opinion' and to 'keep him from falling into bad hands'. When one of Hapgood's articles suffered a similar rejection to that of Gleason, the journalist complained to Butler with injured innocence, 'I believed I could improve the very bad Irish situation in America if I were allowed to present facts vividly, showing the discontent in a way that would make the British mismanagement of the affair seem more natural.' As a compromise, the News Department tried to ease the transmission of Hapgood's more acceptable articles by circumventing the usual censorship channels, but this drew a stiff reminder from the Censor that all articles should be sanctioned before publication.[14]

Meanwhile, the Foreign Office continued its practice of sending lecturers on the British war effort to tour America. Such emissaries frequently found themselves confronted by the Irish issue, but most of them studiously avoided the subject whenever possible. For example, Ian Hay Beith, whose work in America was universally praised,[15] later stated that he gave about 800 lectures and 'never once entered upon political ground – or so much as mentioned the name of Ireland'.[16] On the other hand, Alfred Noyes, the poet, who had served briefly in the News Department but was now proving a valuable publicist in America, actively embraced the question. Although, in his memoirs, Noyes asserted that he scarcely mentioned Ireland during his tour, his progress reports at the time suggest otherwise:

> We want much more indirect propaganda on Ireland – something more about what England has done for Ireland in recent years. Nobody knows here, for example, that Irish people are drawing old age pensions. Even our best wishers look sheepish when the subject of Ireland is raised. . . . We are 'up against' Ireland first, last and all the time, and it may be the deciding factor between peace and war. There is only one motto, on both sides of the water, if we are to swing the country into the war and that is *look out for Ireland*.[17]

Despite the complementary activities of British lecturers in the United States and American journalists in Ireland, the Foreign Office was finding it increasingly difficult to counteract the enormous increase in scurrilous Irish-American propaganda. Henry Duke therefore asked Charles Masterman at Wellington House to arrange for regular publication in America of accurate reports on Irish conditions, while H. M. Whitten, one of Duke's staff, stressed that defamatory Irish-American statements should be referred to the Irish Office as quickly as possible, since 'contradictions must be speedy in order to be effective'. In reply, Masterman, one of the few Home Rule sympathisers within the British propaganda organisation, pointed out that day-to-day newspaper material was the province of the Foreign Office News Department, whereas Wellington House dealt with the distribution of books, pamphlets and articles by leading public figures. Nevertheless, if Dublin Castle could provide 'authentic stuff', Masterman would be only too anxious to ensure United States circulation in the interests of Anglo-American relations:

Nothing, as you may imagine, has caused us more anxiety than the question of dealing with Irish opinion in the United States. It is not too much to say that the rebellion, the executions, and the subsequent failure of the Home Rule negotiations, caused a most disastrous change of opinion throughout the whole of America (not only among the Irish) and that the Irish question stands in the forefront today among the things which are alienating America from this country.[18]

These developments coincided with a growing controversy regarding the organisation of British propaganda and particularly the role of Wellington House. In February 1916, Geoffrey Dawson had written that the 'Masterman–Gilbert Parker outfit is a real scandal. If the organisation of that office were exposed it would crumble in a moment', while H. A. Gwynne, the *Morning Post* editor, argued that the job could 'only be done by a newspaper man'. Lord Northcliffe repeatedly tried to convince leading politicians of the need for a reorganised and more forceful propaganda and warned Lloyd George that the pro-Allies in America needed support, since 'what we are winning by projectiles, we look like losing by lack of propaganda'. In fact, the new Prime Minister, with close ties in Fleet Street, had already accepted a plan by Robert Donald of the *Daily Chronicle* to amalgamate the various propaganda agencies – Wellington House, the News Department and the Press Bureau – into one building and under one head.[19]

This assault on the existing propaganda organisation was deeply resented at the Foreign Office, which believed that propaganda should be formulated in conjunction with the dictates of diplomacy. It was also feared that more aggressive propaganda schemes for influencing American opinion would, as Masterman had warned the Cabinet some months earlier, 'bring their own ruin'. Lord Hardinge foresaw a 'revulsion of feeling' against Britain, while Robert Cecil typified Foreign Office contempt for Lloyd George's cronies with a caustic epigram: 'It is curious how these "men of action" believe in words!' When Germany's declaration of unrestricted submarine warfare led, in February 1917, to the rupture of diplomatic relations between the United States and Germany, Hubert Montgomery considered it 'a vindication of the policy of restraint in matters of propaganda' and asserted, 'The only thing which might have prevented the Americans taking the decision when the moment came was a "raging, tearing propaganda" on our part which would have given them the impression that we wished to push them in.'[20]

The struggle between the journalists and diplomatists temporarily abated on 20 February, when the War Cabinet established a Department of Information, with the novelist John Buchan as Director. Even so, Montgomery and his colleagues achieved one success by ensuring that the new department was lodged at the Foreign Office, albeit with semi-independent status.[21] This new body was to initiate and direct most of the Irish propaganda in America in the years ahead, and from it eventually emerged the Ministry of Information in 1918.

II

By early 1917 the Home Rule movement was a spent force, and Irishmen on both sides of the Atlantic turned increasingly towards Sinn Fein and its claims for the recognition of Ireland at a future peace conference. To this end, Irish propagandists made great play of English hypocrisy in preaching the rights of small nations while Ireland was still in bondage. This spurred Alfred Noyes, who arrived in the United States while such demands were in vogue, to ask Butler, 'Is it wise – so far as America is concerned – to give them quite so much about the "small nations"? The Irish have fastened on this idea, and they are using it against us in their own perverted form.' Laurence Whibley, an official at the new Department of Information, agreed that the 'small nations' theme could have dangerous propaganda repercussions if used excessively, and remarked sharply that it would be more to the point 'if something could be done to show that Ireland is a spoiled child still crying for the moon'.[22]

Claims for peace conference representation loomed large in campaigns by Sinn Feiners and Home Rulers. In early 1917, with Sinn Fein contesting its first by-election, this insistent demand was heard throughout Ireland. The Republicans' chief ally at Westminster, Lawrence Ginnell, MP for North Westmeath, informed the Commons defiantly that, regardless of the British Government's wishes, Ireland would go to the peace conference because it 'no longer admits that its inalienable right to absolute and exclusive independence is a domestic question for any country but itself'. The Commons had already been rebuked by John Dillon, deputy leader of the Home Rule Party, in a forthright warning of international factors:

> How can you face Europe? How can you face America tomorrow, and pose as the champions of oppressed nationalities? What answer will you have when you are told, as you will be told, at the Peace Conference: 'Go home and put your own house in order.'

Dillon's stance was fortified by an assurance from Shane Leslie that President Wilson's 'small nations' principle could be 'Ireland's international card', and that, 'the more Ireland is regarded as an international and not as a domestic problem, the better for us all'. The crucial moment to press for a settlement, he suggested, would be just after America entered the war, when Spring-Rice could advance the measure as being essential for effective wartime co-operation.[23]

Lloyd George would undoubtedly have welcomed a workable scheme, having been warned by Lord Wimborne, the Viceroy, that it would be unwise to underestimate the peace conference agitation, and by Professor W. G. S. Adams, of the Prime Minister's 'Garden Suburb' secretariat, that an Irish solution would 'strengthen our influence generally at the settlement of international affairs'. However, as always, the introduction of such external factors was controversial. The Times, for example, urged Irish Nationalists to be more constructive, since 'an Irish debate is always apt to develop into sham sentiment about small nationalities and grotesque comparisons with Belgium and Poland'. In the House of Commons, the eloquent Tory Hugh Cecil dampened the atmosphere of Wilsonian idealism by casting cynical doubts on whether the peace conference would 'trouble its head about Home Rule for any portion of the world', adding in amplification, 'I do not suppose that this country will dictate to Russia what form of Home Rule is to be given to Poland, and I am quite sure that Russia will not dictate to us what form of Home Rule should be given to Ireland.'[24]

With an eye to Allied and neutral opinion, Lloyd George's Irish declarations increasingly employed the fashionable terminology of 'self-determination'. Thus, during the Commons Irish debate on 7 March, he emphasised that the part of Ireland which clearly demanded Home Rule would receive it, but that Ulster had a right to be treated as 'a separate nationality' from the rest of Ireland and could not be coerced. This argument, intended as it was for

American consumption, provoked an outburst from John Redmond, who asked, 'How did America deal with minorities when they attempted to stand in the way of the unity, the prosperity, and the liberties of their country? We all know the doctrine of rule by the majority . . . is probably the one held most sacred there.' As it was clear that the Government was now committed to Ulster exclusion, Redmond dramatically led his party out of the House in protest at the Government's policy. This turbulent incident prompted the Liberal MP Frederick Guest to warn sombrely that the exit of the Nationalists had 'probably been flashed by now all over the world' and that Britain's critics would jibe that 'we who are fighting for small nations have brought our own state of affairs to such a pitch that the representatives of Ireland have been forced to leave the British House of Commons'.[25]

On the day following his Commons walk-out, Redmond issued a manifesto, with copies to President Wilson and the Dominion premiers, exhorting Irish-Americans to pressurise the British Government to 'act towards Ireland in accordance with the principles for which they are fighting in Europe'.[26] The Liberal press welcomed the manifesto, but the *Belfast News Letter* spoke for many Unionists when it contended that involving Wilson was 'an invitation to him to embarrass Great Britain at the most critical stage of the war'. However, the President would ignore this, since 'it would be contrary to international courtesy to do anything else'. On the following day the *News Letter* argued that many American politicians had 'ceased to ask for or desire the Irish-American vote', and Wilson himself had 'treated it with contempt at the last election'. In any case, the newspaper concluded, 'the government of Ireland is not an international question, and no interference by any other nation, even the most friendly, will be tolerated'.[27]

In addition to irritating Unionists, the manifesto marked the end of any lingering Foreign Office or D of I co-operation with Redmond and his party. On the day of its issue, Ronald Roxburgh underlined the change in official attitudes when he suggested that, to counter the manifesto, an interview be arranged to impress upon Americans that 'Ireland could have Home Rule if it would exclude Ulster'. Indeed, realising that the Redmondite cause in America had, in Joyce Broderick's words, 'practically passed out of existence', the D of I increasingly leaned towards the Unionist cause as a new propaganda counterweight to Irish-American extremism. This may have stemmed from the largely Unionist complexion of the new

Coalition Government and the advent as Foreign Secretary of Arthur Balfour. It would also have been stimulated by Spring-Rice's reports to Balfour that the Unionist argument was 'little understood and never presented' and that the Irish difficulty was viewed solely as a conflict between England and Ireland rather than as a dispute between the opposing Irish parties. Balfour, who despaired of 'educating' Americans on the subject, minuted wearily that 'the ignorance of the Americans about the Irish Question is what theologians describe as invincible'.[28]

The need to 'educate' Americans on the Home Rule problem was also exercising officials at the D of I. Laurence Whibley, concerned that the American view was 'obscured by ignorance and prejudice', drafted the framework of an article which might be given to a writer 'for amplification and illustration'. The draft argued that Home Rule would encourage Sinn Fein's demand for total separation, which, as Americans who had fought a civil war against secession would realise, was an unacceptable threat to national unity. Unionism, contended Whibley, was 'a more natural solution' and Ireland had prospered in recent years as a result. Moreover, having been exempted from the burden of conscription, Ireland had been 'treated with indulgence . . . a spoilt child, who doesn't know what she wants and won't be happy till she gets it'. In Whibley's opinion, the Home Rule issue was now a purely Irish affair between Ulster and the South, but an all-Ireland parliament was impracticable, since Ireland was, in effect, 'two nations', with marked differences of race, religion and economic structure. Even the cry of self-determination was invalid, since 'the very arguments which can be advanced for Home Rule for the rest of Ireland justify the exclusion of Ulster'. The Cambridge historian Dr Joseph Tanner, who was chosen to convert the draft into a finished article, reproduced all Whibley's key points: Ulster's right to self-determination, the benefits of Union, and Ireland's position as the 'spoilt child of the partnership'.[29] The Tanner–Whibley combination – similar to that in June 1916 between Arnold Bennett and Raymond Needham – illustrates that many of the articles which appeared in the foreign press as the work of leading academics and writers were not only officially inspired but largely moulded by lesser-known officials from British Government departments.

A further indication of the revised D of I approach to the Irish dilemma came on 12 March, when Geoffrey Butler queried whether

Ulster could undertake 'a little propaganda of her own' in the United States, and added,

> The Ulster case goes by default though there is a fair body of moderate, non-Irish opinion in the country which would be open to reason. . . . From our point of view we want to encourage the idea that it is a question of Ulster v. the South, not England v. Ireland. Ulster has quite a chance of appearing as the injured small nationality and 'No Popery', despite what one might imagine, is no bad cry in the U.S.A., which is filled with more obscurantist Protestantism than any other country except Australia.[30]

Thus, Butler was proposing major innovations in Irish propaganda: a cynical exploitation of the anti-Catholic bigotry which had been rampant in the 1850s, and furtherance of the Ulster cause by dint of self-propaganda in America. It is probable, however, that he was less concerned with the Ulster cause itself than with using the 'Orange card' as a propaganda weapon against the claims of Irish-American extremists. Indeed, although he was subsequently Conservative MP for Cambridge University, he claimed by the end of the war to support Home Rule for Ireland.[31] Since, in addition, he was 'intolerant of any conception of conservatism which was not concerned to secure reforms',[32] the picture of him which emerges is of a progressive Tory of the pragmatic school, rather than a traditional Unionist such as Newton, Nicolson or Montgomery. Significantly, Butler's lucid exposition of Conservatism in his book *The Tory Tradition* contained no mention of the importance of the Union.[33] Like Miles Lampson and Eustace Percy, he had close connections with the United States,[34] and these possibly led him to view the Home Rule question from an imperial rather than a domestic point of view.

Hubert Montgomery, as a staunch Ulster Unionist, considered Butler's suggestions for publicising the Ulster cause to be 'sound' and he referred them to John Buchan, the Director of the D of I. Buchan had stood unsuccessfully as Conservative candidate for Peebles and Selkirk in 1911, but later succeeded in winning the Scottish Universities seat for the party. Although he described himself as only a 'weak-kneed Conservative', he had been profoundly at odds with the Asquith Government over its handling of the pre-war Home Rule crisis and later confessed that its 'blundering treatment of Ulster roused some ancient Covenanting devil in my blood'. Indeed, in a speech in 1912, he had defended the Unionist Party's strong stand:

> We are standing for . . . a universal truth in politics – the principle that Union is strength, that the rights and duties of the whole cannot be sacrificed to the selfishness and vanity of the part. This was the principle for which Abraham Lincoln stood, the cry which echoed on a thousand platforms and a hundred blood-stained fields of the American Civil War. Gentlemen, it is a principle which cannot die.[35]

It was, however, typical of Buchan's independent code of beliefs that he asserted in his memoirs that he agreed with 'nine-tenths of the Liberal creed' and had been a 'federal Home Ruler' after the fashion of his friend F. S. Oliver, the Conservative publicist. Nevertheless, his strong sympathy for Ulster's stand was revealed in his reaction to Butler's proposals:

> Nothing would be more useful than to have a discreet Irishman sent to the States, who could point out in articles, in conversation, and if necessary in public addresses, that the Irish question is now a purely domestic question for Ireland – that Britain will accept any settlement to which the whole of Ireland will agree – and at the same time will show the difficulties of Ulster's position. Such a man would spike a lot of hostile guns.

Edward Carson proposed an Ulster colleague, Bryan O'Donnell, for the task, but Buchan, fearing that O'Donnell would be 'too much of an ordinary Ulster politician', secured the services of Joseph Fisher, who had already written 'some of the best and most moderate articles on the Ulster question'.[36] After some administrative delay, Fisher finally left for the United States after its entry into the war.

There is little doubt that the new policy more accurately reflected the convictions of most D of I officials. However, one leading propagandist who found the new departure difficult to accept was Charles Masterman, to whom Ireland was 'a sort of second patriotism'. Masterman had viewed the formation of the Lloyd George Coalition with 'a good deal of dismay', partly because his own influence diminished with his subordination to Buchan and partly because 'the presence of a solid anti-Home Rule block made him feel that Irish affairs were likely to go against everything that he desired'. Not surprisingly, Masterman found it difficult to justify the Government's Irish policies, as he complained to A. P. Magill of Dublin Castle:

> All the British authors well known in the United States whom I have asked to write on the subject always ask questions which I cannot answer. – Each one says 'Am I to justify the executions. . . . Am I to assert that the future of the Irish question is still open? How far can I deal with these large political questions, unless I know what the real opinion of the Government is on the matter?[37]

Ironically, just as Masterman's Home Rule sympathies appeared to be increasingly out of place at the D of I, the Cabinet was compelled by American pressure to renew its search for an Irish settlement. American support for Home Rule was highlighted in March by a memorandum from William Wiseman, a British Secret Service agent who, from December 1916, acted as an unofficial but key liaison between President Wilson and the British Government. The memorandum, which was circulated to the Cabinet as representing the views of Wilson and the American people, described the Irish Question as an obstacle to full Anglo-American co-operation should the United States enter the war.[38] As if to reinforce this message, the American Ambassador in London, Walter Page, warned Balfour that Britain would remain unpopular as long as the Irish grievance endured, and added, 'You've had that problem at your very door for 300 years. What's the matter that you don't solve it?'[39]

Although, in his Commons speech of 7 March, Lloyd George had announced his Government's adherence to the partition principle, an alternative scheme to refer the problem to an Irish Conference or Convention received strong backing from some of the Prime Minister's private secretariat of advisers – notably Philip Kerr, Leo Amery and Professor W. G. S. Adams. They believed that the Government could shed much of its responsibility if it gave Irishmen the task of working out their own salvation,[40] and it seemed the perfect way for the Government to convince Americans that it was honouring the 'small nations' principle. At the same time, it avoided the turmoil which would almost certainly have followed any attempt to impose a settlement on Ireland.

While the Convention proposal steadily gained support in

Britain, President Wilson was moving closer to an American declaration of war against Germany. A month after the suspension of diplomatic relations, Congress passed a bill which authorised the arming of merchant ships. Significantly, the thirteen Congressmen who voted against the bill were 'mainly composed of representatives from German districts or anti-British Irishmen',[41] while those who organised anti-war demonstrations and bombarded Congress with protest telegrams received aid from both German and extremist Irish organisations.[42] Despite this opposition, Wilson finally took America into the war against Germany on 6 April. Wilson's motives for taking the decisive step, and the importance of the Irish-Americans in influencing this decision, have been the subject of much debate. An English MP, J. Allen Baker, informed Balfour that, according to Colonel House, American entry would have been greatly accelerated by 'the consummation of Home Rule'. This view was later echoed by Lloyd George, who wrote that without the Irish problem 'it was by no means impossible that America would have come much earlier into the war, and by so much shortened its duration'.[43] However, such claims exaggerated the strength of the Irish-American lobby, which had little influence on either Wilson's decision or its timing. It was the failure of the peace moves in December 1916 and January 1917, followed by Germany's declaration of unrestricted submarine warfare, which primarily decided the issue. Nevertheless, the mood of Irish-Americans served to temper the enthusiasm of America's entry into the war and was to play a notable part in shaping the extent and nature of America's role as a belligerent.

8
America Enters the War; the Balfour Mission (April–June 1917)

I

America's entry into the war was of great importance to the Irish Question, but it had a different significance for each of the factions involved. To the Irish-American extremists, it was a curb on their pro-Germanism and it weakened their position vis-à-vis the pro-Ally moderates. To Nationalists in Ireland, it was, by contrast, a boost to their varying interpretations of self-determination. To the diehard Unionists, however, it brought increased pressure from Lloyd George and his Cabinet for acceptance of Home Rule – a denial of the Unionist argument that domestic questions should be unaffected by foreign opinion.

The Irish extremists in America – now damned by their sympathy with Germany – sought to escape censure by combining their campaign for Irish independence with a display of unequivocal allegiance to the United States. However, in the patriotic atmosphere created by the war, it became increasingly difficult for extremists to gain a hearing, and subscriptions to extremist organisations plunged to a ruinous nadir. It has been argued that America's entry was also a blow to the Sinn Feiners in Ireland, for 'it wrecked their hopes of any intervention by Washington in their favour'.[1] In truth, America's role as a belligerent enabled Wilson to intercede more freely than hitherto and enhanced the Nationalist claim for representation as a 'small nation' at the peace conference.

The Home Rule Party made the maximum capital from American entry into the war. John Dillon reminded the Commons that in the American forces Irishmen would proportionately outnumber 'the record of any other race' and that, consequently, 'at the Peace Conference we shall have a friend who will not desert us'. Privately, however, many Nationalist MPs were less sanguine. Stephen Gwynn considered that international arbitration would inevitably endorse partition, since 'from a European Peace Conference point of view, there is no answer to Lloyd George's speech of last March. It is far easier . . . to demonstrate by argument the existence of two nationalities in Ireland than of one Geographic unity.' Indeed, Horace Plunkett later recorded that, by 1917, Ireland faced permanent division, 'with a majority and a minority each relying upon the doctrine of self-determination to settle the Irish Question according to its own desire'.²

The Cabinet realised that Ulster exclusion was anathema to Nationalists, but persevered in the hope that its efforts would at least indicate 'the Government's desire to reach a fair settlement'. However, the *Irish Independent* bluntly predicted that a partition scheme would never placate opinion in Ireland or America, while C. P. Scott typified radical reaction by dismissing the proposals as a 'bare makeshift to tide over the immediate future and spare us the shame of a revolted Ireland at the moment of the Peace Conference'. Such criticisms were bolstered by the conviction that, with America as a belligerent, more favourable terms could now be extracted than in the previous summer. Arthur Lynch, the Irish Nationalist MP, wrote to Redmond that the March Revolution in Russia and America's entry into the war had led to a 'modification of war aims in favour of the freedom of oppressed Nationalities', and that, if the Home Rule Party returned to the 'humiliation' of a partition scheme, it would 'stand before the Irish people in a ridiculous posture'.³

An important factor in the new situation was the changed attitude of *The Times*, which had formerly been a distinguished champion of the Ulster cause, but which by now supported Home Rule. Although the newspaper's editor, Geoffrey Dawson, was pro-Unionist, he had by 1917 come to accept 'the importance of a liberal and sane settlement of Irish affairs as a main factor in improving British–American relations'. In so doing, he acknowledged the force of Arthur Willert's warnings that, until the Home Rule problem was solved, there would always be 'a danger of a rift appearing in the lute' and of President Wilson being unable to 'weld his countrymen together behind a vigorous prosecution of the war'.⁴ On 11 April the newspaper began a strong Home Rule campaign based largely on the need to placate American opinion. It expressed hopes that American entry would inspire a solution and so induce fresh Irish recruits to fight alongside their Irish-American brethren. An approving Lord Northcliffe praised the editorial staff in his customary review: 'Profoundly glad to see Ireland to the front again. Knowing the United States as I do, I greatly fear that the Irish canker will eat into the rose of the alliance.'[5]

So concerned was Northcliffe about the 'canker' that he invited leading Americans to voice their views in *The Times*. The appeal gained a wide response, stimulated by the efforts of Shane Leslie, John Quinn and others, who induced contributions from former presidents Roosevelt and Taft, as well as from Cardinal Gibbons and New York's Mayor Mitchel.[6] Without exception, the contributors made strong pleas for a settlement as a stimulus to Anglo-American co-operation, and several cited the American Civil War as demonstrating their country's belief that, although a majority should not coerce a minority, the minority's rights should 'not be permitted to dismember a nation'.[7] The solution lay in an all-Ireland parliament, with generous safeguards to the Ulster minority against religious or economic oppression, and with rights equivalent to those of an American state legislature vis-à-vis the Federal Government in Washington.[8]

The Times's apparent deference to American opinion triggered a storm of Ulster wrath. The *Belfast News Letter*, indignant that Northcliffe was now leading the 'conspiracy to organise Home Rule opinion in the United States', queried,

> What would Mr. Roosevelt, Mr. Taft, Cardinal Gibbons, and the other Americans who have been inveigled into this controversy say if British statesmen followed their example and instructed President Wilson how he should deal with his domestic problems?

Such irritation was echoed by Hugh Montgomery, who, mindful of Lloyd George's tactics in 1916, commented tartly that much of the alarm about American opinion was 'as baseless as the yarns we were told, about America and munitions, at Belfast this time last year'. The implied threat to national sovereignty drew a sharp counter-attack in Parliament from Ronald McNeill:

> I believe too much in the robust common sense of the American people to think that they will take offence at our wishing to guide

our domestic policy as they do their own, for their own reasons and independent of foreign criticisms.⁹

Southern Unionists were no less critical. Richard Bagwell, a Tipperary Unionist, accused *The Times* of being 'a Home Rule organ of the worst kind masquerading as an Imperial patriot', while J. Mackay Wilson inquired of Bonar Law whether it was conceivable that 'the descendants of Abraham Lincoln, who sanctioned the flowing of rivers of blood to save the Union, are now to dictate the abandonment of the Union between Great Britain and Ireland'. The *Irish Times*, mouthpiece of Southern Unionism, diplomatically passed over the 'propriety' of American interference but warned that such pressure might induce Britain 'to find momentary relief in a bad and hasty settlement', with the Government 'bullied' into violating its Ulster pledges. The historian Professor Alison Phillips remonstrated with *The Times* as to 'how little the problems involved in this question are understood in the United States'. He asserted that the federal system favoured by the American contributors bore no relation to the Nationalist belief in 'Ireland a Nation' – a concept which, 'as the Civil War proved once and for all, the Americans would never admit in their own case'. Phillips later criticised not only the failures of successive British governments to grasp the nettle of the Irish Question, but also the American people, 'whose sense of their own exceptional righteousness is apt to lead them into blundering interference in the concerns of other nations'.¹⁰

Resentment against transatlantic pressure was not confined to Irish Unionists. Although some Tory newspapers, such as the *Observer* and *Daily Express*, accepted the need to placate America, the diehard press remained staunchly opposed to outside intervention. The *Morning Post*, for example, commented severely that 'the government of Ireland is a British question, for which the United Kingdom has the entire responsibility', and added bitterly that, 'while the voice is the voice of America, the hand is the hand of Lord Northcliffe'.¹¹ The *Morning Post* spoke for Unionist bodies such as the Imperialist Unionist Association, originally formed to fight the Lloyd George scheme of 1916. In April 1917 its Chairman, Lord Salisbury, warned Lord Curzon that, although the Association was loth to issue statements which might 'militate against the success of the Alliance', the Cabinet should understand that 'American interference would be received by Unionists with considerable resentment'.¹²

Opposition to the *Times* campaign often cut across party divisions. Even the former Prime Minister, Asquith, counselled the Liberal Eighty club that it was dangerous to encourage false optimism abroad, since success would be more elusive than imagined by 'theorists and benevolent outsiders' – advice eagerly seized on by the *Belfast News Letter* as a 'gentle rebuke to the eminent public men in the United States who have been so misguided as to interfere in the internal affairs of the United Kingdom'.[13]

The *Times* campaign, whilst increasing the pressure on the Government, provided Lloyd George with extra leverage on the recalcitrant Unionists. As War Cabinet members, Bonar Law, Milner and Curzon were already committed to Home Rule, and the Prime Minister held strong hopes of Balfour, who had recently gone to America as head of a British War Mission and would there encounter the renewed Home Rule clamour sparked by the *Times* campaign. Although Balfour stressed to Americans that he had no brief to deal with Irish affairs, Lloyd George's *War Memoirs* state that Balfour 'undertook to make special enquiry' into the importance of the Irish problem in Anglo-American relations. On the day of Balfour's departure Bonar Law confided to a colleague, 'There is hope that the entrance of America into the struggle may make the Irish situation easier but it is a very vague hope.'[14]

The greatest obstacle to a Home Rule settlement was Edward Carson, who, as Ulster Unionist leader and newly appointed First Lord of the Admiralty, suffered a personal conflict of loyalties. Since partition was reportedly unacceptable to American opinion, Ulster's stubborn insistence on exclusion was constantly under attack as obstructionist and unpatriotic; on the other hand, Carson could not risk alienating his Ulster supporters with further concessions such as those of 1916. In mid April, however, Lloyd George was presented with the perfect means of winning over both Carson and Balfour. President Wilson, impressed by strong Congressional feeling over Ireland, instructed Ambassador Page to urge the Prime Minister unofficially that the Irish impasse was the only obstacle to 'an absolutely cordial co-operation' between the United States and Britain. This, once achieved, would show that 'the real programme of government by the consent of the governed has been adopted everywhere in the anti-Prussian world'.[15] Page's subsequent report to Wilson described the Prime Minister's opportunist reaction to the message:

A short while ago he [Lloyd George] dined with me and, after dinner, I took him to a corner of the drawing room and delivered your message about Ireland. 'God knows, I'm trying', he replied. 'Tell the President that. And tell him to talk to Balfour.' Presently he broke out – 'Madmen, madmen – I never saw any such task', and he pointed across the room to Sir Edward Carson, his First Lord of the Admiralty – 'Madmen. But the President's right. We've got to settle it now.' Carson and Jellicoe came across the room and sat down with us. 'I've been telling the Ambassador, Carson, that we've got to settle the Irish question – in spite of you.'[16]

Unionist historians have criticised President Wilson for intervening in Irish affairs. Alison Phillips condemned the 'almost complete ignorance' in America of Irish conditions, while Alfred Gollin contemptuously described the President's message to Lloyd George as the product of 'that bland arrogance which enabled him to interfere in the most private affairs of other countries'. Many contemporary observers, however, appreciated that Wilson's intervention was encouraged for tactical reasons by the wily Lloyd George. Significantly, at the Guildhall a few days later, the Prime Minister exhorted, 'If I appeal for the settlement of Ireland, it is because I know from facts which are driven into my mind every hour from America . . . that it is one of the essentials of a speedy victory.' Ireland, he declared, was 'the one menacing spot in the whole horizon' – a far cry from Edward Grey's reference at the outbreak of war to 'the one bright spot'.[17]

When Balfour and the British War Mission disembarked at New York on 22 April, they were confronted with a growing Home Rule campaign which, spurred by Northcliffe's efforts, soon assumed compelling proportions. Although Wilson had been asked by Lloyd George to press Balfour on the need for settlement, he deliberately left it to Lansing to warn the Foreign Secretary of the failure to satisfy 'the intense longing of the Irish for the freedom of Ireland'.[18] Meanwhile, Northcliffe 'raised little less than an agitation in Washington' by telegraphing that Balfour had the power to settle the Irish Question.[19] Thus encouraged, John Quinn led a deputation of moderates to the British statesman to emphasise strong Irish-American opposition to any partition scheme. Balfour was a model of courtesy and charming evasion, complimenting the deputation on the presentation of its case but stressing that he was in America solely to represent the British Cabinet on war issues; as regards the Irish Question, he had 'no authority whatever to speak upon it' and 'not the least conception' of how matters stood in Britain. However, he pointed out that, under the Union, Ireland enjoyed benefits and freedoms which contrasted, for example, with Germany's exploitation of the Poles and which left Irishmen 'as free as any American citizen or wherever free institutions on the British model have existed'. It was Ulster's devotion to the Union, rather than fear of religious 'persecution' from the Catholic South, which explained its resistance to Home Rule. Balfour ended the meeting by assuring the deputation that only the extreme difficulty of the situation, rather than any 'obstinacy or prejudice' on the Government's part, prevented a settlement.[20]

Balfour cabled a brief résumé of the interview to Lloyd George, commenting that the Irish Question was 'apparently the only difficulty we have to face here' and that its settlement would 'greatly facilitate the vigorous and lasting cooperation of the United States Government in the war'. However, he concluded with a 'most secret' coda: 'Shane Leslie has stated confidentially that, though the deputation had to reject any scheme involving partition, if such a scheme was all that could be agreed to, a considerable portion of Irish moderate opinion here would rally to it.' Balfour had long appreciated that American pressure required a settlement, but, as the telegram coda showed, he had not accepted that a successful scheme must, of necessity, be based on an undivided Ireland. Contemporary opinion varied as to whether Balfour's meeting with the Irish-Americans served to promote goodwill towards Britain. Cecil Dormer, one of Balfour's entourage, claimed that Quinn and the delegation 'were enormously pleased' at Balfour's receiving them, while Arthur Willert later recalled that they were 'well satisfied . . . and got to work on their co-racialists in Congress and elsewhere'. However, Shane Leslie reported that Irish-Americans would not accept Balfour's claim to have no brief regarding the Irish Question: 'Either, they say, he has been sent in contempt of them or to make a dramatic reconciliation between the Irish and English peoples as the climax of his mission.' Although Balfour made no such 'dramatic reconciliation', Leslie considered that the Foreign Secretary had at least been saved from 'the error of supposing that Irish opinion can be over-ridden in this country'.[21]

Balfour was further confronted with the Irish problem when he was invited to address Congress in person – the first Englishman to be accorded the honour. About 200 Congressmen cabled to Lloyd George that America would be 'deeply stirred and their enthusiastic efforts enlisted if Britain would now settle the Irish problem in accordance with the principles announced by President Wilson'.[22] Fears that hostile disruption would prevent Balfour's speech were dispelled when Irish Congressmen went *en bloc* to the Speaker and requested that Balfour should speak as arranged. Discord was confined to the fruitless distribution of leaflets which demanded, 'Ask Mr Balfour: Why are you called "Bloody Balfour"?' When Arthur Willert taunted the leading demonstrator, Medill McCormick, 'So that is the worst your tough friends can do', the Congressman replied candidly, 'Your man has disarmed us. He is some salesman.'[23]

It was much the same story when Balfour visited New York a week later. Willert reported in *The Times* that 'those responsible for law and order had been nervous about the possibility of Irish or other hostile demonstrations. But the worst that the Irish did was to scatter abusive broadsheets among the waiting crowds'. However, Irish-American antagonism played a large part in preventing Balfour from visiting Chicago, despite a contemporary account which merely claimed that 'there was too much to be done in Washington and New York to make the trip possible'. Balfour's subsequent report to Lloyd George emphasised that Chicago was a city where German and Irish influences were 'most hostile' and the non-German population 'most indifferent':

> It is there that any good effect which the Mission might have on public opinion would be most valuable: and for the same reason it is there some contretemps was most to be apprehended. The State Department came to the conclusion that the risks outweighed the benefits, and strongly urged us not to go. I think they were wrong; but evidently we had no choice but to acquiesce. Their main reason was the possibility of a hostile Irish demonstration.[24]

Irish-American discontent was deplored by pro-Ally journalists such as Frederick Dixon, who, throughout the Mission, supplied Robert Cecil with analyses of American opinion. On 27 April his newspaper, the *Christian Science Monitor*, attacked Nationalist suggestions that Wilson should make Home Rule a condition of American co-operation, since this would be 'an interference in a purely domestic matter, of a kind which he [Wilson] would be the first to resent if the conditions were reversed'. In forwarding this article to Cecil, Dixon advised bluntly that 'you cannot pacify the Irish out here because they have no intention of being pacified'. Whatever concession was made, he believed they would want more; better therefore to 'face the Home Rule question without paying any attention to these gentlemen out here, and take it on its merits in the United Kingdom'. Dixon's views were certainly shared by Cecil, who was openly opposed to the new Home Rule initiative. In fact, when Balfour had telegraphed the Foreign Office for information as to the Government's plans, Cecil had passed the inquiry to Lloyd George with a curt and pointed minute: 'A reply must be sent to this based on materials from some other member of the Government. I know nothing about it.'[25]

Resentment against Irish-American pressure was exhibited by at least one member of the Balfour Mission – Ian Malcolm, Balfour's Parliamentary Secretary and Unionist MP for Croydon. When campaigning for the December 1910 election, Malcolm had strongly attacked Irish-American interference in terms strikingly similar to those used by Gilbert Parker in the same campaign:

> The United Kingdom has its own Monroe Doctrine. 'Hands off, foreigners.' Our Kingdom does not belong to the Irish of the United States; the United Kingdom will not suffer the Mother of Parliaments, to which she has looked up through all these years, to be degraded, to be bought and sold, by American dollars, collected from Fenians and rebels.

Thus it was hardly surprising that Malcolm, when reporting to Cecil on the progress of the Balfour Mission, should complain irritably at the Irish-American agitation:

> We don't worry them about any of their domestic affairs, but they are thinking about their own damned politics all the time, and don't care if they do make things difficult for the head of our Mission. However, they haven't got much 'change' out of him so far and he has on each occasion scored a heavy personal success. Some of us trace the Irish activity to the machinations of Northcliffe rightly or wrongly and feel rather bitter about it.[26]

Another member of Balfour's staff, Cecil Dormer, had previously served as secretary to the British Legation at the Vatican and was, in his own words, 'a kind of courier' for the Mission. Dormer, a Catholic, had no personal antipathy towards the Home Rule agitation and seems to have believed that Irish-American unrest was less troublesome than expected. On 6 May he wrote to a colleague in London that the existing animosity was 'based more on old history than on the Irish Question'. Nevertheless, Ireland aroused 'a terrific amount' of discussion, and the Mission had received 'shoals of letters' about it, mostly friendly in tone and taking the view that a Home Rule settlement would 'sweep away the last obstacle to a perfect unity between the US and us'. In a letter to the author written almost sixty years later, Sir Cecil gave a modified view:

> Irish-American influence in the U.S. in 1917 was dormant. It was naturally a very important factor in the Mission's work but I think only as a background. If it was discussed by Mr. Balfour, which I doubt, for it [the Mission] was dominated by the Jewish influence in the U.S., it would have been only in casual conversation. Mr. Balfour would not have dreamt of consulting me or anyone in the F.O. on Irish policy – he had no need and the F.O. had nothing to do with it. Some of the F.O. men had their prejudices over Ireland, but that no more affected their F.O. work than, say, the Women Suffrage question.[27]

Perhaps the most striking point in Dormer's letter is his claim that, although some officials 'had their prejudices over Ireland', the Foreign Office 'had nothing to do with' Irish policy. Such a defence of the traditional non-partisan ethos of the Civil Service clearly does not tally with the attitude of several Foreign Office officials over Irish matters. Sir Cecil's recollection that the 'Jewish influence' was of greater importance to the Mission's work is a useful corrective to the tendency of Irish historians in particular to ascribe disproportionate weight to the Irish-American lobby at this time. Nevertheless, in some respects the letter reveals the fallibility of memory long after the event, for it is clearly an exaggeration to claim that Irish-American influence in 1917 was 'dormant'. Indeed, another Mission official, General Thomas Bridges, recalled in his memoirs that, soon after Balfour's arrival, the Irish Question 'raised its Hydra head against us in the Press and by leaflets'. The most important confirmation, however, lay in Balfour's own report to Lloyd George, following his return to England:

The Irish question looms very large in the minds of United States politicians. From the domestic as well as the international point of view they are deeply concerned that no solution has yet been found for this ancient problem. From the international point of view they regard it as the one obstacle which stands in the way of a close friendship between their country and ours. From the point of view of domestic politics . . . , even a settlement which satisfied the majority of Irishmen both in Ulster and the South (were such a thing possible) would scarcely satisfy the Irish-American 'boss'. The interests of so many wirepullers of the lowest sort are involved in the maintenance of the Irish-American party that, if the existing Irish question were solved, a new one would have forthwith to be invented.

Thus, although admitting the importance of the Irish Question, Balfour was at pains to impress upon the Prime Minister that a Home Rule settlement would not extinguish the Irish-American agitation. Nevertheless, he warned that if a settlement was not found, the Irish-American extremists, who were now 'silently watching the course of events', would regain the initiative from the Redmondites and 'do their utmost to cause dissension and mistrust between the United States and Great Britain'.[28]

In addition to reports from the Balfour Mission, London was kept informed of the Irish-American situation by British lecturers such as Alfred Noyes, who had written to Geoffrey Butler in early April,

The Irish over here are perhaps the chief danger in the world at the present moment to the British Empire; and they may just dash the cup of complete triumph from our hands at the critical moment. . . . It may be the turning point of our history. Certainly, if the Irish situation can be smoothed out, you remove at once a gigantic fetter that is holding America back from striking with her full force at Germany.[29]

Noyes was representative of a new breed of roving ambassadors – comprised of politicians, writers and businessmen – who augmented and often by-passed traditional diplomatic channels. This new style of diplomacy assumed striking proportions after America entered the war, and reached danger point in many eyes when, in June 1917, Lord Northcliffe succeeded Balfour as head of the British War Mission. Since practitioners of the new diplomacy were not civil servants, they were less responsible to authority for their actions and were unfettered by the Civil Service ethic of political neutrality. Ian Malcolm's Unionist hostility towards Irish-American pressure was one example of this tendency. Another was the D of I sponsored mission of Joseph Fisher, formerly editor of the Belfast *Northern Whig*. Through the years, Fisher had done 'excellent work in defending the interests of the Loyalists and Protestants of the North',[30] but, unlike most Ulstermen, he was convinced that propaganda work in America was essential to the Unionist cause. His mission, which stemmed from the D of I decision to publicise Ulster's cause in America, began in May and embraced New York, Washington, Chicago and Boston. In New York, he visited most of the city's newspaper offices and collaborated with the New York *World* in producing a cartoon which put the British case over Ireland 'in a nutshell' and which attracted considerable attention. In Washington, Fisher met Medill McCormick, leader of the Home Rule campaign in Congress, who gave him introductions to prominent politicians and whom he found 'very clear on the distinction between the legitimate demand for Home Rule and the Sinn Fein demand which amounts to a demand for secession'. Travelling on to Chicago, he encountered 'a good deal of grumbling' against Lansing for blocking Balfour's visit, and was surprised to find more interest in the war than in Irish affairs: 'It is rather odd after New York to find how much Ireland takes a back seat.' Fisher's final report, written on the way home to England, emphasised the apparent weakening of the Irish extremists and the unexpected signs of increased goodwill towards Britain:

> In New York on the day of landing I saw what even ten years ago would have provoked the shrillest clamour – the American and British flags displayed side by side in the most conspicuous position over the City Hall, and the Mayor, by whose orders this was done, was John P. Mitchel, the grandson of an Irish rebel.

Such impressions, contrasting markedly with the pessimism of Alfred Noyes a few months earlier, were doubtless coloured by Fisher's Unionist sympathies, as were his views on Irish-American influence:

> What has struck me most during my present visit is the change

that has gradually been coming over Irish opinion in America and over American opinion on the Irish Question. When I first visited the United States – in the Eighties – the extremists had it all their own way. . . . Now all that is changed. Local Government and Land Purchase have taken most of the poison out of the Irish Question. Home Rule is still looked on as an act of administrative reform and as something for the Irish to settle for themselves not as an anti-English revolution. The extremists are still active and noisy, but they are becoming identified more and more with the Socialist revolutionary element – Russians, Poles, South Italians and so forth – who are feared and detested by all the orderly elements in the country.[31]

In addition to Fisher's mission, the D of I continued its complementary policy of arranging Irish visits for American journalists. 'It is very important', Buchan stressed, 'to get the real situation as to Ireland understood in America – that it is a matter for the Irish to decide and that England is only too willing to ratify their decision.' Special pains were taken to secure introductions among Nationalists for Robert Sloss of the Chicago *Daily News*, who was 'highly thought of in the Foreign Office' and had 'proved himself a very good friend to the Allied cause'. Even so, publication of one of his first interviews – with the Sinn Fein leader, Arthur Griffith – was held up by discomfited officials. Horace Plunkett, who was organising the introductions, protested to Buchan that Sloss had to present 'all sides of the situation' to an American public which was quite capable of taking 'the proper measure' of Griffith's views. Trust to the journalist's discretion, argued Plunkett, for, 'if the lid is to be put on', Sloss might abandon his Irish tour altogether.[32]

When Sloss moved on to Ulster, F. S. Oliver, the Conservative publicist who was temporarily assisting at the D of I, arranged with Pemberton Wicks, an Ulster sympathiser at the Admiralty, that the journalist should see 'only common-sense people in the North', since 'the more reasonable they are and the less fiery – especially on religious matters – the better impression they will make on him'. Oliver stressed reassuringly that Sloss held 'very reasonable views' and was 'not in the least under any illusions as to the justice of the Ulster contentions'. Richard Dawson Bates, Secretary of the Ulster Unionist Council, accompanied the American throughout Ulster and later assured Wicks, 'I saw quite a lot of Sloss and I think he went away well satisfied.'[33]

The problems of chaperoning visiting journalists increased in proportion to the numbers involved, acting as a brake on more ambitious schemes. Such a difficulty arose when Colonel Hutchinson of the War Office proposed an Ulster visit by a party of American pressmen to inspect American naval flotillas and, in the process, interview leading Ulster politicians. This would enable the journalists to 'grasp that there is a large moderate party in Ireland and that the problem of Ulster really exists'. However, as it would also create the danger of correspondents 'wandering unshepherded throughout Ireland', the scheme was eventually rejected by the D of I, as Hubert Montgomery explained:

> The difficulty seems to me that if they are *not* carefully shepherded they will probably hear views and see a state of affairs which would do more harm than good, while if they *are* so shepherded they will realize at once that they are not getting a proper view of the situation.[34]

II

The *Times* campaign and the Balfour Mission stimulated American expectation, for, as Arthur Willert reported, it was widely believed that *The Times* would not have published leading American opinion 'had not a settlement been pretty well assured'. In truth, the Government was still confronted by Ulster's obduracy, but had been encouraged by Balfour's secret assurance that Irish-Americans would reluctantly accept partition, and by Willert's opinion that moderate Irish-Americans would be 'appeased with a settlement in which the projected Ulster (except for the Catholic countries) would remain separate till after the war'. The Cabinet, therefore, continued to think along partition lines until, in a last-minute decision on 16 May, the Irish Convention alternative was proposed by letter to the various Irish leaders. This proposal lifted British prestige in America, where, according to Willert, it produced a 'far healthier atmosphere than any of its predecessors'. Americans, he reported, increasingly accepted Ulster's 'right to be heard' and were impressed by the readiness of English Unionists to 'sink their convictions' so as to make British policy 'square with the ideals for which we are fighting'.[35]

Redmond grasped at the Convention straw in preference to partition, and when the Ulstermen also agreed – albeit with suspicion – Lloyd George was able to announce the development to the Commons. In a corresponding announcement in the Upper House, Lord Curzon deprecated the fact that Ireland was a 'weakness to the common cause' and claimed that an immense impetus would be given to the American war effort if 'this single rift in the unity of the Allies' could be sealed. He then risked diehard anger by taking these international factors a stage further:

> Who can doubt that a contented Ireland will be an asset of immeasurable value in future settlement of the interests of the British Empire. Who can doubt that Great Britain will be a more powerful figure at the Peace Conference, when we get there, if she can speak with the united voice of all her sons. And projecting our gaze a little further into the future, may not such a consummation pave the way for that world cooperation of the three greatest liberty-loving nations on earth – namely, France, the United States of America, and ourselves . . . the settlement of the Irish question emerges as a great world factor of capital importance that may affect both the fortunes of Great Britain in the war itself and the destinies of mankind for generations to come.[36]

Curzon's conversion to such imperial arguments signified a more pragmatic Tory approach to the Home Rule problem. The conversion of Lord Lansdowne, former leader of the House, was even more striking. While Curzon had vacillated during the 1916 negotiations, Lansdowne had resolutely opposed both Lloyd George's schemes and his use of the 'American bogey' – thereby significantly contributing to the abortive outcome. More the surprise, then, when Lansdowne declared his support for the Convention, contending that, realistically, American pressure had to be accepted as the 'great actuality of the moment'. It was no longer sufficient, he argued, to protest that American opinion should not influence British domestic affairs; rather it was a duty to ease 'the task of those who are our friends in America and by so doing to advance our common cause'.[37] It is quite possible, of course, that Lansdowne's apparent change of heart concealed a shrewd tactical appreciation that the Convention would be unproductive and merely act as a temporary sop to American opinion. Consideration of hidden motives spotlights two opposing expedients: throughout the war, many calculating politicians with little personal belief in the 'American argument' used it to promote Irish policies of which they strongly approved; conversely, other politicians paid lip service to Irish policies for which they entertained little hope of success but which might placate American opinion. These opposing tendencies were in evidence during the 1916 negotiations and again during the Convention, but it should also be stressed that many public figures genuinely sought a lasting Irish settlement which would, at the same time, place Anglo-American relations on a firmer footing.

At the other extreme, there remained strong diehard elements who disliked both the Convention scheme and the increasing deference to American opinion. Lord Selborne spoke gravely in Parliament of the many Britons 'who resent deeply the idea that we are to change our Constitution because of the force of American public opinion'. The Southern Unionist leader, Lord Midleton, while accepting the Convention as a last resort, contended that a settlement would merely be retarded if Southern Unionists were asked to surrender their birthright 'at the instance of persons who, by their very utterances, show that the real condition of Ireland and of affairs there has not reached them'. In a subsequent history of Ireland, Midleton repeated his condemnation, claiming that 'geographical isolation had made Americans impervious to the liabilities and restraints of foreign politics', as a result of which 'their spasmodic incursions into questions of world interest have not been always wise or consistent'. As regards Ireland, Midleton wrote that a deep-rooted but misplaced conviction of 'British tyranny and Irish sufferings' was responsible for 'the mistaken judgement formed by America, and for the many breaches of international comity which resulted from it'. Most Southern Unionists shared this dislike of American interference, but some, such as J. Mackay Wilson, now believed that a 'little more enlightenment' would soon show Americans that the Union was 'the only medium by which Ireland can be saved from ruin and chaos'. It was partly for such reasons that the Southern Unionists, after much heart-searching, finally decided to attend the Convention.[38]

Ulster Unionists were even more wary, being concerned lest the Government might use international pressure as an excuse to force Home Rule on their province. The *Belfast News Letter* warned that such pressure would 'imperil the unity of the Allies and therefore their victory', which could only be secured 'if each of them will refrain from interfering in the internal affairs of the others'.[39] There persisted, in fact, a strong suspicion that the Convention was 'intended as window-dressing for the Americans and a diplomatic move on the part of Lloyd George to shift the responsibility from the House of Commons to Ireland'.[40] Not surprisingly, although the Ulster Unionist Council backed the Convention, they were 'never under the delusion that it could lead to anything in Ireland' and considered it to be a 'bone thrown to a snarling dog' at a critical period of the war.[41]

Similar suspicions that the Convention was 'window-dressing for the Americans' helped to decide two of the principal Nationalist groups against attending. William O'Brien, suspecting that the Convention was designed 'for Anglo-American war purposes', protested to Lloyd George on behalf of the All for Ireland League that to blame Ireland for the Convention's certain failure would be a 'gross imposition on the credulity of friendly nations abroad'. Sinn Fein, whose power had grown enormously in the year since the rebellion, argued that the planned composition would give the British Government the 'opportunity of declaring to its Allies, to the U.S. and to the neutral powers that England had left the solution of the Irish question to the Irish themselves [and] that the Irish were unable to solve it'.[42] Thereafter, to the scorn of Unionists, Sinn Fein concentrated on its 'fantastic claim to be independently represented at the Peace Conference after the war'.[43] With many important groups missing at its inception, the Convention was hampered in its claim to speak for the Irish people. However, as Balfour reported, the proposal created 'a most favourable impression' in the United States and emphasised to the thinking portion of the American public that the solution lay with the Irish themselves, while in America Joseph Fisher found that the proposal was 'recognised generally as the offer of a "square deal" '.[44]

Many historians have attributed the Convention scheme to President Wilson's message to Lloyd George,[45] but some credit must also be given to the *Times* campaign. Northcliffe evidently believed so and congratulated Dawson on stimulating the new departure, which was 'demonstrating to the world that Home Rule is not an Anglo-Irish question, but a purely Irish one – an all-important aspect of the case in view of our American Ally'. Can it, however, be argued that the Convention was merely a time-wasting device? House of Commons lobby talk certainly welcomed the development, because it 'put the Irish controversy outside Parliament for a time'. Perhaps more significantly, Lloyd George's Private Secretary noted that the Prime Minister was 'hopeful that peace may reign for a few months at least in that quarter, although I do not known whether he has any hopes of the Convention ultimately solving the Irish puzzle'. It would be naïve to overlook Lloyd George's penchant for the cynical stratagem, but in this instance the Cabinet turned to the Convention as a last-minute alternative because Nationalists strongly opposed partition. Moreover, Redmond himself contributed to the outcome when, some days before the Cabinet offer, he privately informed Lord Crewe that he would prefer a Convention to partition.[46]

It was at this juncture, marking an important watershed in Irish affairs, that a new development occurred in Anglo-American relations. As Balfour was returning to England, the Cabinet nominated the controversial scourge of English politics, Lord Northcliffe, to succeed him as head of the British War Mission – a post which he assumed after arriving in America on 11 June 1917.

9
The Northcliffe Mission; the Irish Convention and British Propaganda in the United States (June 1917–April 1918)

I

Lord Northcliffe's mission to America marked the zenith of the new-style diplomacy in America. Balfour's own visit had already illustrated the 'twentieth century vogue for ministerial diplomacy',[1] but the Foreign Minister himself was, nevertheless, a product of the traditional school of statesmanship. By contrast, Northcliffe, whose newspapers had frequently castigated the Foreign Office, was regarded as a 'business hustler' and a 'self-advertiser' and the Foreign Office was acutely aware that he was distrusted by many Americans, including President Wilson.[2] Considerable disapproval therefore followed when the Cabinet rushed through Northcliffe's appointment – apparently against Balfour's wishes and while he was sailing home – in what was seen as a move to silence possible criticism of the Government by Northcliffe's newspapers.[3]

Northcliffe's principal biographers have suggested that the War Cabinet may have taken into account the value in America of his Irish extraction. This attribute would have been underlined by the *Times* campaign, which seemed to show concern both for Ireland and for American sensitivity. By contrast, Robert Cecil contended that Northcliffe's indiscretions might incur 'serious trouble with the anti-war section of American opinion'. Northcliffe himself was only too aware that the 'Fenian' and pro-German pressmen would make intense efforts to 'discover material for anti-British attack', and instructed his *Daily Mail* editorial staff to avoid criticism of the

United States during the mission. On arrival in America, he advised Lloyd George that the Irish were more powerful than he had anticipated and 'hurt us in all kinds of ways that are not apparent in England'. Apart from their power in the press, they were, for example, involved in munitions, and the Secretary of the Interior, Lane, had predicted that a 10 per cent increase in war production would follow an Irish settlement.[4] Spring-Rice, who shared the Foreign Office distrust of Northcliffe,[5] nevertheless agreed with him that a breakdown of the Convention might cause 'serious consequences' among Irish-Americans, since 'some of the more desperate and those in German pay will try to organise draft riots as they did in the Civil War'. He reported that 'Sinn Feiners' were instigating strikes and that priests were urging cooks not to economise on food 'because it would help the English'.[6]

Although the main details of the Convention had been settled by June, an amnesty for the remaining Sinn Fein prisoners was widely advocated so that the assembly could meet in a constructive atmosphere. Such advocates placed great emphasis on the importance of the two new influences on world diplomacy – Russia and the United States. The release of political prisoners by the new Russian Government was cited by Liberal and Irish MPs as a humanitarian example to follow, while Horace Plunkett advised Lloyd George that American criticism was only withheld 'out of unwillingness to give comfort to the enemy'. Accepting that amnesty would give 'confidence to onlookers abroad', the Government finally yielded to cumulative pressure and in mid June announced the release of the remaining prisoners.[7]

The decision inevitably roused Unionist ire, and Ronald McNeill likened the gesture to 'playing a penny whistle to conciliate a cobra'. The *Belfast News Letter* predicted that Sinn Fein would be emboldened to press its 'insolent' peace-conference claim, and this was soon confirmed when Arthur Griffith asserted that Sinn Fein would present Ireland's case 'before an unpacked jury of the nations of the world and before a tribunal that England could not coerce or cajole – the Peace Conference'. Sinn Fein's critics, such as the Redmondite *Freeman's Journal*, were quick to jeer that 'the plan of "ourselves alone" needs international support'. It is indeed a paradox that the new movement, whose ethos was self-reliance, should adopt as its principal policy an appeal to the international community; but it is equally paradoxical that the Home Rule Party, which had traditionally sought overseas support, should seek a solution of the Irish Question by a purely internal mechanism. Even John Dillon, the most internationally minded of the Home Rulers, argued that, before resorting to 'the sympathy of foreign nations', it would be infinitely better to settle the problem domestically, since Ireland's reliance in the past on overseas aid had invariably 'met with hideous disaster'. Horace Plunkett also attempted to 'prick the bubble of the Peace Conference' by suggesting that Irishmen should 'turn to the Convention and see whether that bird in the hand does not offer a better solution than this doubtful bird in a distant bush'. However, despite these efforts to present the Convention as a more valid expression of Irish self-determination, the groundswell support for the peace conference scheme grew inexorably, leading William O'Brien to observe that the Government's policy of 'packing' the Convention had 'made the Sinn Feiners with their Peace Congress programme the masters of the situation'.[8]

British spokesmen were naturally anxious to gain American backing for the Convention. This concern prompted Spring-Rice to recommend a Government statement of its intention to give Ireland the 'advantages of self-government', but simultaneously to 'maintain unimpaired' the unity of the Empire for defence purposes. Many Foreign Office officials were, indeed, keen to persuade Americans that 'unimpaired' imperial unity was crucial against German aggression, but there was much less enthusiasm to affirm the 'advantages of self-government' in Ireland. Ronald Roxburgh deemed this unnecessary, since Irish-American extremists, 'if given enough rope, will hang themselves', while Robert Cecil minuted tersely, 'I am not going myself to say that I am in favour of Irish self-government.' As a permanent civil servant, Hubert Montgomery could not officially express such political opinions and merely voiced an inexplicit doubt: 'I do not see how any official statement can be made and I should not think it is at all desirable.' However, a private letter to his father clarified his real objections:

> I quite agree with you about the perniciousness of the statement that everyone will be glad to give Ireland any form of Home Rule that all Irishmen agree about, but presumably what makes it comparatively harmless amusement for anyone who likes to air that view is that there is practically no danger of 'all Irishmen' agreeing to any form of Home Rule.[9]

A week later, Montgomery and Cecil were more receptive when

a further Spring-Rice telegram omitted all reference to the 'advantages of self-government' and suggested, instead, a statement to show the 'great progress made in Ireland' under the Union. This would expose the 'falsity and absurdity' of accusations by Irish-American agitators, 'who constantly speak and write without contradiction as if penal laws were still in force and religious and civil liberty were non-existent'. Spring-Rice's switch of emphasis to the benefits of Union transformed the D of I's tepid indifference into warm support, and Montgomery, casting aside previous reservations, arranged for Joseph Fisher to write an article for American distribution.[10]

In addition to Fisher's article, the D of I compiled for America a fresh selection of pamphlets which embraced both the role of Catholics within the British Empire and Irish valour in the war.[11] Stories of Irish valour had become such a staple of British propaganda that there was a danger that oversaturation would invite derision. Geoffrey Butler, who had gone to America to take charge of a British Publicity Bureau in New York, warned that journalists in the New York *World* office 'were rather laughing at the device of writing up the Irish (Ulster and the South) charging side by side'.[12] Indeed, although many Irishmen fought in the belief that their sacrifices would earn Home Rule, British propagandists interpreted their achievements as indicating not only a united war effort but also continuing satisfaction with British government.

D of I attitudes towards one of the pamphlets, Thomas Kettle's *Ways of War*, demonstrated how the ingrained prejudice against Irish Nationalists – even those fighting in France – often exercised an unjust influence. In transmitting a request from Shane Leslie for Kettle's tract to be subsidised, Geoffrey Butler commented that, although Kettle was 'an Irish rebel', the pamphlet was pro-Redmond and worthy of support. The description 'rebel' immediately alienated the D of I, where Roxburgh termed the idea 'doubtful' and Montgomery minuted darkly, 'A proposition in which Shane Leslie and an Irish rebel are involved had better be handled with caution.' It was typical of Montgomery's prejudice that he should cast aspersions on the reliability of Leslie, whose work in America received widespread praise and whose only transgression could have been his advocacy of Home Rule. Buchan, however, was quick to defend Kettle against the 'rebel' label: 'He died fighting for Britain in France. His work is a very good one, and I am all for supporting it.' Although the pamphlet was then sanctioned, it is clear that without Buchan's intervention it would have been rejected because of its Irish Nationalist origins.[13]

Coincidentally, a similar situation involved Shane Leslie when a law firm asked the Foreign Office whether his activity in the United States was Government work, since, if so, he stood to gain financially from a trust fund. The D of I knew of no important duties keeping Leslie in America, while the Metropolitan Police chief, Basil Thomson, known for his antipathy towards Irish Nationalism, reported that Leslie had been 'associated with Casement . . . in the formation of the Irish Volunteers' and was, at that time, 'an advanced Nationalist'. It is difficult to escape the conclusion that, had Leslie been a Unionist, he would have been spared this rigorous investigation. As it was, the Foreign Office would doubtless have disowned him had it not been for Eric Drummond's assurances that he was 'tried and trusted' and often supplied Spring-Rice with useful information. Although reluctant on security grounds to admit any connection with Leslie, the Foreign Office finally decided to acknowledge his activities in strictest confidence.[14] Despite Redmond's patriotic stance throughout the war, it is clear that Home Rulers were still viewed with suspicion by many officials. In Leslie's case, the innuendo of disloyalty was particularly undeserved, since he had been a 'valuable go-between and source of information' on Irish-American matters and, in the process, had incurred considerable animosity from Anglophobes in the United States.[15] The D of I's ignorance of his activities is surprising, for they were highly valued by Spring-Rice in particular; indeed, Arthur Willert later wrote that Leslie helped the Ambassador to 'keep straight' on Irish-American and Catholic affairs, and, 'though independent and unpaid . . . , was the nearest approach to a secret propagandist that we had in the United States'.[16]

Pamphlets which covered the role of Catholics in the British war effort were considered of great importance in view of the Church's sway over Irish-Americans and because, unlike their counterparts from the Central Powers, British diplomats found rapport with American Catholics difficult. In Leslie's view, the Church hierarchy in America disliked Northcliffe and had 'no touch with Springy or the F.O.'. Spring-Rice's remoteness from the Catholic Church may have encouraged his stated belief that, while the hierarchy officially backed recruiting, many priests were co-operating with Sinn Feiners in dissuading American soldiers from going to France. 'The attitude of the Catholic priests here', he advised Drummond, 'raises a very dangerous and difficult question, that of political opposition to the policy of the state.' The leading Anglophobe within the hierarchy was Boston's Cardinal O'Connell, of whom Frederick Dixon reported that, although publicly seeming to bless Irish recruiting, O'Connell was in reality 'cursing it between every line of his pronouncements'. As a result, there was 'not a man around here who would willingly enlist. I have talked to dozens of them, and they all regard it as being sent to the other end of the world to be shot by Germans.'[17]

In the summer of 1917, the D of I considered various publicity schemes to mollify American Catholics. Geoffrey Butler believed that the increasing willingness of some priests to help with Catholic propaganda indicated that, with the growing fear of pro-German stigma, the Irish agitation was 'no longer an acute one, so far as Anglo-American relations are concerned'. Moreover, he opposed suggestions for a secretly controlled Catholic Publicity Bureau as giving 'excellent ammunition' against Britain at a time when the Irish were 'slowly hanging themselves'. D of I attitudes towards the bureau scheme were mixed. Ronald Roxburgh agreed with Butler that Britain had 'too many enemies among Catholics in the U.S. to make any secret arrangement desirable', while P. F. Willson, a junior official, minuted stiffly, 'Too much of the "hole and corner" about it. . . . It does not sound quite cricket.' In the event, at the suggestion of Alec Randall, a D of I expert on Catholic matters, an open bureau was established, 'outwardly independent but with subterranean communication with this Department'. The bureau head, H. Christopher Watts, an English Catholic journalist with two years' experience on the Jesuit journal *America*, regularly obtained D of I material showing that 'Catholicism is by no means to be identified with the Teutonic side in the war'. While agreeing with Butler that America's entry into the war had moderated outward Catholic attitudes in the United States, he nevertheless believed that the American Church was still 'as anti-British as it can be' and that its purpose was 'to crab the war'. Although, in Watts's view, Butler appeared not to recognise 'what a power is exercised by the Catholic press in America', religious channels were increasingly used as a more subtle means of placating Irish-Americans than political propaganda.[18]

Most of the propaganda so far discussed was essentially defensive, with conciliation as its aim. With America's growing involvement in the war, however, 'hyphenism' was becoming increasingly unpopular, thereby opening up possibilities of more aggressive combined action against Irish-American extremists. Anti-hyphenate feeling is frequently glossed over by historians. Edward Roberts, for example, subsequently proclaimed that, with the advent of war, 'Irish-Americans forgot all save that the country of their adoption or birth had drawn the sword.' How different was the view of Tom Spring-Rice, the Ambassador's cousin, who wrote ruefully of the antipathy aroused by 'mischief-makers', whose one object was 'to perpetuate trouble' and make a settlement impossible:

> They are by degrees making themselves pretty unpopular with the general public here, and people are forming societies to combat the activities of the street orators, who preach treason to the U.S. and advocate resistance to the draft law on the ridiculous plea that the American troops would be fighting England's battles. . . . But it does make one sick to see what a bad name all the Irish get, owing to the shouts of the extremist minority. The voices of the reasonable majority simply are not heard.[19]

The principal attacks on Irish-American 'disloyalty' began in September 1917, when the United States Government belatedly published many of the documents captured in the von Igel raid of April 1916. The most sensational revelation was an unsigned, typewritten note to the German Foreign Office, to the effect that the Irish extremist Judge Cohalan had recommended German fleet and submarine action in the North Sea to coincide with the outbreak of the Easter Rising. Cohalan at once publicly denounced the document as a British-inspired forgery. Citing evidence received from an Irish-American, William J. Maloney, he referred to an alleged discussion at the British Embassy in May 1917 between Eustace Percy, Shane Leslie, Maloney and others, at which Leslie talked of evidence which might 'silence' Cohalan. Ignoring a warning from one of those present that such a vendetta would 'prove to be a boomerang', Leslie reportedly conspired with Spring-Rice to persuade the State Department to 'destroy' the Judge's reputation. There seems to be no evidence, either in the Foreign Office archives or in the memoirs of British officials, to substantiate this allegation, and Spring-Rice dismissed Cohalan's accusations as merely 'entertaining'. However, John Devoy subsequently claimed that the typed note was 'surreptitiously added to the von Igel Papers to furnish a pretext for attacks on Judge Colahan'.[20]

William Wiseman, who acted as British liaison with President Wilson, considered that the revelations had created an 'excellent impression' and had disgraced the pro-German elements. However, the 'boomerang' danger now materialised, for many Irish-Americans resented the release of the von Igel material seventeen months after the raid itself, and only after Germany had become an enemy. Arthur Willert, who had been temporarily seconded to the British War Mission, warned Northcliffe that 'several well-meaning Irishmen' had hinted of trouble among Irish-American recruits and a lessening of war work unless the Wilson Administration stopped 'dragging Irishmen in the dirt'. Willert's steadfast Home Rule convictions surfaced again in his conclusion: 'In the long run, can anything except an obviously good Home Rule settlement scotch the pest of the professional Irish-American?'[21]

The mutinous reaction of Irish-Americans finally crystallised in November 1917 at the New York Mayoral election, when the incumbent Mayor, John P. Mitchel, attacked Tammany Hall's Irish candidate, John F. Hyland, over his alleged alliance with disloyal elements. Colville Barclay reported that many Irish-Americans interpreted Mitchel's 'injudicious' attack – coinciding as it did with the von Igel revelations – as 'a general anti-Catholic and anti-Irish campaign' inspired by Britain. As a result, the Irish polled heavily for Hyland, whose resultant victory was seen by discomfited British officials as the success of a pro-German puppet. The significance of the reversal was reflected in subsequent recommendations to the D of I. Barclay urged that *The Times* in particular be warned to 'drop all reference to Irish-Americans'; dismissing Cohalan as 'not worth powder and shot', he recommended that British newspapers should focus instead on the loyalty of the great body of Irish-American Catholics to their government's war policy. Hubert Montgomery duly passed on Barclay's warning to *The Times*, but the damage had already been done. Both the British and United States governments absorbed the lesson, and, when further revelations were planned six months later, neither was anxious to assume responsibility for disclosure.[22]

Although treading warily against Irish-Americans, British propagandists were not averse to damning extremists in Ireland. Such an opportunity arose when American sailors on shore leave in

Cork proved a 'vogue' with local girls, leading to 'scandalous reports' of their activities and an 'offended sense of propriety' among the townsfolk. Sinn Feiners also took umbrage at the presence of Americans as Britain's allies, 'contrary to the Irish tradition that the question of Ireland would keep England at enmity with the United States'. With the encouragement of the clergy, Sinn Fein leaders organised groups of vigilantes, who 'marched about the streets in large numbers and interfered between sailors and women whenever they saw them together'. Clashes were inevitable and one local man was killed during an argument.[23]

Both Government propagandists and Ulster Unionists used the Cork confrontation to demonstrate that Sinn Fein was anti-American and undeserving of sympathy in that country. A highly coloured account from the *Freeman's Journal*, spotlighting the local clergy's encouragement of the vigilantes, was forwarded by the D of I to Butler, who arranged reproduction in the *New York Times* and *Tribune* and subsequently reported its 'great effect on public opinion'. Meanwhile, Hugh Montgomery calculated that the need for Ulster concessions at the Irish Convention would disappear once America was 'more thoroughly in the war and a few more American sailors have been mishandled by Irish patriots'. Indeed, Spring-Rice found the Washington naval authorities already alarmed that Sinn Fein had 'attacked the U.S. Navy', while Theodore Roosevelt later heard of Irish-American sailors 'declining to take shore leave at Cork because of their bitter feeling as to the Sinn Fein outfit'.[24]

Another line of attack discussed by the D of I was that, under Home Rule, Sinn Fein would soon gain effective control of Ireland and would permit a German naval base on the west coast – thus threatening both British and United States security. Spring-Rice noted that such a fear was already prevalent in United States naval circles and in the country at large, while Hubert Montgomery, writing privately to his father, referred to the American unease with obvious satisfaction:

> I hear that it has now dawned on some Americans that the sort of Home Rule which most of their Irish friends want would provide the Germans with a nice handy naval base particularly convenient for dealing with America and some of them are beginning to wonder whether Home Rule is a good idea after all. If this idea will only get a good hold, there will be a good deal less silly rubbish talked.[25]

In view of changing American attitudes, the Navy League – a British organisation which claimed political neutrality but was, in fact, Unionist-oriented – sought D of I permission to publish a pamphlet in the United States, urging that any settlement emerging from the Convention should safeguard Irish harbours and sea communications; otherwise, this 'Heligoland of the Atlantic' could menace the American east coast. However, the D of I considered that the time was not yet ripe for the circulation of such a pamphlet and advised the Navy League that it would be more acceptable once America was 'roused with the anger of the war'. As a compromise, the League agreed to revise the pamphlet into 'an American interpretation which could be circulated without being attacked as British activity'.[26]

With America now firmly in the war, Irish extremism on both sides of the Atlantic was under sharp attack. Revolutionary Irish-Americans could no longer pursue their activities with impunity, while Sinn Feiners in Ireland were also losing the popularity they had once enjoyed in America. The Foreign Office attributed this unpopularity in large measure to the publicity surrounding the Cork incidents and also to the revelations of alleged Irish intrigue with the Germans.[27] From the Foreign Office point of view, therefore, the autumn of 1917 marked an important stage in the struggle to win over American support on the Irish Question, for, with the United States now in the war, British propagandists felt able to conduct a more aggressive campaign against the iniquities of Irish extremism.

In addition to the propaganda work of the New York Publicity Bureau, the D of I increased the flow of visiting lecturers to the United States. In keeping with the Department's policy, these visitors were usually warned 'not to criticise anything American, and not to mention Ireland'.[28] Nevertheless, even Northcliffe, who prided himself on his 'excellent terms' with the Irish-Americans, was frequently compelled to tackle the Irish problem. One of his own speeches, in Atlantic City, bore this out:

> There was only one dissentient voice in the course of a speech of an hour's duration – 'What about Ireland?' The question was received with a good deal of applause by many present but I 'put it over them' by replying: 'I can hardly be expected to eulogise the country in which I had the honour of being born. Its deeds speak for themselves.' The Irish question is the very devil here. One is up against it in all sorts of unexpected places.[29]

As a result of such experiences, Northcliffe favoured greatly increased British propaganda to counter the German–Irish claim that Britain was 'getting all the money and . . . doing little of the work' in the war.[30] Northcliffe's 'propensity to propagandise', which irritated President Wilson and worried British officials such as Wiseman, Willert and Spring-Rice, contributed to the Government's decision in August 1917 to appoint Lord Reading as overall head of the British War Mission.[31] Indeed, when Northcliffe, after a short visit to England, planned to resume his propaganda activities in America, Eustace Percy warned him that this would be unwise in view of hostile Irish and pro-German influences.[32]

Controversy also surrounded a lecture tour by F. E. Smith, the brilliant and colourful Attorney General. Both Reading and Northcliffe favoured the tour, which was organised by Buchan and Edward Carson (newly appointed as Cabinet minister superintending the D of I).[33] There were, however, doubters, such as the federalist Moreton Frewen, who foresaw trouble arising from Smith's connection with the pre-war Ulster campaign against Home Rule. 'It really appeals to my sense of humour', wrote Frewen to Balfour, 'that you despatch to bound around over there my friend "Galloper Smith", his chief title to fame [being] that he was Carson's aide de camp! C'est magnifique, mais ce n'est pas la guerre.' It is ironic that, almost as Frewen wrote these words, Smith gave an interview to the *Boston Post* newspaper which created a storm amongst Irish-Americans. After allegedly stating that 'nothing ever gave me greater delight than the execution of Casement', the Attorney General disclosed that he had threatened resignation from the Cabinet when it showed signs of 'wobbling' over the death penalty. Turning next to the Convention, he advocated that the ideal course would be to prolong its life: 'Let them keep on talking. If they don't agree, it's the fault of the Irish and not of the English, for there is not one Englishman in the Convention. It's an Irish problem and not an English problem.'[34]

After hurriedly travelling to Toronto, where Smith was then speaking, Geoffrey Butler obtained a denial of the offending remarks, in which Smith stressed his long-standing desire to 'conciliate the Nationalist Party both in Great Britain and the U.S.'. Moving on to Boston, Butler found the Irish still 'very much perturbed' by the original interview and noted that it had 'driven together the extremists and the moderates'. The Anglophobe Cardinal O'Connell, denouncing the interview as the irresponsible outpourings of drunkenness, advised Butler against the issue of any denial. 'Leave it alone', he urged, 'and tell your Government that the only decent thing they can do is to call him home in disgrace.' Butler, however, dismissed O'Connell's advice as indicating 'the powerful weapon which such a denial would form'. In the event, the denial was 'poked away in a corner' of the *Post*, prompting Colonel Arthur Murray, Assistant British Military Attaché to lament, 'Two thirds of the people who read the original will probably miss reading the denial.' British officials were dismayed at Smith's apparent folly. Spring-Rice considered that Smith had 'put his foot into it pretty considerably', whilst Arthur Murray believed that 'the root of the mischief lay in the fact that he gave the interview at all'. Verbal interviews in America were always liable to misrepresentation, but one given by 'an individual of F.E.'s Ulster record in a hotbed of Irish-Americanism' was bound to be misrepresented.[35]

Following Smith's return to Britain in February 1918, Foreign Office hopes that the controversy would die down were dashed by suggestions that he had been recalled prematurely because of his indiscretions. The New York *World*'s London correspondent, for example, telegraphed that, in view of Smith's 'undergraduate bumptiousness' and 'invincible self-esteem', his 'accelerated homecoming' was no surprise. The D of I entreaties for this 'deplorable' article to be withdrawn were rejected by the correspondent, and, with America now an ally, enforcement of such requests was difficult. Robert Cecil summed up Foreign Office feeling on the episode by minuting curtly, 'Silence is golden.'[36]

A similar contretemps terminated the activities in America of Lord Aberdeen, former Viceroy of Ireland. Although Aberdeen had toured America on Irish charity work since 1915, he had also made periodic statements on Irish political issues,[37] and in the eyes of Irish-American extremists he symbolised English overlordship of Ireland. Problems arose in May 1918, when Aberdeen organised a fund-raising benefit at New York's Carnegie Hall and advertised Charlie Chaplin as the chief attraction. According to Aberdeen's subsequent account, the comedian was then 'induced to keep away' from the function by German–Irish extremists and, while Aberdeen himself remained 'in the dark' about the development, the New York press and District Attorney's Office had been carefully primed as to Chaplin's non-appearance. Aberdeen was criticised in the press for falsely billing Chaplin and was questioned by the District

Attorney both for this and for accusations of misappropriated funds. The perplexed peer regarded the affair as a German–Irish 'plan of reprisal' and considered it 'the most extraordinary experience of my now rather lengthy life, that the failure of a youthful comic actor to keep an engagement should have been manufactured into material for a campaign of calumny'. British officials were none the less irritated at Aberdeen's lack of political guile, and Stephen Gaselee, a Government propagandist, suggested that official intervention was scarcely warranted, 'so entirely discredited is Lord A.'.[38]

While the problems facing the likes of Smith and Aberdeen in America were considerable, those for Redmondite missions were even more daunting, since the Irish-American community, once the financial lifeline of the Home Rulers, was 'no longer on speaking terms with the Irish party'.[39] Even so, America's entry into the war had stirred new hopes among Redmond and his lieutenants that the party could regain lost influence and obtain desperately needed funds. On Shane Leslie's advice, an Irish Commission under T. P. O'Connor was sent to America in July 1917, but its reception shocked O'Connor, who found himself 'living in an atmosphere of violent anti-English hatred' from the moment of his arrival:

> The Sinn Fein papers opened a bitter campaign against me and every mail brought letters of horrible abuse, in which Judas Iscariot was the mildest term applied to me, and in which there was the universal suggestion that I was a highly paid corrupt agent of the British Government.[40]

To prevent taunts of being a British agent, O'Connor avoided contact with the British Embassy.[41] He was nevertheless assisted by officials such as Arthur Murray who, apart from being Assistant Military Attaché, was also a Liberal MP and convinced Home Ruler. In October, Murray informed Eric Drummond that O'Connor was beginning to win over American support with his argument that, 'so long as the Sinn Feiners rule the roost in Ireland, that country is to all intents and purposes a portion of the German Front'. Indeed, the Attaché claimed to have stressed to wealthy Americans that, 'from the point of view of the British Government, it was of essential *war* importance that the constitutional party should maintain the upper hand'.[42] Murray, who wanted to see the Irish sore removed from Anglo-American relations, clearly considered it vital to sustain the

Home Rule party wherever possible, and his activities showed that the mission received at least some official support.

Notwithstanding O'Connor's efforts and the assistance of sympathisers such as Murray, the time was inopportune for fund-raising in America. As O'Connor's travelling-companion, Richard Hazleton, explained to Redmond, the war fever which had eclipsed Irish-American extremism had simultaneously diverted the average American mind from the Irish problem: 'Where we can get people to listen to us they are interested, but Ireland is a side-issue with most of them, about which they cannot bother just now.' To combat such apathy, O'Connor was forced to base his appeal on an anti-German war platform, which he believed made him 'champion for the moment of the sane, patriotic Irish-American against the turbulent and disloyal enemies'. It is ironic that, after years of denouncing British governments to American audiences, O'Connor should be compelled by the climate of opinion in the United States to link the Home Rule movement with the British cause and adopt a similar stance to that of official British lecturers. This laid him open to jibes such as William O'Brien's that he was the British Government's 'Ambassador in America to misrepresent us'.[43]

Despite his considerable difficulties, O'Connor was able to despatch a modest sum to Redmond by December 1917, thus ending a period in which his 'haunting terror' had been that the Convention would break up before he could send anything. By past standards the mission had been a failure, which was no surprise to Spring-Rice, who regarded the Redmondites as 'hopelessly discredited'. O'Connor himself attributed the situation to the failure of so many Home Rule schemes and warned Redmond that, unless the Convention gave some defensible settlement, 'our mission as a party is at an end'.[44]

By the autumn of 1917, however, prospects of a settlement through the Convention looked remote. The Ulster Unionists, who had never disguised their reluctance to attend, cited America's growing intolerance of Irish extremism as proof that the 'imperial argument' for settlement was dissipating. Nevertheless, they raised no objection when proceedings were protracted by various committees, for, as Hubert Montgomery told an Ulster delegate, 'you are not losing time as your deliberations give the Americans an opportunity of revising their opinion about Home Rule'. The Government, too, was well satisfied with the continuing deliberations. Maurice Hankey, indeed, acknowledged that the likelihood of a solution emerging was 'questionable', but still considered the Convention a 'real asset' for the British cause in the United States, Russia and the Dominions:

> By many people abroad it is understood . . . as a real earnest of the intention of the British Government to seek a solution to the Irish difficulty and, so long as it can keep steadily at work, this happy state of affairs should continue.[45]

Sensing that the Convention was becoming a mere delaying-tactic, Redmond warned the delegates that, while the Irish problem persisted, Americans would distrust British pretensions to champion the rights of small nations. This had become the 'chief cause of America's apathy today' and might even lead the United States Government to make a premature peace on terms 'which we could not accept'. Consequently, 'all connected with our foreign affairs' were 'feverishly anxious as to the result of our deliberations'. Ulster Unionists were unimpressed as ever. The *Belfast News Letter* countered that, despite constant warnings that America would not enter the war without an Irish settlement, she was now a belligerent 'with her whole heart and resources'. The newspaper, therefore, scorned the claim that Home Rule was necessary 'to obtain American support or to shorten the war'.[46]

The situation at the Convention was further complicated when the Nationalist delegates split into two factions, both claiming American sympathy for their own conception of a settlement. The more extreme faction, headed by the Bishop of Raphoe, demanded control of customs and excise as the main step towards Dominion status, arguing that the Government would be forced to concede this, since Irish-Americans would no longer tolerate the limited Home Rule acceptable to Redmond.[47] This led Lord Midleton, the Southern Unionist leader, to introduce a compromise scheme, whereby an Irish parliament would control internal taxation, including excise, while customs would remain an imperial responsibility. This scheme – acceptable to the Redmondites and thus providing a bridge between them and the Southern Unionists – was the nearest that the Convention came to a settlement. Paradoxically, however, it eventually proved to be another rock on which constitutional Nationalism was to founder, since it heralded the subsequent parting of the ways between the Redmondites and the Raphoe faction. Hopes for compromise were not helped when a redefinition of war aims by the British and United States Governments focused renewed attention on the principle of self-determination and thereby encouraged the more advanced Nationalists to believe that they could wring greater concessions from the British Government.

II

At the onset of 1918, both Lloyd George and President Wilson chose to issue fresh statements of their war aims. The British Premier, desperately needing fresh troops for the spring campaign, sought the support of the Trades Union Congress for a wider measure of conscription. Having been forewarned by William Wiseman of Wilson's planned statement, he decided to move first to avoid pre-emption. The situation was complicated by the negotiations between the Bolsheviks and Germans, during which the Bolshevik Foreign Minister, Trotsky, appealed to Britain to show her sincerity by including self-determination for Ireland, Egypt and India in her war aims – as Russia had done for Finland and the Ukraine.[48] In Cabinet, Robert Cecil argued that such comments made the moment 'particularly favourable' for a British declaration that these countries were 'governed for the benefit of the governed'. Accordingly, he drafted a statement stressing that British rule in Egypt and India had brought great benefits and had allowed considerable participation in local government. The Irish case, he contended, was particularly clear, since the task of reforming Irish administration had been given to a Convention, 'admittedly as representative as it was possible to obtain'; any difficulties, therefore, were entirely owing to 'the unfortunate fact that the Irish themselves are not agreed on what they desire'.[49]

Most of Cecil's draft was incorporated by Lloyd George into his speech delivered to the trades unions on 5 January. However, concern from Walter Long and Maurice Hankey about possible repercussions within the Empire led to emphasis on self-determination being replaced by the less inflammatory slogan 'Government by the consent of the governed.' Moreover, mention of Ireland was severely curtailed, Lloyd George merely stating that Redmond as spokesman for Irish Nationalism had already 'made clear what his ideas are as to the object and purpose of the war'. By contrast, President Wilson's 'fourteen points' declaration of war aims, made only three days later, was seen as an unequivocal commitment to 'self-determination' and therefore received greater acclaim. Indeed, as Henry Duke noted, the Irish Question was now 'notoriously involved in the definition of our war aims and those of the United States'.[50]

This dual affirmation of war aims renewed newspaper pressure for implementation of any settlement produced by the Convention. Prominent in this campaign was Lord Northcliffe, who privately urged leading politicians that Ulster should be coerced if it blocked a settlement, since threats of industrial action in Belfast could be dealt with if necessary, whereas a 'downing tools' in America if Ireland was denied justice would be fatal to the Allies. Northcliffe's private overtures were reinforced by *Times* editorials and by despatches from Henry Noble Hall, Willert's deputy as Washington correspondent. Hall reported that rumours of a Convention breakdown had created 'great anxiety' in American Government circles and that President Wilson was 'known to sympathise most deeply with the aspirations of the Irish people for the fullest measure of Home Rule'. In Hall's view, lack of progress would stimulate anti-British resolutions in Congress, where, with forthcoming Congressional elections in mind, even Republicans were prepared to push the Irish cause in order to win votes. Northcliffe deemed Hall's despatch to be of vital importance, since it was 'obviously sent by the wish of the President, with whom Noble Hall is intimately acquainted'.[51]

Many Unionists resented the constant pressure of the Northcliffe press and called on the proprietor to 'bring to an end a press campaign, the most outrageous and the most misleading that perhaps has ever taken place'. The Belfast *Evening Telegraph* condemned Noble Hall's assessments as 'engineered and manufactured', while the *Belfast News Letter* complained that the correspondent was 'pushing this anti-Ulster convention campaign for all he is worth'. Harking back to past reports from Hall's predecessor, Willert, the *News Letter* jibed at 'how clever' he had been in 'finding just the sort of news that will best serve the purpose which his journal for that moment has decided to champion'.[52]

In addition to the *Times* reports, the Government received similar warnings from a committee newly formed to monitor the Irish-American situation and comprising Geoffrey Butler, Arthur Murray and Arthur Willert. Butler warned that Americans would regard an unproductive Convention as 'disastrous', while Murray predicted a 'deplorable effect on public opinion'. Willert went further by suggesting that, should the Convention fail, Americans would applaud if the Government 'simply coerced Ulster into accepting something like the old Home Rule measure'. Professional diplomats supported the committee's view. Colville Barclay telegraphed that future Anglo-American relations might be 'gravely jeopardised' by failure, while Spring-Rice reminded the Foreign Office that, with so many Catholics in the American forces, an abortive outcome would 'gravely weaken the American war-effort'.[53]

Unanimous though they were, these warnings provoked little response at the Foreign Office. Eric Drummond considered that the clamour following a collapsed Convention would 'not be as serious during the war as is sometimes feared', while Robert Cecil cautioned that Irish-Americans were 'first-rate agitators' and were 'trying to make our flesh creep at the prospect of a breakdown of the Irish negotiations'. Balfour's Private Secretary, Ian Malcolm, condemned Butler's messages as 'hysterical', while Rowland Sperling's penchant for cynical calculation was again to the fore:

> If the failure of the Convention can be deferred till U.S. troops are in serious fighting, less attention will be paid to Irish matters in the U.S., and less sympathy will be wasted on those who embarrass the Allied military effort.[54]

Despite its lack of concern over Ireland, the Foreign Office functioned as transmission agency for a two-way flow of information between Ireland and America. President Wilson received copies of Plunkett's secret Convention reports to the King, while Plunkett, in turn, was supplied with current Irish news from America.[55] The D of I decided, however, that, since the Convention was 'the only thing about which the average American now cares', propaganda on Irish matters was futile until that body reported. 'The problems are problems of statesmanship and policy rather than propaganda', minuted Ronald Roxburgh. 'Propaganda can ease the situation, but cannot cure it.' When asked by Roxburgh how the D of I should approach the Convention issue, Robert Cecil replied with an unmistakably partisan viewpoint which laid the whole weight of imminent failure on Irish shoulders:

> The Irish Convention is slowly drifting to its inevitable failure, and the hopes which have been excited about its results must end

in corresponding disappointment. Personally, I should like to take and emphasise the point that the British Parliament is now and has always been perfectly ready to accept any solution of the Irish problem which the Irish as a whole approve; that the Government are not prepared, especially during war-time, to coerce any important section of the Irish to accept a settlement which they resent, nor are they prepared in the midst of all their other anxieties to try to pass through Parliament a highly controversial measure of Irish Government. If therefore the Irish Convention fails the whole question will be necessarily hung up till the end of the war.[56]

Coinciding with this hardening of attitudes towards the Convention, the D of I continued its efforts to present the Ulster case to Americans. A fact-finding tour of Ulster was arranged for a group of American journalists by Nigel Lindsay, who had been attached to the D of I whilst invalided from the Western Front. Significantly, Lindsay was the son of an Ulster Unionist MP, and, since the Ulster leader, Edward Carson, was now the minister superintending the D of I, the *Freeman's Journal* saw the project as proof that the Department was being 'used for purposes of Unionist propaganda' and the 'undermining of American sympathy with Ireland'. This 'monstrous outrage', it argued, was a further stage from the Department's original purpose of justifying British war aims and threw 'a sinister light upon the policy of the so-called War Cabinet'. Even the less partisan Horace Plunkett suspected that the tour had been organised with a Convention breakdown in mind, so that American journalists could be 'educated in the gospel of Saint or Sir Edward'.[57]

Such accusations were strenuously rejected by the Unionist press. The *Morning Post* claimed that 'independent inquiry would be encouraged', while the Belfast *Northern Whig* found it 'easy to understand the alarm of the Nationalists', since they had been 'spoon-feeding the American public for thirty years with their own brand of information'. An investigation by 'fair-minded strangers from across the Atlantic' would soon discover 'what law-abiding, loyal, honest and industrious men can do, and they will understand why we do not want to go under a Dublin Parliament'. The *Belfast News Letter* wrote accusingly that the Nationalists had 'induced too many Americans, including some men of political prominence, to believe that the Irish people are almost unanimous in demanding

Home Rule'. While reaffirming its traditional view that UK internal affairs were 'not matters which directly concern the citizens of the United States', the *News Letter* now welcomed American interest as heralding a better understanding of Ulster.[58]

This tactical switch towards wooing the American press exasperated the *Manchester Guardian*, which complained that only those newspapers which were 'least sympathetic to the Irish cause', such as the Chicago *Tribune* and the *New York Times*, had been invited to Ulster. Piqued by the accusation, the D of I protested to the *Guardian* editor that the journalists had all been selected by ballot and that the tour was complementary to a similar one in Southern Ireland. In truth, however, although it may only have been correcting an existing imbalance towards the Nationalist viewpoint, the tour clearly favoured the Ulster cause. Indeed, Lindsay subsequently reported that the journalists, after previously regarding Ulster as a 'small and insignificant part of Ireland', could now 'see the Ulster point of view. Ulster had put her back into it and . . . was entitled to have some consideration.'[59]

This episode was only one of many in 1918 when British propaganda was accused of Unionist bias. The Nationalist MP T. J. Harbison asserted in Parliament that one of Carson's aims during his period as 'Minister of Propaganda' had been to 'spread his doctrines far and wide over the world', while the *Freeman's Journal* attacked British lecturers in America as 'the agents of British Die Hards', aiming to 'range the American people in open hostility to the Irish race'.[60] Although many British propagandists periodically sniped at Irish Nationalism, the allegations against Carson himself seem unfounded, since he neglected his propaganda duties[61] and, judging by Departmental minutes, never participated in policy decisions. Moreover, his propaganda responsibilities lasted only four months. He resigned in January 1918, when, with Ulster's prospects in jeopardy, he felt that his place was with his followers in the struggle to come.

Nationalist touchiness regarding British propaganda was largely owing to the delicate balance of the Convention and the increasing influence on its deliberations of foreign opinion. The *Times* reports, together with the war-aims declarations, were used by Nationalists of all shades to reinforce their own particular claims. Speaking for Sinn Fein, Eamon de Valera proclaimed that Wilson and Lloyd George were 'hypocrites' if, after their talk of 'self-determination', they refused independence to Ireland. At the other end of the

Nationalist spectrum, however, supporters of the Midleton compromise claimed that it, too, was 'a striking embodiment of the principle of self-determination' and, as such, would impress America, Russia and other nations.[62] Horace Plunkett, despite his position as Convention Chairman, unreservedly supported the Midleton compromise and made a last-ditch but vain effort to convince Raphoe that it was 'by far the most generous advance England has ever made to Ireland' and that he was 'haunted' by 'what the world will say if we adopt an intransigent attitude'.[63]

Unfortunately for the prospects of any compromise, the more advanced Nationalists had also been encouraged to cling to their demands. Indeed, Plunkett considered that, owing to the 'extraordinary psychology of the Convention', the war-aims speeches had 'made all patriots crazy on self-determination'. Moreover, it was now freely voiced at the Convention that Wilson was applying pressure which would compel the British Government to grant Ireland full fiscal autonomy. As a result, Joseph Devlin and several other Nationalist delegates deserted Redmond and voted with Raphoe against the Midleton compromise – thus signalling the final eclipse of moderate Nationalism in Ireland.[64]

Throughout late 1917, many Ulstermen had feared that the world tide towards 'self-determination' was so strong that it was tactically expedient to use the new catch-phrase to their own advantage, as the *Belfast News Letter* did when it asked, 'On what principle is Ulster to be denied the right of self-determination?' However, with the Southern Unionists rejoining the Unionist fold after the failure of the Midleton compromise and with Irish extremism increasingly unpopular in America, Ulster attitudes hardened once more against any form of Home Rule. Joseph Fisher, for example, considered the cry of 'Ulster self-determination' to be undesirable, for it implied acceptance of Home Rule for the Nationalist areas. It had, in fact, only been adopted 'as a second line of defence', and the province had 'never asked for it or accepted it for its own sake'.[65]

This tactical reversion affected the usage of American Civil War parallels. Hitherto, Ulster's demand for exclusion had been likened to West Virginia's refusal to be coerced into the Confederacy.[66] Now, Hugh Montgomery and his colleagues, increasingly concerned that the parallel might be counter-productive, urged the need to show Americans that the seceding rebel was 'not Ulster from the rest of Ireland but the rest of Ireland from the U.K.'[67] Thus, in Unionist newspapers, Sinn Fein policy became increasingly identified with the path followed by the Confederacy in the American Civil War, while the Unionist stand was compared with Abraham Lincoln's efforts to preserve national unity.[68] Indeed, the Ulster delegation's report at the close of the Convention illustrated, by its use of this parallel, how far Ulster had set its face against concessions:

> The U.S. established, at the cost of much blood and treasure, national unity when the Confederacy claimed (like the Irish Nationalists) to set up an independent Government. With this and other examples before us we cannot help feeling that the demands put forward, if conceded, would create turmoil at home and weakness abroad.[69]

The Government was acutely aware that Americans expected some kind of settlement to emerge from the Convention. When, in early January, the Midleton compromise had looked as if it might secure a 'substantial majority', Lloyd George wrote anxiously to Bonar Law on the urgent need for Ulster to 'show that it places the Empire above everything' by implementing such an agreement. Otherwise, Americans would accuse the British Government of 'sacrificing the interests of the war to that of a small political section', while President Wilson's position, 'with Germans and Irishmen on his flank, would become untenable'. The Prime Minister warned that 'if America goes wrong we are lost' and that, as a last resort, it might become necessary for the Government to compel acceptance of a majority decision by the delegates.[70]

With the defeat of the Midleton compromise, Lloyd George tried to persuade a Nationalist deputation to be content with American state rights (i.e. no customs or excise powers) and forgo their claim for Dominion Home Rule. He pressed the same solution on Sir Hugh Barrie, the leader of the Ulster delegation, particularly with a peace conference in prospect: 'Shall we go there', asked the Prime Minister, 'with Ireland unsettled and possibly in a state of coercion? If so, it will seriously impair our influence in that Council of Nations.'[71] The sincerity of Lloyd George's exhortation is questionable, since President Wilson had already assured him that he 'would not allow Ireland to be dragged into the Peace Conference'.[72] Indeed, although other War Cabinet ministers, such as the South African leader Jan Smuts, considered that Britain must not enter the peace conference with 'this skeleton in the cupboard' and that it was essential to find a solution beforehand, the Prime Minister later minimised this factor in private conversations.[73]

With John Redmond's death in March, the last slim hope of a moderate settlement disappeared. On 5 April the Convention adopted a diluted Home Rule scheme, with no customs and excise powers, by an unconvincing majority of forty-four votes to twenty-nine; but, with the Ulster delegates and several prominent Nationalists voting against it, the Government's stipulation that 'substantial agreement' be reached as a precondition of legislation was not fulfilled. This negative outcome nullified preparations by both the D of I and Plunkett to publicise the Convention's anticipated achievements. Although Plunkett ensured circulation in America for the final Convention report and stressed the near-success of the Midleton compromise, little could be done to dissuade Americans from believing that the Convention had merely been a method of shelving the Irish problem for nine months.[74]

It is ironic that foreign pressure, directed as it was towards a Home Rule settlement, should arouse such exaggerated hopes among advanced Nationalists that it ultimately constituted the greatest factor thwarting 'substantial agreement' to a moderate compromise. It is also ironic, and typical of the hydra-headed nature of government, that the Cabinet discreetly pressed for compromise, whereas the D of I worked against it, in effect, by sponsoring American journalists to absorb the Ulster viewpoint. At this critical juncture, the Cabinet's dilemma was aggravated by the repercussions of a new crisis on the Western Front. The German spring offensive achieved a breakthrough, provoking demands in Britain for an extension of conscription and, in particular, its application to Ireland. It was this proposal, long resisted by the vast majority of Nationalists, which produced the last major Irish crisis of the war.

10
The Conscription Crisis; the Last Months of the War (April–December 1918)

I

Although the problem of Irish conscription reached its climax in April 1918, it had arisen initially as early as autumn 1915, when Tory ministers in the Asquith Coalition pressed unsuccessfully for Ireland's inclusion in the Military Service Bill. The issue thus became a rallying-cry for Irish extremists on both sides of the Atlantic, prompting John Dillon to warn Parliament that Ireland's inclusion would destroy 'the moral effect that has been created in the United States of America and throughout Europe by the unexpected union between England and Ireland in this war'. After the Easter Rising, recruiting in Nationalist Ireland ground to a halt and the issue was raised anew in Cabinet. However, the proposal was again dropped after memoranda from both Maxwell and Duke pointed to its many drawbacks. Indeed, Maxwell argued that, apart from encouraging Sinn Fein, the measure would 'raise a storm among the Irish-Americans and play into the hands of German propaganda and intrigue'. When Lloyd George took office two months later, he confided to Lord Riddell, the newspaper proprietor, his fear that Irish conscription would cause 'a possible rupture' with America, with whom relations were 'hanging in the balance', and 'serious disaffection' in the Dominions, which would demand, 'What right have you to take this little nation by the ears and drag it into the war against its will?'[1]

Once America entered the war, the climate of opinion began to change. Having accepted conscription as a patriotic duty, Americans increasingly resented Ireland's exemption from the measure. The *Irish Times*, a persistent advocate of conscription, warned 'shirkers' in Ireland that they would receive a cold welcome from their 'fighting kinsmen' in the United States. Irish-Americans, it declared, had set aside their ancient quarrel and had rallied to the Allied standard, thereby placing Ireland in 'an inglorious isolation'. Querying whether Ireland's 'magnificent traditions as a fighting race' were to be maintained from America alone, the newspaper declared, 'America has given much to Ireland in the last sixty years. She will give Ireland the greatest boon of all if she leads her to her rightful place in the forefront of the war.'[2]

Not surprisingly, when the conscription issue became paramount in March 1918, it was to America that many heads turned to ascertain likely United States reaction to Irish conscription. Lord Reading, who had succeeded Spring-Rice as British Ambassador in February 1918, cabled that any serious unrest in Ireland following enforced conscription might 'disturb the unanimity of the war spirit now prevailing'. When the Prime Minister informed the Chief of Imperial General Staff, General Henry Wilson, that this indicated the President's personal concern, the General was disgusted and noted that Lloyd George had 'fastened on this sort of excuse for leaving Ireland out'.[3]

In fact, there was uncertainty within the War Cabinet whether Reading's telegram represented the President's views or merely the Ambassador's personal opinion. When Balfour cited Spring-Rice's past messages as indicating that 'the Irish question always loomed very large in the mind of the British Ambassador', it was decided that the Foreign Secretary should telegraph the President's confident, Colonel House, to seek 'an unbiased expression of the American view'. Balfour's telegram explained that British opinion would no longer tolerate further man-power demands while young men remained exempt in Ireland. Against this, Irish conscription would unite the various Nationalist factions and could only be enforced at the risk of 'serious disorder and, possibly, even of bloodshed'. To sweeten the pill, continued Balfour, the Government planned to introduce simultaneously the Home Rule scheme adopted by the majority at the Convention; but, with Ulster opposing Home Rule and the Nationalists resisting conscription, the 'war situation, to express it mildly, will not be bettered'. Balfour apologised for detailing 'apparently purely domestic' difficulties, but suggested that their ramifications might seriously affect the United States. However, unable to gauge 'the exact part that [the] Irish question takes in American politics', he requested House's own views.[4]

This consultation with House alarmed F. S. Oliver, a severe critic of American politics, who was now acting as Milner's assistant at War Cabinet meetings. Oliver was convinced that certain ministers, including 'the goat' (his malicious name for Lloyd George), would be relieved if President Wilson were to oppose Irish conscription and promise instead 'vast unrealisable monthly reinforcements, which will be worth just as much as any of his windy undertakings'. Oliver urged Austen Chamberlain that Wilson be presented with a 'chose jugée', since, if he was consulted beforehand, 'either his advice must be taken, or he will be justified in taking umbrage, which he will certainly proceed to do with his customary impeccable hypocrisy'. Simultaneously, Oliver urged his chief, Milner, that he 'must not allow the Cabinet to ask Wilson and House to make up their minds for them', and warned that, as Reading was 'no fighter', it was necessary to be 'even firmer with him than with another kind of Ambassador'. After seeing Balfour's completed message, Oliver was appalled by 'such a document as I never thought to see an English statesman put his name to' and was convinced that the Foreign Secretary had deliberately sought a pessimistic response since he 'sets out the arguments "con" with great lucidity and the arguments "pro" with great economy'.[5]

When House passed Balfour's telegram to President Wilson, the latter scribbled in reply that Irish conscription would 'accentuate the whole Irish and Catholic intrigue'. House then incorporated this phrase verbatim into his reply, which one historian has described as the 'one most feared by the British'[6] but which, according to Oliver, would have been welcomed by several ministers as an escape from their dilemma. By way of a second opinion, Eric Drummond obtained William Wiseman's assessment that, in fact, neither House nor Wilson felt deeply on the matter, being merely anxious to avoid Irish-American agitation. Believing that Americans would judge Irish conscription largely by the way it was explained in the United States, Wiseman deemed it a propaganda matter in which suggested 'bad effects' in America should not influence the Cabinet's decision. An even firmer negation of the House–Wilson view came, oddly enough, from the American Ambassador, Walter Hines Page. A strong Anglophile, Page called on Balfour and urged unofficially that, if conscription were not applied to Ireland, when it had been 'accepted practically by the whole of the English-speaking world', American resentment would be 'deep and strong'. Although aware that these were not White House views, Balfour passed them to Lloyd George as being 'so emphatic and . . . so unexpected that I thought you would like to be told'. Heartened by such recommendations, the Cabinet decided to press on with their dual scheme of Irish conscription linked with self-government, since the United States 'would view with the greatest disfavour any attempt to apply conscription without Home Rule'.[7]

The penchant for American Civil War parallels was again to the fore when Bonar Law and Unionist publicists such as Joseph Fisher and St Loe Strachey cited Abraham Lincoln's wide-ranging conscription measures and his uncompromising treatment of those who resisted them. The *Spectator* focused attention on Lincoln's tough handling of the Irish draft rioters in New York and suggested that Lincoln's laconic instruction on that occasion of 'Apply the draft' should be an example for the British Government to follow. Indeed, according to the newspaper, once the New York riots had been put down, the draft was applied to Irishmen with very little trouble.[8] This fondness for citing Lincoln arose in part from the need to justify British policy in terms which Americans could understand and became almost an obsession with many British politicians. (Indeed, during the subsequent 'Black and Tans' campaign, the Prime Minister justified his repressive measures by arguing that Lincoln had 'not shrunk from employing force to secure unity, though at the time he was reproached as violating democratic principle'.[9])

The Home Rule party reacted fiercely to the Government's proposals,[10] prompting Arthur Murray (who had returned to the Foreign Office to handle the flow of information from William Wiseman) to cable Reading for his assessment of American opinion. Reading replied that the press and most politicians – understanding the need for more troops – were 'favourable' towards the intended measure. However, lest Irish-Americans, backed by the powerful Catholic lobby, should 'turn in fury against England', the Ambassador urged that conscription should not be enforced until Home Rule became law and that the Government should, in fact, stake its existence on the immediate application of the measure. Indeed, with Anglo-American relations now 'improving daily', it was desirable to avoid any outcry which would revive 'dying prejudices which now mainly subsist upon grievances of discontented Irish'. Moreover, with Congressional elections due in November, President Wilson would be better able to resist political pressure if Home Rule had already been passed.[11]

A slightly more optimistic assessment was received from Hubert Montgomery, who had gone to America as Reading's assistant. He believed that, if American opinion was 'properly handled' and not 'misled by injudicious utterances at home', it would support Lloyd George's policy. Indeed, having accepted conscription themselves, Americans would demand that the Irish at home should be called upon to make the same sacrifice. Nevertheless, Montgomery echoed Reading's advice that Home Rule should accompany conscription, since another postponement would provoke a 'more critical attitude amongst Americans in general towards Irish policy'. In view of Montgomery's strong Unionist beliefs, his concluding advice doubtless reflected an official stance to which he felt obligated. However, his support for Irish conscription was beyond doubt. In August 1917 he had expressed hopes to his father that 'somebody would start a really good agitation for conscription in Ireland'. He could not imagine why the Government 'go on funking it', since 'there must be enough troops in Ireland to cope with any organised resistance'. Nor did he foresee any strong opposition from America, 'not that it matters what any other country does think on the point'.[12]

Although Robert Cecil argued that Reading was unduly pessimistic and failed to recognise that the Irish 'will endanger their American position if they resist', the Ambassador's message had a 'decisive effect' on the War Cabinet's deliberations.[13] The warning of a 'dangerous reaction in America' to any further hesitation over Home Rule stiffened the Cabinet's resolve to persevere with Irish conscription and Home Rule in tandem. A committee was therefore set up under Walter Long to formulate a Home Rule Bill based on the Convention's majority decision and therefore 'considered fair by both British and American opinion'. On the same day, during the final reading of the Military Service Bill in the Commons, Lloyd George asserted that American opinion, which was 'vital' to Britain at that moment, supported the Bill, provided self-government was offered to Ireland. The dual policy was the best way to secure a 'full measure of American assistance' and would be widely seen as expressing 'that principle of self-determination for which we are ostentatiously fighting'.[14]

II

Lloyd George's proposals failed to assuage Irish bitterness on either side of the Atlantic. Moderate Irish opinion in America was reported as accepting conscription, provided that it was passed in conjunction with Home Rule. However, as the Boston editor Frederick Dixon reported to Reading, this support was frequently a veneer to avoid the taint of disloyalty: 'The real feeling of the Irish, the great mass of whom are still living with the background of the Famine before them . . . , is utterly opposed to conscription and entirely in favour of the Sinn Fein element.' The 'real feeling of the Irish' was perhaps revealed in Chicago, where, according to the British Consul, Horace Nugent, even moderate Irish-Americans regarded the measure as the 'greatest possible blunder' and believed that a Home Rule parliament was the only body entitled to conscript Irishmen. After talking to many Irish-Americans, Arthur Vincent, the Chicago representative of Geoffrey Butler's Publicity Bureau, believed that recent events had rekindled their latent 'hatred of England'. It was widely felt that England had 'placed Ireland before the world in an utterly false position by cunningly representing her as unwilling and loth to join the other nations in fighting humanity's battle'. This had renewed Irish suspicions of the 'dirty English way of doing things' and had encouraged the belief that the only way to gain self-government was to 'thwart England in every direction' until it was carried out.[15]

Opinion in Ireland itself was even more hostile to the Government's 'dual policy'. At a Mansion House meeting, the various Nationalist factions joined forces in a rare show of solidarity and announced their intention to send a statement of Ireland's case to President Wilson.[16] Ulster Unionists, however, shared Lord Londonderry's conviction that nothing would now lessen the 'part which united America is determined on playing in this great war', while the Belfast *Northern Whig* took the point a stage further by alleging that Bonar Law in particular had 'allowed himself to be hypnotised by Mr Lloyd George and his tales about American opinion'. The Ulster MP Edward Archdale, on the other hand, attributed much of the Cabinet's indecision to Reading's 'frantic wires' to London, which, in turn, arose from T. P. O'Connor's calculated 'priming' in the Washington Embassy's 'inner circle'.[17]

O'Connor certainly paid Reading many visits at this time, warning him of the 'evil effect in America' of Irish conscription.

However, contrary to Archdale's insinuations, Reading was by no means O'Connor's puppet and, in fact, assured Lloyd George that conscription was feasible in conjunction with Home Rule. Americans understood the justice of conscription, contended the Ambassador, but 'the subject at present gets confused with the wrongs of Ireland'. According to Arthur Murray, it was this warning which finally dispelled any temptation in the Cabinet to enforce Irish conscription before a new Home Rule Bill was passed. Not surprisingly, therefore, Unionists continued to complain of Reading's Home Rule bias (as they had previously done with Spring-Rice). Joseph Fisher described the Washington Embassy as a 'centre of Home Rule propaganda' and complained that Reading, 'with *The Times* correspondent in his pocket and with T. P. O'Connor as agent in advance, has everything his own way'.[18]

Meanwhile, with Irish Nationalists strenuously opposing any partition scheme and Ulster Unionists hostile towards an all-Ireland parliament, Long's Committee increasingly favoured a federal system for the whole United Kingdom, with an Irish assembly as one element. This had long been a popular idea with those young Conservatives who considered that, in view of the international situation, full maintenance of the Union was no longer tenable. It was this solution which, in 1910, J. L. Garvin had fruitlessly suggested to both Austen Chamberlain and Arthur Balfour as an escape from potential 'Imperial difficulties' over Irish Home Rule. Lloyd George clearly believed federalism to be a long-term answer to the Irish impasse, for he told a Nationalist delegation that it offered the equivalent of American state rights and would therefore be considered fair by most Americans.[19] F. S. Oliver, normally hostile to any 'Yankee placation', now made a particular virtue of the argument that Americans would support Long's scheme, 'because, in their ignorance of our political struggles, they believe federalism to be exactly what Ireland has been asking for all the time and vainly striving to obtain'. Long himself discarded his previous objections to the introduction of American opinion, urging the Prime Minister that a federal solution would attract the support of American Home Rulers, and that without it Irish conscription would 'greatly outrage sentiment in the U.S.A.'.[20]

Although federalism had Lloyd George's tentative support, it was strongly opposed by Balfour, Lord Curzon and Bonar Law, all of whom foresaw great difficulties in establishing such a system in wartime, and by Tory diehards such as Lord Salisbury, who condemned the scheme as a 'sort of reflection of the self-determination which is occupying the whole stage in international politics'. Pressured from so many directions, Long's Committee, in Arthur Murray's assessment, 'swayed this way and that' but, eventually, deviated from the majority decision of the Convention by giving concessions to Ulster which were, 'to say the least, generous'. However, by reserving customs-and-excise powers for the Imperial Government, the Committee planned to make the Bill consistent with a 'federal solution at a later date'. Meanwhile, discussions dragged on in the hope that uncompromising attitudes would mellow.[21]

With Long's Committee making 'heavy weather' of formulating a Home Rule agreement, the Cabinet sought to justify the delay in carrying out the 'dual policy' by again focusing attention on pro-German conspiracy in Ireland. This campaign had its origins on 12 April, when a member of Casement's Irish Brigade was captured after landing from a German submarine on the west coast of Ireland. Since he admitted receiving German instructions to communicate with leading extremists and spoke of a German expedition to Ireland,[22] Tory Cabinet ministers were furnished with the perfect excuse to demand the arrests of prominent Sinn Feiners. They were supported in this by a newly appointed and more vigorous Irish Administration of Field Marshal Lord French and Edward Shortt MP, replacing, as Viceroy and Chief Secretary respectively, the more conciliatory partnership of Wimborne and Duke.

The Cabinet's major concern was to ensure that the so-called 'German Plot' would be accepted as justification for the Sinn Fein arrests. This task fell largely to Admiral Reginald Hall, who throughout the war had been responsible for the Admiralty's interceptions of German code messages. When Hall queried the likely American reaction to arrests based on 'definite proofs that Sinn Feiners had been in close communication with Germany', Lord Reading replied tersely that any such move would be 'injurious'. Nevertheless, Austen Chamberlain, Long and other Unionists continued to press the Government for immediate action, Chamberlain arguing that, if the proofs were as good as the von Igel revelations, 'then, although it may be insufficient for a jury, it will be sufficient for America'. Although some ministers, such as Bonar Law and Smuts, were concerned at the paucity of hard evidence, the Cabinet eventually agreed that it was 'on safe ground' in accusing

Sinn Feiners of 'treasonable relations, not only with the enemies of England, but with the enemies of the United States, France and Belgium'.[23]

After Admiral Hall had given copies of the incriminating documents to Walter Page, Lloyd George pressed the Ambassador for immediate American publication 'in the interests of the Allied cause'. The Prime Minister suggested that, since all such previous disclosures had been made by the United States, an 'appearance of consistency' would be preserved if President Wilson were to make the contents public himself or, alternatively, sanction a British statement that the information originated from the United States Government.[24] However, when Long telegraphed Lord Reading that, with the arrests imminent, it was 'absolutely essential that the documents should appear as emanating from the U.S.', he revealed that the principal motive was to safeguard British intelligence sources. Long wanted the 'widest publicity' for the disclosures, and he urged Reading to stress that, with Sinn Fein agents communicating with German submarines off the Irish coast, 'American transports were endangered'.[25]

On 17 May, de Valera, Arthur Griffith and other Sinn Fein leaders were arrested, closely followed by a Government proclamation accusing Sinn Fein of 'communication with the German enemy'.[26] Meanwhile, Lansing advised the President that it would be 'impolitic' to assume responsibility for publishing the documents, since this would be construed as direct assistance to Great Britain and would 'involve us in all sorts of difficulties with the Irish in this country'. Wilson, in fact, was irritated that the British Government should 'use us to facilitate their fight for conscription in Ireland', and Reading advised London of the President's annoyance at premature press reports that the United States Government intended to publish the evidence. Moreover, as Lansing explained to Reading, most of the disclosures related to incidents before America entered the war, and 'this alone made it impossible to act'. It is ironic that Wilson condemned the British Government for using the German Plot as an excuse to *enforce* conscription, when in fact the plot was used to *postpone* the dual policy. When the President's reply was shown to Basil Thomson of the Metropolitan Police, Thomson was not too dispirited, having anticipated 'difficulties with the President', who was 'afraid evidently of influencing the Irish vote'. Thomson assumed that Wilson would not object to the disclosures themselves as long as the British Government would 'take all the responsibility'. The evidence was therefore issued without mentioning the United States Government.[27]

Supporting evidence was, indeed, vitally necessary. Noble Hall reported rumours that the plot was 'a concoction designed to mislead the American Government', while H. A. Goode of Butler's New York Publicity Bureau feared that, without 'substantial evidence', the plot would merely be seen as an excuse for the arrests. Within the Cabinet, however, Curzon and Smuts doubted whether the evidence would stand up to public scrutiny, while Lloyd George was reported by Maurice Hankey to be depressed by 'evidence of the most flimsy and ancient description'. However, Admiral Hall reported that 'absolutely reliable' evidence did exist, but that its disclosure would endanger the Government's intelligence sources. Thus, the evidence published on 25 May consisted of the German–Irish communications preceding the Easter Rising of 1916, together with unsubstantiated allegations of de Valera's plans for another German-aided rising in 1918. No supporting documents were produced and none of the arrested Sinn Feiners was ever tried, but, according to the Anglophobe historian Charles Tansill, the 'Government's cheap stratagem of smearing the Irish leaders and thus destroying American sympathy for the cause of Irish independence had worked to perfection'.[28]

American sympathy had indeed been eroded. Laurence Lowell, President of Harvard, considered it 'pathetic' to see Sinn Fein 'throwing away the sympathy of America which is one of their greatest assets'. The *New York Times* wrote scathingly that most Americans were 'weary of and disgusted with Sinn Fein folly', while the Philadelphia *Public Ledger* tolerated the lack of hard evidence in the belief that there were 'many good reasons for withholding it for the present'. Lord Reading reported that, while Irish-American extremists were 'excited to a pitch of frenzy' by the arrests, moderates were trying to protect their good name by 'drawing a distinction between the Sinn Fein faction and the loyal Irish-Americans' and by publicly demanding that Home Rule 'should be obtained by constitutional methods and not by opposing the war'. Consequently, within a few weeks, Irish rumblings were reported to have quickly disappeared.[29]

In Britain, Unionists were jubilant at the adverse effect on the Nationalist cause and at the 'changed opinion of the U.S. towards traitors in time of war'. The *Spectator* observed scathingly that 'the manner in which the American Government treat Irish undesirables' was in stark contrast to the 'timidity' of Britain, and that it was 'almost incredible' that the Government had hesitated to enforce law and order in Ireland 'owing to an entire misapprehension of what would be said and thought in the U.S.'. Nationalists, however, were furious with what they deemed an excuse to shelve Home Rule and an expedient to 'poison American opinion' against them. In the Commons, Tim Healy condemned the broadcasting of 'falsehoods' throughout the United States, while Joseph Devlin thundered that, through its propaganda, the Government had endeavoured to 'besmirch the fair name of our country' and to 'dub us as pro-Germans'.[30]

Nationalist resentment against the German Plot found more concrete form in an anti-conscription manifesto to President Wilson in June 1918. The idea had originated at the tripartite Mansion House Conference on 18 April, when it was decided that the Lord Mayor of Dublin, Laurence O'Neill, should personally present the appeal to the President. *The Times* typified most non-Nationalist opinion by predicting that Wilson would give the Lord Mayor 'a piece of the world's mind which would shatter Ireland's soul-destroying illusions', while the *New York Times* declared that 'the Chief Burgomaster of Berlin would be exactly as welcome and popular a personage here'. Horace Plunkett, although broadly sympathetic with the appeal, feared that it would appear to Americans 'dangerously alike that for which the Civil War was fought'. Since it would also spotlight Ireland's opposition to conscription and thereby 'retrieve the Government's mistake' in adopting the measure, the Nationalists, he believed, had 'blundered' and were probably 'praying that the passports would be refused'.[31]

Meanwhile, Walter Long telegraphed anxiously to Reading that the mission should 'not be encouraged' by Wilson. In fact, the President had already informed the State Department that, although there was no way to 'head off' O'Neill, 'if he knew how little he was going to get out of the trip he would stay at home'. At this juncture, Balfour made a tactical error by stipulating that any documents carried by the Lord Mayor should be 'essential for the purpose of the voyage' and should be vetted by the Irish Office. The Nationalists, profiting from this tactical naïvety, rejected the stipulation and forwarded the manifesto via the American Embassy in London. Horace Plunkett remarked that the Government, by its bureaucratic caution, had lost 'the opportunity to put the

Conference in a hole' and, as a result, the Sinn Fein leadership 'duly seizes the lifebelt which has been thrown to them and swims ashore'.[32]

The manifesto itself, which argued that the British Government had attempted to 'poison the wells of American sympathy', vehemently contested the 'insinuation that the Irish coasts, with native connivance, could be made a base for the destruction of American shipping'. As regards conscription, it claimed that, 'while self-determination is refused, we are required by law to bleed to make the world safe for democracy in every country except our own'. The document ended by appealing to 'the tribunal of the world' and by seeking the President's understanding of Ireland's resistance to conscription.[33] Although making no effort to suppress the manifesto, Balfour arranged with the United States Embassy that it should receive no publicity in America and, for its part, the White House quietly shelved it without replying.[34] Moreover, the British military authorities were quick to intercept copies of the manifesto sent to newspapers in America and Europe, for, as Stephen Gaselee minuted, 'Comparatively little of this "letter to the President" has at present appeared in the neutral and hostile press, and the subject is more or less "dead" – it would all be revived again if these copies were allowed to go through.'[35]

Far from accepting that the subject was 'dead', Ulster Unionists planned their own 'counterblast' letter to Wilson. In order to emphasise that Ireland was 'two nations', the Lord Mayor of Belfast was selected as chief signatory to match the Nationalist choice of the Lord Mayor of Dublin. The letter argued that Unionist Ireland regarded the Nationalist claim to escape conscription as tantamount to a declaration of secession. The principal opponents of conscription were men who had 'twice been detected during the war in treasonable traffic with the enemy', whereas Ulster was more concerned with supporting the Allied war effort 'at a time when the very existence of civilization hangs in the balance'.[36]

Through his contacts at the American Associated Press, Joseph Fisher gained good coverage for the Ulster letter throughout America. He was convinced that it was 'a big success on both sides of the Atlantic' and that the Nationalists were 'wild' at the prominence it received in the United States. Nevertheless, Fisher was greatly concerned that, in general, Ulster's propaganda in America was ailing. Not only had Lord Reading and T. P. O'Connor 'arranged everything on the other side' for the Home Rule cause, but a Nationalist MP, Hugh Law, was now in charge of Irish-American propaganda at the Ministry of Information (which, under Lord Beaverbrook, had replaced the D of I in February 1918). This meant that Ulster was 'blocked in every way' and the Ministry's American Department was 'entirely in Nationalist hands'.[37] Law's appointment was inevitably an irritant, since he had already criticised conscription, had cast grave doubts on the German Plot, and was a strong advocate of Irish self-determination.[38]

Ulster suspicions of official prejudice also applied to the Foreign Office. An Ulster sympathiser at Cambridge University, Professor Ridgeway, complained to Carson that his attempts to send copies of Ulster's 'counterblast' to an influential academic friend in New York had been blocked by Foreign Office censorship. It was, he claimed, very difficult to organise effective propaganda in America, and he attributed this to the many Catholics working at the Foreign Office. Although the inference of anti-Ulster bias was – as earlier chapters have shown – largely unjustified, it is nevertheless a fact that the Foreign Office contained in its ranks a high number of Catholics, who were generally less hostile towards Irish Nationalism than their colleagues. Lord Colum Crichton-Stuart, for example, when standing for Cardiff East as a Coalition Conservative in the December 1918 election, appealed to local Irish voters as a Catholic and a Home Ruler, while throughout the last year of the war Eric Drummond, a Liberal Home Ruler, acted as the principal Foreign Office ally for the activities of Arthur Murray and Shane Leslie.[39]

It is ironic that, while the Ulstermen were accusing the M of I of falling into Nationalist hands, the Nationalists were bitterly denouncing the Ministry for alleged Unionist bias. Joseph Devlin was angered at yet another sponsored visit to Ireland by American journalists, who were 'shepherded by a Tory propagandist' from the M of I and fed 'strong anti-Home Rule speeches'. He largely attributed this state of affairs to Ian Hay Beith, who had taken temporary charge of the Ministry's American Department in the summer of 1918, and whose study *The Oppressed English* had, according to the author, been widely circulated in America to show that 'Ireland was in no sense an oppressed or enslaved country'. However, Devlin denounced it as 'a tissue of falsehoods from beginning to end' and complained sourly that its sentiments were 'expressed as the official views of the Propaganda Department'.[40]

Despite Nationalist accusations, Beaverbrook's ministry was

composed of a very different type of propagandist from the traditionalists who had dominated the Foreign Office News Department earlier in the war. In fact, following Beaverbrook's appointment, many officials had resigned rather than serve under a press baron, and had returned to the more formal atmosphere of the Foreign Office.[41] Cecil Spring-Rice's horror at the appointment typified such reactions: 'The Lord Deliver us . . . M.A. [Max Aitken] is one I simply loathe and consider a wrong-'un of the wrongest.' Nevertheless, accusations of Tory bias at the M of I prompted Beaverbrook to write a defence of the Ministry's political complexion, in which he claimed that 'among the higher officials every shade of political opinion is represented'. As illustration, he pointed to the presence of Liberals such as Charles Masterman (Library Director), Lord Rothermere (Northcliffe's brother, who headed the American Section for a while) and Arnold Bennett (head of the French Section). Beaverbrook himself was no enemy of Irish Nationalism, but he had long been Bonar Law's friend and supporter and, 'as a Presbyterian, was ready to champion the demand of the Ulster Protestants not to be put under Rome rule'. Indeed, he later complained that the attempt to conciliate America over Irish self-government was the first in a series of unnecessary concessions to America. 'If we made peace with Ireland', he later wrote to Winston Churchill, 'we were to enjoy for ever and ever the favour of America. We did what we were told. But it brought no comfort in Ireland and little credit in America.'[42]

While the M of I continued its efforts to improve the Irish situation by propaganda in America, the converse policy of bringing American politicians, journalists and other influential figures over to Ireland was now greatly extended. This policy of entertaining, which Beaverbrook considered a most 'effective avenue for propaganda', had a dual aim: to flatter the visitor and thereby convince him that British rule in Ireland was less harsh than depicted by Nationalists; and to awaken greater Irish enthusiasm for the war effort. The latter idea – using Americans to win over Irish 'shirkers' – was an innovation conceived after the Cabinet, alarmed at 'the entire absence of any organised system of propaganda in Ireland', left Beaverbrook and Walter Long to remedy the deficiency between them. Throughout the remainder of the war, Long was active in encouraging American journalists to visit Ireland, while Beaverbrook, for his part, insisted that Americans were 'the only possible general advocates of the allied cause in Ireland', since they could 'fairly ask Irishmen to accept burdens they have accepted themselves'.[43]

The principal instrument of such a campaign was to have been the American soldier. Indeed, suggestions for training and parading American soldiers in Ireland, and even forming Irish brigades under American command, were received from many influential sources.[44] However, the War Minister, Lord Milner, rejected the idea as impractical, although the principal factor was probably 'the great danger of undesirables coming over who could act as agents and messengers for the Clan na Gael, and the difficulty of removing such men if found here'.[45] Despite this 'small-minded and short-sighted' rejection,[46] the proposal was indicative of a great change in British propaganda. Whereas in the early years of the war there had been many schemes for sending Irish Nationalists to America to win support for the British cause, the emphasis now was on Americans visiting Ireland to win over the alienated Irish Nationalists.

III

By June 1918 the British Government had reached an impasse in Irish affairs and could make little progress with either Home Rule or its conscription plans. Consequently, with the German Plot as justification, Lord Curzon announced in Parliament the indefinite postponement of the 'dual policy' and a return to voluntary recruiting. In America, this virtual abandonment of Home Rule aroused a good deal of indignation, especially since Lord Wimborne in the same debate denied any knowledge of a German plot during his period as Lord Lieutenant. Lord Reading prophesied that old antagonisms would return, since 'once more it will be said that the British Government has broken faith with Ireland', while Consul-General Leay in Boston suggested that the lesson to be learned was that fresh proposals should only be announced when their implementation was certain.[47]

In the months following the Government's announcement, Allied victories in Europe distracted attention from Ireland, but by the autumn of 1918 the prospect of an imminent peace conference prompted fresh efforts by British officials in America to shake this complacency. Arthur Willert predicted that Irish-Americans were 'ready to shed the muzzle imposed by war conditions', and William

Wiseman estimated that 90 per cent of the United States population still regarded British treatment of Ireland as a 'blot on civilization'. Lord Reading, fearing that the Cabinet was increasingly ignoring the Irish problem, warned that American tolerance of the Government's inaction would not continue in peace time, when the Irish would again 'make themselves felt at elections'. Indeed, the Irish would 'probably join with other discontented sections of the US population' to pose a 'serious obstacle' to future Anglo-American co-operation (a prophetic warning in view of the subsequent defeat of Wilson's League of Nations crusade).[48]

On several occasions during the last months of the war, the Irish Parliamentary Party used the threat of British disgrace at the peace conference to revive the Home Rule issue in Parliament. In July, John Dillon moved that the Irish Question should be settled in accordance with Wilson's principle of self-determination, and that the President himself should arbitrate to prevent a situation in which 'Ireland would stand at the door of the Conference of Nations as an incalculable barrier'. On the eve of the armistice, T. P. O'Connor warned that, even if Ireland failed to gain recognition at the peace conference, she would nevertheless be present, 'not in body perhaps, but in the spirit'. Her case would be a constant reproach for British hypocrisy in preaching self-determination for small nations while withholding it from Ireland. Indeed, O'Connor's Nationalist colleague Richard Hazleton avowed that Ireland would 'hammer and hammer on the door of the League of Nations' until the British Government was 'shamed before the civilized world'.[49]

Unionists were now confident that the Nationalist eloquence was based on unwarranted optimism rather than firm substance. Lord Salisbury contended that American support had been completely 'demoralised' by the German Plot, while Ireland's Lord Chancellor, James Campbell, attributed this to 'Ireland's failure to recruit'. Similar convictions were inevitably voiced at the Foreign Office. When, on Armistice Day, Colville Barclay reported that Irish-Americans were mounting a fierce campaign for Irish recognition at the peace conference, Rowland Sperling displayed all his own scorn towards Irish Nationalism: 'Considering Ireland's record during the war, it is hard to believe that Home Rulers will find much support in the U.S.' However, should the issue be raised by the United States Government, it could, argued Sperling, be shown that self-determination was 'not applied by the U.S.G. to its own smaller and incompetent neighbours' in Central America. Underlining his own Unionist principles, he concluded that, in any case, any self-determination argument would 'apply equally to Ulster' and thus prevent a settlement.[50]

By this stage, the Government's attitude towards the Irish Question had perceptibly hardened. Edward Shortt, the Chief Secretary, asserted in Parliament that, as Ireland had, in effect, been given self-determination by the Dublin Convention but had failed to reach agreement, the matter would now have to be settled by the British Government. In the same debate, Bonar Law continued this reversion to old arguments by describing the Irish problem as a 'domestic question', in which Britain would not listen to the 'dictation of people outside the British Empire'. Another striking indication of this shift in Government thinking was provided by Walter Long. As recently as July 1918, Long had warned Lord French that an abandonment of the dual policy would provoke 'considerable trouble' in the United States. By October, however, he was advising Reading that no scheme could be found to overcome the obduracy of Ulster and simultaneously satisfy the demands of the Nationalists. Partition, concluded Long, was the only remaining option, but, since this would be 'violently resisted' throughout Nationalist Ireland, the obvious course was to govern Ireland strongly, restore law and order and hope that a settlement might be found in due course. He accepted Reading's contention that the Irish Question would be 'really troublesome' during the peace settlement, but believed that President Wilson, once he knew the facts, would understand the Government's policy.[51]

Any hope of a solution materialising before the peace conference met was rudely shattered when the Lloyd George Coalition issued its manifesto for the December 1918 election. Although paying lip service to the need for a settlement, it asserted that, 'in the present condition of Ireland, such an attempt could not succeed and . . . must be postponed until the condition of Ireland makes it possible'.[52] To the Irish people, this statement was the final nail in the coffin of constitutional Nationalism. The inevitable consequence occurred at the General Election, when the Irish Parliamentary Party suffered political annihilation and was replaced as Nationalist Ireland's representative by Sinn Fein. The newly elected MPs refused to attend Westminster and reaffirmed their intention of demanding representation at the peace conference, with a view to the establishment of an independent Irish Republic.[53]

In the meantime, leading Sinn Feiners were appealing for financial and moral support from America, where, as Reading had forecast, Irish-American agitation had become voluble immediately the Armistice was signed. The Roman Catholic Church featured prominently in this agitation, and Cardinal O'Connell, perhaps its most powerful figure, privately informed Colville Barclay that he would be unable to hold the Irish in check unless the British Government carried through a generous measure of self-government. Otherwise, he argued, such pressure would force the President to raise the Irish Question at the peace conference, after which Irish opinion would be 'permanently alienated'. Barclay urged that the Government should 'nip this movement in the bud' with a new Home Rule scheme before Irish-Americans were again 'thrown into violent opposition to England'. However, despite mass meetings which portended a 'great outburst of activity' by Irish-Americans, Barclay reported little indication that Ireland had regained 'any of the popularity which she undoubtedly lost in the eyes of the average American owing to her attitude in the war'.[54]

Despite the Irish-American resolutions and the persistent lobbying of Congressmen, President Wilson was well aware that intervention over the Irish Question might severely diminish British co-operation in schemes such as the League of Nations. He therefore 'preferred to regard the solution of the Irish Question more as a factor in home politics than as an integral part of the new European settlement'.[55] Nevertheless, the importance of the Irish vote dictated that he should be non-committal in public, and this raised doubts at the Foreign Office, where Maurice de Bunsen minuted, 'It remains to be seen how far President Wilson will allow himself to be moved by these appeals from the American Irish.' In truth, Wilson's concept of the rights of nationalities – idealistic though it was – posed countless dilemmas, as Robert Lansing reflected in his diary:

> The more I think about the President's declaration as to the right of 'self-determination' the more convinced I am of the danger of putting such ideas into the minds of certain races. It is bound to be the basis of impossible demands on the peace conference, and create trouble in many lands. What effect will it have on the Irish, the Indians, the Egyptians. . . . The phrase is simply loaded with dynamite. It will raise hopes which can never be realised.[56]

In regard to Ireland, the British Government's diplomatic and propaganda activity had largely prevented the problem from burgeoning into a matter for Anglo-American diplomacy. However, in many respects this was a Pyrrhic victory, since Ireland's failure to gain a hearing at the peace conference created new and greater dangers. The realisation that Wilson would not raise the Irish Question in Paris spurred many Irish-Americans to play a leading part in preventing America's entry into the League of Nations,[57] while Ireland itself, with the 'collapse of all the hopes she had based on peace . . . passed into a stage of savage revolt'.[58] On reflection, British politicians and civil servants might well have asked themselves whether their efforts to preserve the domestic nature of the Irish Question had warranted the high price that had been paid.

11
Conclusion

During the period 1914–18, the Irish Question was transformed from an essentially domestic problem into one occupying the stage of international politics. This arose from two main issues: Ireland's possible effect on the European balance of power up to August 1914 and, subsequently, her growing role in Anglo-American relations. The theory that the Ulster stance had influenced German strategic calculations in the months preceding the outbreak of war became almost a commonplace, although there is no firm substantiation for this. Nevertheless, obsession with the Irish tangle clearly blunted British appreciation of the European danger in the crucial weeks after Sarajevo. Paradoxically, a sudden awareness of the ramifications involved led to a closing of ranks in Ireland and to Grey's reassurance that she was the 'one bright spot' in the war situation. With the onset of war, Ireland largely ceased to be a factor in the European crisis, although Germany, with the connivance of Roger Casement, attempted to make cynical capital from her grievances.

In America, however, with the powerful Irish-American community a constant source of pressure on successive administrations, the Irish Question was sure to play a more sustained part. Unfortunately for British interests, the seeds of future trouble were sown by the suspension of the Home Rule Act in September 1914 and by Redmond's unpopular advice to Irishmen to fight the Central Powers 'wherever the firing line extends'. Following this, constitutional Nationalism began its inexorable decline in America. It was this drift, accelerated by the introduction of Unionists into the Asquith Coalition in 1915 and by criticism of War Office policy towards Irish regiments, which prompted the beginnings of Foreign Office propaganda on Irish matters.

Despite growing Irish-American hostility during 1915, it was only after the Easter Rising that the problem in America assumed menacing proportions. Specifically, it was the executions following the suppression of the Rising which achieved the end result sought by Casement: namely, the elevation of the Irish Question into the realm of international affairs. Contrary to Casement's prediction, however, this was brought about not by German intervention but through pressure of American public opinion. Moreover, the Rising marked the first occasion on which the idea of tailoring Irish policy to placate American opinion was discussed both at the Foreign Office and within the Cabinet (even though it was summarily dismissed by outraged Tories in each instance).

With British prestige in America at its lowest ebb after April 1916, the anxiety of diplomats and other observers based in America was largely wasted on the Foreign Office, which took the traditional view that Irish matters had no place in foreign affairs. There was also a recurring tendency to dismiss warnings from the 'man on the spot' as undue panic, and this affected the credibility of Spring-Rice's recommendations and, to a lesser extent, those of Lord Reading. Significantly, both Spring-Rice and Reading were Home Rulers, whereas events clearly showed the underlying Conservative – and frequently Unionist – bias of what Maurice Hankey described as 'the finest civil service in the world'. Indeed, the attitude of many Foreign Office and Wellington House officials casts grave doubts on Asquith's contention that the Civil Service, 'performing as it does in a country where party divisions often cut deep . . . has never incurred even the suspicion of corruption or of bias, and is carried on with rare disinterestedness'. The Ulster partisanship and ingrained Unionism of Nicolson, Montgomery and Sperling does not bear out this 'rare disinterestedness' in major domestic controversies. Even those officials with less fervent attachment to the Union (such as Hardinge and Butler) favoured a strong hand against Irish unrest during the war and thereby typified the 'social and professional conservatism of the Foreign Office'. Indeed, the attitude of senior Foreign Office officials was aptly summarised by Stephen Gwynn's contention that 'the man who says he has no politics is in practice almost invariably a Conservative'. Moreover, many of the officials who were drafted in to staff Foreign Office and Wellington House departments were Conservative politicians such as Newton and Parker who were untrammelled by the Civil Service ethos of party-political neutrality. The presence of such men, coupled with the advent in 1915 of the uncompromising Unionist Robert Cecil as Parliamentary Under Secretary, must have set a tone which the comparatively small number of Home Rulers at the Foreign Office could do little to change.[1]

Edward Grey and his secretary, Eric Drummond, although Liberal Home Rulers, were not fervent supporters of Irish Nationalism. Nevertheless, the aftermath of the Rising made Grey regard the appeasement of Irish-Americans as essential to future Anglo-American co-operation in world affairs. Thus, in Cabinet meetings, he joined Lloyd George in urging the American argument for a Home Rule settlement, while Drummond, also pursuing a conciliatory path, worked closely with Home Rulers such as Shane Leslie and Arthur Murray. Concern for Anglo-American harmony also persuaded some of the more pragmatic Conservatives of the younger generation, such as Percy and Lampson, that every effort should be made to conciliate Irish-Americans. Such men looked to America with hope and friendship, whereas many Tory traditionalists exhibited contempt for America and her increasing incursions into world affairs. A parallel divergence of opinion extended even to the Conservative members of the Cabinet: Austen Chamberlain, Balfour and Bonar Law appeared to accept the American argument, whereas, for most of the period under review, Walter Long, Lord Lansdowne and Robert Cecil maintained a rigid intransigence. Indeed, like their spiritual brethren at the Foreign Office, the diehards considered Irish-American influence to be ephemeral and, in any case, a challenge to British sovereignty over its own affairs.

United States entry into the war marked a major change in the position of the Irish Question in Anglo-American relations. Thereafter the British Government was increasingly urged by influential American figures (including President Wilson himself) to bring about a solution. It is indicative of the contradictory forces at work in Government policy that, while Lloyd George responded by applying pressure on Carson, the D of I was simultaneously attempting to buttress the Ulster cause by propaganda and sponsored missions. It was the impossibility of reconciling Nationalist and Ulster claims which led the Government to set up the Irish Convention. This effectively shelved the problem for almost a year and muted American criticism at a key period in her war preparations. Moreover, by appearing to give Irishmen the responsibility for devising their own settlement, the Government could claim to be fulfilling its own 'small nations' pledges and, also, Wilson's principle of self-determination.

It was the latter concept which increasingly governed discussion of the Irish Question in the last year of the war. As Kevin Leys, a member of the Irish War Aims Committee, commented in late 1918, Ireland had been 'miserably ignorant' of international politics in 1914, and yet 'the Irish mind now bites and feeds on foreign affairs and relates them to domestic politics closer than the English mind does'. In subsequent Irish debates, the Government emphasised the imprecision of concepts such as 'nationality' and 'self-determination', but it was fighting a losing battle against the fashionable philosophy of the age. By 1920, Balfour had to admit that 'our Home Rule policy has been largely influenced by our desire to shew the world that the principles which we apply to other peoples are those we accept for ourselves'. Although, in this way, many Unionists reluctantly accepted the new philosophy, this often disguised a tactical realignment to their second line of defence: the demand that Ulster had a right to 'self-determination'. Such use of Wilsonian concepts, however, had now made British Unionism less tenable than hitherto. As Shane Leslie later wrote, 'the lesson of all propaganda is that it is self-destroying . . . the British propaganda roused and made the Irish Question alive'.[2]

Although Leslie claimed that such propaganda was 'self-destroying', he himself was a key figure in its ever-increasing volume. This upsurge in propaganda activity was all the more surprising since, in the early years of the war, such a policy had been deprecated by Spring-Rice, Grey and most News Department officials. As Augustine Birrell recalled, it had 'always been the tradition . . . of the F.O. to hold itself aloof from publicity and to move in a mysterious way'. This changed, first, when the publicity-minded Lloyd George came to power and, secondly, when the entry of America into the war made increased propaganda more viable. In the event, British propaganda in America proved to be more subtle and effective than its more clumsy German counterpart. Geoffrey Butler, whose New York Publicity Bureau had carried out much of this work, believed that it had served a useful function and that its termination after the war merely gave a 'free hand to the revival of Irish and German propaganda'.[3]

The return of peace ended hopes that the taint of pro-Germanism had destroyed Irish Nationalist influence in America: the Irish-Americans were as vocal as ever, while Americans in general continued to support Home Rule. In fact, the United States dimension of the Irish Question plagued Anglo-American relations severely for another three years until December 1921, at which time Lord Curzon admitted, 'There has not been a Foreign Minister in this country during the last fifty years who has not felt, and indeed often stated, that the strength of England was diminished and her moral influence jeopardised by the unsolved position of the Irish Question.'[4]

It was generally assumed that the Anglo-Irish Treaty of December 1921 had finally put an end to this irritant, but the old maxim 'History repeats itself' is as applicable to the Irish Question as to any other subject. The partition secured by Ulster and its supporters in 1921 merely extended the Irish problem and, over sixty years later, is still creating discord in Anglo-American relations. The parallels between the two periods are, indeed, striking. In the pre-1921 period, Irish Nationalists sought financial and political aid in the United States; this process still continues, with IRA agents causing Whitehall 'considerable concern'[5] by their fund-raising activities in America. Just as the missions of Balfour and Northcliffe in 1917 tried to curb such support, so in 1985 the British Prime Minister, Margaret Thatcher, in a personal address to Congress, appealed strongly for Americans to avoid financing Irish terrorism.[6] In 1916 the leaders of the Easter Rising were hailed as the Irish equivalent to America's founding fathers; in 1979 the same claim was made of the IRA leaders by Fred Burns O'Brien, a leading figure of the Irish-American lobby group, the Irish National Caucus.[7] Similarly, American ill-feeling towards the Easter Rising executions was, in part, attributed to the 'inherited American feeling for any rebel against the British crown', while as recently as 1985 the *Daily Telegraph* admitted with resignation, 'The truth is that we are not just up against the historic memories and myths of Irish-Americans, but also the anti-colonialist myth itself, under the terms of which Ireland today is a symbol for the American colonies before 1776.'[8]

Throughout much of the present century, Britain has shown itself to be highly sensitive to accusations of human-rights violations in Ireland. Soon after Lloyd George came to power, the *Belfast News Letter* argued that it was 'absurd to talk of the oppression of the Irish people as if they were the Poles of Prussia, the Slavs of Austria, or the Christian subjects of the Sultan'. This is echoed with uncanny similarity in a recent British press riposte to American attacks: 'It is pure fantasy to speak of the Province . . . as though it were comparable with Hitler's Germany, Stalin's Russia or even South Africa under apartheid.'[9] In both periods, it has been feared that United States administrations would participate in political initiatives over Ireland for 'vote-catching' purposes.[10] However, successive American presidents have followed Woodrow Wilson in officially refusing to involve their office in Irish matters. Wilson considered that an intervention would be 'inexcusable' and would cause 'serious international embarrassment', while President Carter's Secretary of State, Cyrus Vance, asserted, 'For us to intrude ourselves into the Irish Question would not be wise. I think it would be resented by the parties concerned.'[11] British ambassadors in the United States continue to be especially sensitive to the effects of the Irish Question. In 1979, Peter Jay caused some consternation when, on relinquishing the Washington Embassy, he claimed that the Irish situation had not been well explained to Americans and that the ultimate solution lay in the reunification of the thirty-two counties.[12] However, advice on Irish matters – whether from Cecil Spring-Rice during the First World War or from later ambassadors – has never been well received by Tory politicians or journalists.

In the pre-1921 period, the Irish problem was often explained by British officials as a matter for the various parties to determine for themselves, with England acting merely as an 'honest broker'; in the 1970s and 1980s, the Government's policy has generally been to allow Ulster 'self-determination' and not to coerce her into concessions aimed at a united Ireland. 'If ever there were to be a majority in favour of change,' declared Mrs Thatcher to the American Congress, 'then I believe that our Parliament would respond accordingly.' However, typical of the ambivalence which has surrounded the problem throughout the years has been the converse argument that Ireland's future is very much a British concern for security reasons: in 1917 the Navy League viewed it as 'a fortress that guards the main routes of the world'; in 1974 a study group of the Conservative Monday Club faction deemed it 'a potential Achilles heel of British defence'; while in 1979 it was seen as threatening 'the strategic unity of mainland Britain . . . the triflers who make political mileage in America should look at a map of the Eastern Atlantic some time'. During the First World War such concern centred on possible German infiltration, while in 1979 the fear was that, in the event of a civil war in Ulster, there was 'every prospect that the Soviet Union will have bases and harbours across the Irish Sea'.[13]

Perhaps, most significantly of all, many British politicians and journalists are still, as before, hostile to the 'intrusion' of American politicians. In 1916 the *Belfast News Letter* claimed that the Government should not 'tolerate foreign interference in the internal affairs of the United Kingdom'; in 1979 the *Daily Telegraph* warned against any steps 'designed to soothe intrusive and unwanted American dabblers', while the *Observer* denounced Irish-American pressure as the 'poisonous nonsense' of transatlantic 'naggers'.[14] Such resistance to outside interference has also applied at ministerial level. In the Lloyd George Coalition, Arthur Balfour deplored American 'ignorance' over Ireland as 'invincible'; in recent years, Roy Mason, Secretary for Northern Ireland in the Callaghan Government, publicly dismissed Irish-American utterances as 'naïve' and 'ill-informed',[15] while his Conservative successor, Humphrey Atkins, refused to attend a New York summit on the future of Ulster on the grounds that 'the political future of the province is a matter for negotiation between Her Majesty's Government, the Parliament at Westminster and the people of Ulster'.[16] Despite such declarations, it is obvious that, as long as the reunification of Ireland remains the established liturgy of Irish Nationalists, Irish-American concern will continue to embarrass British governments and the pressures thereby engendered will exercise a harmful effect on Britain's foreign relations.

Appendix

Organisation and Personnel of Relevant Sections of the Foreign Office, Department of Information and Ministry of Information

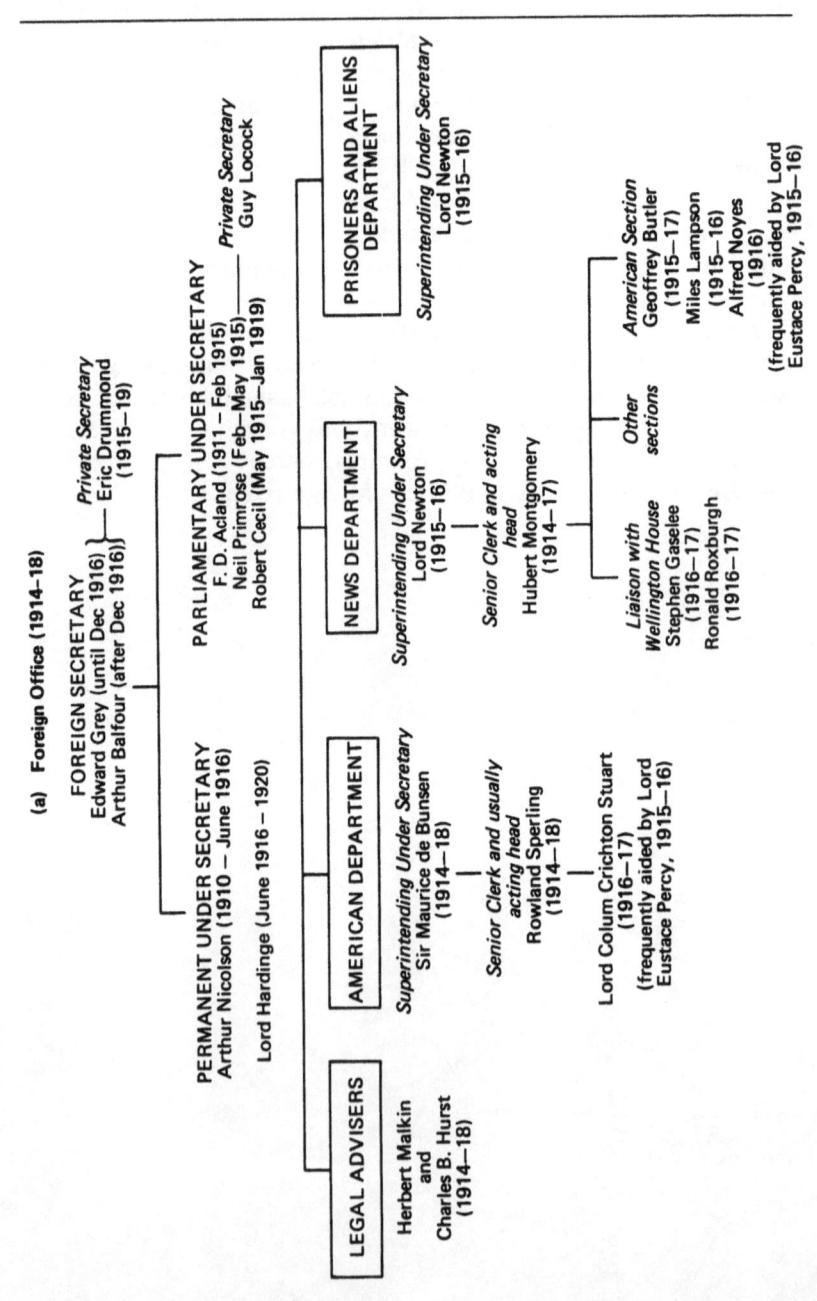

(a) Foreign Office (1914–18)

Appendix 201

(b) Department of Information (Feb 1917–Jan 1918)

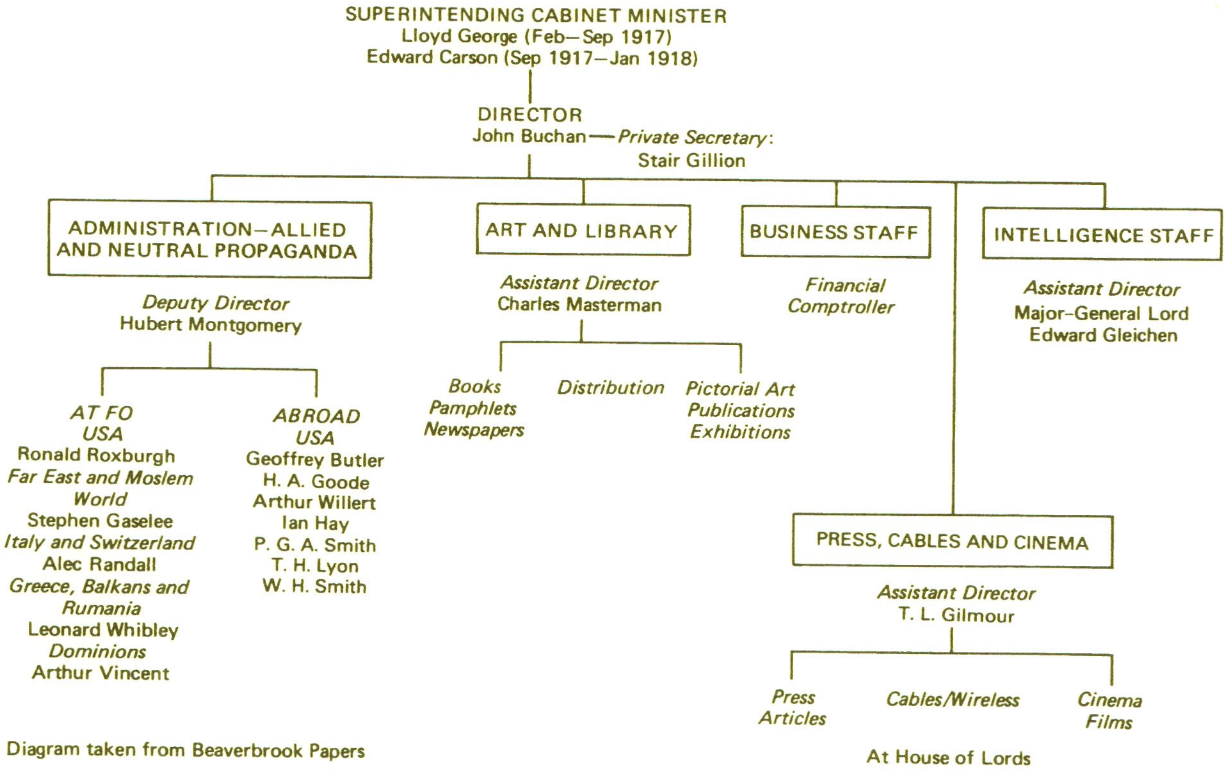

SUPERINTENDING CABINET MINISTER
Lloyd George (Feb–Sep 1917)
Edward Carson (Sep 1917–Jan 1918)

DIRECTOR
John Buchan — *Private Secretary:* Stair Gillion

ADMINISTRATION—ALLIED AND NEUTRAL PROPAGANDA

Deputy Director
Hubert Montgomery

AT FO
USA
Ronald Roxburgh
Far East and Moslem World
Stephen Gaselee
Italy and Switzerland
Alec Randall
Greece, Balkans and Rumania
Leonard Whibley
Dominions
Arthur Vincent

ABROAD
USA
Geoffrey Butler
H. A. Goode
Arthur Willert
Ian Hay
P. G. A. Smith
T. H. Lyon
W. H. Smith

ART AND LIBRARY

Assistant Director
Charles Masterman

- *Books Pamphlets Newspapers*
- *Distribution*
- *Pictorial Art Publications Exhibitions*

BUSINESS STAFF

Financial Comptroller

INTELLIGENCE STAFF

Assistant Director
Major-General Lord Edward Gleichen

PRESS, CABLES AND CINEMA

Assistant Director
T. L. Gilmour

- *Press Articles*
- *Cables/Wireless* — At House of Lords
- *Cinema Films*

Diagram taken from Beaverbrook Papers

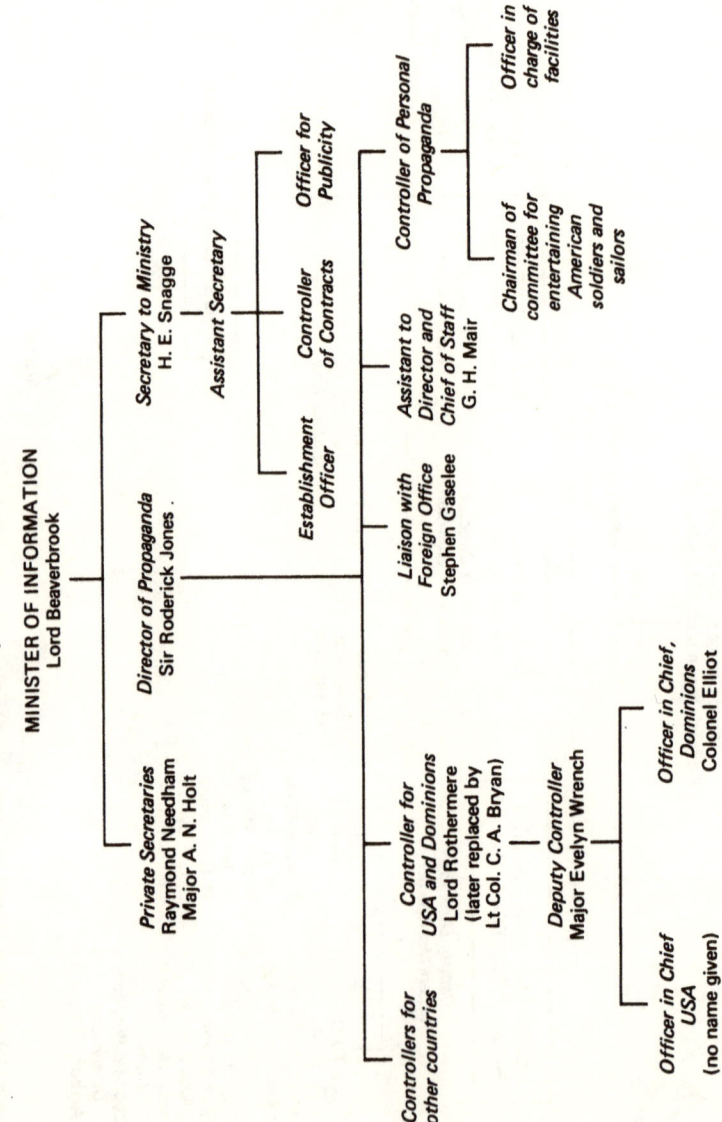

(c) Ministry of Information (1918)

Diagram taken from Beaverbrook Paters F/2A/1

Notes

CHAPTER 1. IRELAND AND PRE-WAR BRITISH FOREIGN POLICY

1. Casement diary, quoted in Rene MacColl, *Roger Casement* (London, 1960) p. 115; Patrick Keatinge, *A Place among the Nations. Issues of Irish Foreign Policy* (Dublin, 1978) chs 1–2.
2. Denis Gwynn, *The Life and Death of Roger Casement* (London, 1931) p. 141.
3. Geoffrey de C. Parmiter, *Roger Casement* (London, 1936) pp. 104–5.
4. Balfour to White, 12 Dec 1900, Balfour Papers, Add. MS 49742.
5. Devlin memorandum, c. Feb 1914, Lloyd George Papers, C/20/2/6; *Hansard*, HC, 19 Mar 1914 (LIX, 2296).
6. Philip G. Cambray, *Irish Affairs and the Home Rule Question*, 2nd edn (London, 1911) p. 133; Garvin to Sanders, 21 Jan 1910, Balfour Papers, Add. MS 49795. Some months later, Balfour assured Garvin that he gave 'full weight' to such 'external influences', but rejected Home Rule as a solution (ibid.).
7. Garvin to Chamberlain, 20 Oct 1910, and Chamberlain's reply, 21 Oct 1910 (copies), Joseph Chamberlain Papers, 27/52/77.
8. Sir Almeric Fitzroy, *Memoirs*, 2 vols (London, 1925) II, 507.
9. A. T. Q. Stewart, *The Ulster Crisis* (London, 1967) p. 226.
10. George Dangerfield, *The Strange Death of Liberal England* (London, 1966) p. 105.
11. *Irish Churchman*, 14 Nov 1913; Felician Prill, *Ireland, Britain and Germany, 1871–1914* (London, 1975) pp. 110, 115, 117; Goschen to Nicolson, 19 Nov 1913, Nicolson Papers, FO 800/371; Alfred Noyes, *The Accusing Ghost or Justice for Casement* (London, 1957) pp. 36–7; Stronge to Hugh Montgomery, 29 Aug 1918, Montgomery Papers, D627/436/37.
12. Evelyn Wrench, *Geoffrey Dawson and our Times* (London, 1955) p. 80.
13. Memorandum by poet, Alfred Graves, 27 Oct 1915, regarding earlier conversation with Carson, Redmond Papers, MS 152.61(2); Tim Healy, *Letters and Leaders of my Day*, 2 vols (London, 1928) II, 558.
14. Prill, *Ireland, Britain and Germany*, p. 113.
15. Harold Nicolson, *Sir Arthur Nicolson. A Study in the Old Diplomacy* (London, 1930) p. 401; Nicolson to Mallet, 30 Mar 1914, Nicolson Papers, FO 800/373.
16. Sir C. E. Callwell (ed.), *The Diaries of Field Marshal Sir Henry Wilson* (London, 1927) I, 139, 141, 146.

17. Nicolson to Goschen, 30 Apr 1914; Buchanan to Nicolson, 2 Apr 1914; Buchanan to Grey, 3 Apr 1914; and Nicolson to Buchanan, 21 Apr 1914: Nicolson Papers, FO 800/373.
18. Zara Steiner, *The Foreign Office and Foreign Policy, 1898–1914* (Cambridge, 1969) pp. 153, 139–40, 152.
19. Hardinge to Nicolson, 28 Mar 1914, Nicolson Papers, FO 800/373; Hardinge to Lord Sanderson, 22 Aug 1912, 13 May 1914, 26 Nov 1912, 17 Aug 1911, 12 Jan 1911, 9 May 1912, 10 Mar 1914 (copies), Hardinge Family Papers, U 927/Zi 19; Hardinge to Nicolson, 19 Nov 1913, Nicolson Papers, FO 800/371.
20. Sir Charles Petrie, *The Life and Times of Sir Austen Chamberlain*, 2 vols (London, 1939–40) I, 342.
21. *The Times*, 11 Mar 1914; Cromer to Milner, 10 Mar 1914, Milner Papers, G17.
22. Sam Cunningham (Ulster Unionist) to Milner, 7 Sept 1914 (reporting Crawford's claim), Milner Papers, G17; Crawford to Montgomery, 8 Jan 1918, Montgomery Papers, D 627/437/17; Montgomery to Bishop John Gunn (Mississippi), Jan 1919 (copy), Montgomery Papers, D 627/438/2.
23. Nicolson to Goschen, 27 Apr 1914, Nicolson Papers, FO 800/373; draft FO telegram to European consuls, FO 371/2185; *Hansard*, HC, 28 and 29 Apr 1914 (LXI, 1590, 1761).
24. Spring-Rice to William Tyrrell (Grey's Private Secretary), 25 Mar 1914; Grey minute, n.d.; Tyrrell to Spring-Rice, telegram, 28 Mar 1914; and Spring-Rice to Tyrrell, 30 Mar 1914: Grey Papers, FO 800/84, 1.
25. Percy minute, 21 July 1914; Bennet to Grey, 25 May 1914; and Birrell to Tyrrell, 11 June 1914: FO 371/2185.
26. Spring-Rice to Tyrrell, 30 Mar and 13 Jan 1914, and Spring-Rice to Grey, 30 Mar, Grey Papers, FO 800/84, 1.
27. Willert to Henry Wickham Steed (European editor of *The Times*), Willert Papers; Percy minute, 15 July 1914, FO 371/2187; John Devoy, *Recollections of an Irish Rebel* (New York, 1929) p. 393.
28. Charles Seymour, *The Intimate Papers of Colonel House*, 2 vols (Boston, Mass., 1926) I, 201; Spring-Rice to Grey, 13 Apr 1914, Grey Papers, FO 800/84, 1.
29. Arthur Willert, *Washington and Other Memories* (Boston, Mass., 1972) p. 54.
30. D. C. Watt, *Personalities and Policies. Studies in the Formulation of British Foreign Policy in the Twentieth Century* (London, 1965) p. 31.
31. Stephen Gwynn (ed.), *The Letters and Friendships of Sir Cecil Spring-Rice*, 2 vols (London, 1929) I, 38, and II, 279; Balfour to Lord Derby, 25 June 1918, Balfour Papers, Add. MS 49743; Arthur Willert, *The Road to Safety* (London, 1951) p. 90; Langley minute, n.d., on Spring-Rice to Grey, 24 Jan 1918, FO 371/2153.
32. Spring-Rice to his wife, 31 July 1914, Spring-Rice Papers, 2/10; Spring-Rice to Newton, 9 July 1914, quoted in S. Gwynn (ed.), *Spring-Rice*, I, 209.
33. Lansdowne to Spring-Rice, 22 July 1914, ibid.; Wrench, *Dawson*, p. 103; G. H. Mair (*Manchester Guardian* correspondent) to his editor, C. P. Scott, 23 July 1914, C. P. Scott Papers, Add. MS 50908.

34. Henry Wickham Steed, *Through Thirty Years, 1892–1922*, 2 vols (London, 1924) I, 392; Reginald Pound and Geoffrey Harmsworth, *Northcliffe* (London, 1959) p. 461; James W. Gerard, *My Four Years in Germany* (London, 1917) p. 63.
35. Denis Gwynn, *The Life of John Redmond* (London, 1931) p. 349.
36. *Lord Riddell's War Diary, 1914–18* (London, 1933) p. 5; David Lloyd George, *War Memoirs*, 2 vols (London, 1938) I, 416; Prill, *Ireland, Britain and Germany*, pp. 132–3.
37. Maurice Hankey, *The Supreme Command*, 2 vols (London, 1961) I, 152.
38. Roy Jenkins, *Asquith* (London, 1964) p. 323.
39. Winston Churchill, *The World Crisis, 1911–18* (London, 1923) p. 193.
40. S. Gwynn (ed.), *Spring-Rice*, I, 210; Blanche Dugdale, *Arthur James Balfour*, 2 vols (London, 1936) II, 114.
41. Lord Beaverbrook, *Politicians and the War, 1914–16* (New York, 1928) pp. 24–5.
42. Asquith to St Loe Strachey, 11 Aug 1918, Strachey Papers, S/11/6/22; Anita Leslie, *Mr Frewen of England. A Victorian Adventurer* (London, 1966) p. 194 (on Grey's denial); Zara Steiner, *Britain and the Origins of the First World War* (London, 1977) pp. 231, 236.

CHAPTER 2. 'THE ONE BRIGHT SPOT'

1. *Hansard*, HC, 3 Aug 1914 (LXV, 1824, 1828–9); Samuel Papers, A/156/466; A. Birrell, *Things Past Redress* (London, 1937) p. 43.
2. *The Times*, 30 July 1914; Redmond to Asquith, 22 Aug 1914, Asquith Papers, vol. 36; O'Connor to Lloyd George, 21 Aug 1914, enclosing Runciman to Percy Illingworth (Liberal Chief Whip), 19 Aug (copy), Lloyd George Papers, C/6/10/10.
3. Donald to Lloyd George, 30 Aug 1914, Lloyd George Papers, C/4/8/8.
4. Leon O'Broin, *The Chief Secretary. Augustine Birrell in Ireland* (London, 1969) pp. 209–10; Asquith's Cabinet report to George V, 12 Sep 1914, Cab 41/35/43; *Hansard*, HC, 15 Sep 1914 (LXVI, 859).
5. Unionist memorandum to Asquith, 7 Aug 1914, Bonar Law Papers, 34/3/16.
6. Bonar Law speech, in Unionist pamphlet, Milner Papers, G17; *Hansard*, HL, 16 Sep 1914 (XVIII, 715–16); Churchill to Chamberlain, 13 Sep 1914, and Chamberlain's reply, 14 Sep, quoted in Petrie, *Sir Austen Chamberlain*, II, 11–13.
7. Gwynne to Bonar Law, 3 Sep 1914, Bonar Law Papers, 34/S/1; Willert, *Washington*, p. 41; Willert to Dawson, 7 and 14 Sep 1914, Willert Papers; Dawson to Carson, 7 Aug 1914, *Times* Irish Papers.
8. Willert to Dawson, 18 Aug 1914, Willert Papers; Redmond to Asquith, 22 Aug 1914, Asquith Papers, vol. 36.
9. Egan to Redmond, 20 Oct 1914, Redmond Papers, MS 15,236(5).
10. Spring-Rice to Grey, 29 Sep and 13 Nov 1914, Grey Papers, FO 800/84, pt 3.
11. See, for example, reports of a New York meeting, FO 371/2225 and 2215.

12. S. Gwynn (ed.), *Spring-Rice*, II, 239–40; Lord Newton, *Retrospection* (London 1941) pp. 211–12.
13. Montgomery to Asquith, 23 Nov 1914, Asquith Papers, vol. 26; Grey minute, n.d., c. Feb 1915, Grey Papers, FO 800/107; minute by Guy Locock, 14 Apr 1915, on Spring-Rice to FO, 1 Apr 1915, FO 371/2559.
14. Healy to William O'Brien, 24 Dec 1914, O'Brien Papers, MS 8556/8; O'Connor memorandum, 3 Apr 1915, FO 371/2560; *Daily Chronicle*, 6 May 1915.
15. Bertie to Grey, 26 Apr 1915; Grey to Bertie, telegram, 27 Apr 1915; and Bertie to Grey, 2 May 1915; Grey Papers, FO 800/57.
16. *Manchester Guardian*, 3 May 1915; Gill to O'Connor, 3 May 1915 (copy), Gill Papers, MS 13,487(3); *Belfast News Letter*, 1 May 1915; Lady Algernon Gordon Lennox (ed.), *The Diary of Lord Bertie of Thame, 1914–18*, 2 vols (London, 1924) I, 213.
17. Crowe minute, 27 Sep 1914, FO 371/2209; Parmiter, *Casement*, pp. 146–9.
18. Brian Inglis, *Roger Casement* (London, 1974) p. 291.
19. Ibid., pp. 293–4.
20. Colum quoted in Robert Monteith, *Casement's Last Adventure* (London, 1953) p. 113; Bernstorff, quoted in D. Gwynn, *Casement*, p. 221; Egan to Redmond, 24 Nov 1914, Redmond Papers, MS 15236(5).
21. Nicolson minute, 21 Nov 1914, and Grey minute, n.d., FO 371/2217; Matthew Nathan memorandum (on Kitchener), 20 Nov 1914, Nathan Papers, vol. 467; S. Gwynn (ed.), *Spring-Rice*, II, 248; Birrell to Nathan, 26 Nov 1914, quoted in O'Broin, *The Chief Secretary*, p. 191; Inglis, *Casement*, p. 297.
22. MacColl, *Casement*, pp. 123, 118.
23. D. Gwynn, *Casement*, pp. 314–19.
24. Birrell to Nathan, 28 Dec 1914, Nathan Papers, vol. 449; Robert Vansittart, *The Mist Procession* (London, 1958) p. 155; O'Broin, *The Chief Secretary*, p. 192; Nathan to Friend, 8 Apr 1915, CO 904/174/2; Percy minute, 30 Nov 1914, FO 371/2225.
25. Devoy, *Recollections*, p. 431; Peter Singleton-Gates and Maurice Girodias, *The Black Diaries* (London, 1959) p. 365.
26. Grant Duff to Grey, 15 Feb 1915, and FO draft reply, 17 Feb, FO 371/2557; Inglis, *Casement*, p. 314.
27. Montgomery minute, 13 May 1915, on Tower to FO, 14 Apr 1915; and Tower to FO, 17 Feb and 23 Mar 1915: FO 371/2553. Peel to FO, 6 May 1915, FO 371/2557.
28. FO draft letter to a correspondent, William Hay, 3 Apr 1915, FO 371/2528.
29. *Morning Post*, 31 July 1915.
30. Willert to Dawson, 4 Jan 1915, Willert Papers; *The Times*, 5 Jan 1915; Dawson to Willert, 25 Jan 1915, Willert Papers.
31. For Percy's views, see Willert to Dawson, 26 Feb 1915, and Dawson to Willert, 8 Mar 1915, Willert Papers; Spring-Rice to Grey, 12 and 26 Feb 1915, Grey Papers, FO 800/85.
32. Percy and Clerk minutes, 29 and 31 May 1915, FO 371/2586.

CHAPTER 3. THE ASQUITH COALITION; THE WORSENING IRISH-AMERICAN SITUATION

1. Bonar Law to Asquith, 28 May 1915 (copy), Bonar Law Papers, 53/6/2; Redmond to Asquith, 7 June 1915, Asquith Papers, vol. 36.
2. *Daily Chronicle*, 7 June 1915; *Manchester Guardian*, 11 June 1915; *Belfast News Letter*, 10 June 1915.
3. Drummond memorandum, 5 June 1915, Grey Papers, FO 800/95.
4. Crewe to Spring-Rice and Spring-Rice's reply, telegrams, both 8 June 1915, Bonar Law Papers, 63/C/55.
5. Percy to Balfour, 6 June 1915, Balfour Papers, Add. MS. 49748.
6. Balfour to Percy, 7 June 1915, Balfour Papers, Add. MS. 49748.
7. Herbert to Arthur Nicolson, 8 Dec 1915, Nicolson Papers, FO 800/380.
8. Arthur Link, *Wilson and the Progressive Era, 1910–17* (London, 1954) p. 166.
9. Spring-Rice to Prince Arthur of Connaught, 18 July 1915 (copy), Spring-Rice Papers, FO 800/241; Willert to Dawson, 23 July 1915, Willert Papers.
10. Retrospective minute by News Department official Miles Lampson, 12 Apr 1916, FO 371/2793.
11. Drummond minute, 9 Aug 1915, FO 371/2571; Grey to Spring-Rice, 13 Aug 1915, quoted in Alan J. Ward, *Ireland and Anglo-American Relations, 1899–1921* (London, 1969) p. 96; Spring-Rice to News Department, telegrams, 15, 17, 23 Aug and Butler minute, 16 Aug 1915, FO 371/2571.
12. Birrell to Redmond, 2 Sep 1915, Redmond Papers, MS 15169(4); D. Gwynn, *Redmond*, p. 439; Spring-Rice to News Department, 25 Sep 1915, Barclay to Grey, 24 Sep 1915, FO 371/2571.
13. Barclay to Grey, 24 Sep 1915, FO 371/2571.
14. Broderick memorandum, n.d., c. Mar 1916, FO 371/2793.
15. Egan to Redmond, 16 Apr and 7 May 1915, Redmond Papers, MS 15236(5).
16. Ward, *Ireland and Anglo-American Relations*, pp. 92–3.
17. George Viereck, *Spreading Germs of Hate* (London, 1931) pp. 77, 210.
18. Broderick memorandum, n.d., c. Nov 1915; Barclay to Grey, 21 Nov 1915; Leslie to Spring-Rice, 18 Nov 1915; and Percy minute, 11 Dec 1915: FO 371/2571.
19. Broderick memorandum, n.d., c. Mar 1916, FO 371/2793.
20. Sperling minute, 29 Feb 1916, on Spring-Rice to Grey, 12 Feb, FO 371/2793; Masefield to Parker, 23 Jan 1916, FO 371/2846.
21. Broderick memorandum, 27 Mar 1916, FO 371/2793.
22. Spring-Rice to Grey, 19 Aug 1915, FO 371/2571; Percy minute, 7 Nov 1915, on Gregory to Grey, 20 Oct, FO 371/2501.
23. Spring-Rice to Grey, 3 Dec 1915, FO 371/2501.
24. Spring-Rice to Grey, telegrams, 17 and 28 Aug 1915, FO 371/2571; J. D. Gregory, *On the Edge of Diplomacy* (London, 1928) p. 100.
25. Leslie to Spring-Rice, 18 Nov 1915, FO 371/2571.
26. Butler, Locock and Montgomery minutes, 2, 3 and 4 Dec 1915, on Spring-Rice to Grey, 21 Nov, FO 371/2571; Montgomery to WO, 24 Feb,

and Wellington House to Montgomery, 25 Feb 1916, FO 371/2836; Montgomery minute, 17 Apr 1916, FO 371/2793.
27. Bennet to FO, 23 Jan, 17 Feb and 27 May, and Leay to FO, 9 June 1915, FO 371/2854; Spring-Rice to Grey, 24 Dec 1915, FO 371/2847.
28. Bennet to FO, 1 Apr 1915, FO 371/2584; Devoy, *Recollections*, pp. 444–7.
29. Bennet to Spring-Rice, 10 and 12 May 1915, and FO to Board of Trade (draft, subsequently cancelled), 30 May 1915, FO 371/2587. For an account of the *Lusitania* sinking, see Horace Peterson, *Propaganda for War* (Norman, Okla, 1939) p. 121.
30. FO memorandum 'German Intrigues in the Far East', FO 371/2586.
31. Poem by Peter Golden of *Gaelic American* in *Ghadr*, 18 July 1915, and *Ghadr* article on Ireland, 30 June 1915, FO 371/2495.
32. C's testimony, n.d., FO 371/2785; Bennet to Grey, 18 June 1915; FO 371/2590; Nathan to John Dillon, 7 July 1915, Nathan Papers, vol. 464; Dunraven to *Morning Post*, 24 Oct 1915; *The Times*, 15 June 1915; Ridgeway to Willoughby de Broke, 12 Nov 1915, Willoughby de Broke Papers.
33. Jodh Singh testimony, FO 371/2791.
34. MacColl, *Casement*, p. 127.
35. See Devoy, *Recollections*, ch. 53.
36. Memorandum on 'Arms to Indian Revolutionaries', FO 371/2786; Captain Karl Spindler, *The Mystery of the Casement Ship* (Tralee, 1965) p. 183.
37. Spring-Rice to Grey, 7 May 1914, FO 371/2152; Barclay to Grey, 6 Sep 1915, FO 371/2495.
38. Charles C. Tansill, *America and the Fight for Irish Freedom, 1886–1921* (New York, 1957) p. 196; S. Gwynn (ed.), *Spring-Rice*, II, 303–4.

CHAPTER 4. THE EASTER RISING AND ITS AFTERMATH

1. For details of the Rising, see Thomas M. Coffey, *Agony at Easter* (London, 1971).
2. *New York Times*, 19 Apr 1916; *Gaelic American*, 29 Apr 1916; Devoy, *Recollections*, p. 469.
3. MacColl, *Casement*, p. 198; Tansill, *America and the Fight for Irish Freedom*, p. 196.
4. Spring-Rice to Grey, telegram, 22 Apr 1916, FO 371/2804.
5. Spring-Rice to Grey, 1 May 1916, FO 371/2847; minute by Sperling, 15 May 1916, FO 371/2797.
6. *New York Herald*, 28 Apr 1916; Ward, *Ireland and Anglo-American Relations*, p. 108; Spring-Rice to Grey, 28 Apr 1916, FO 371/2847.
7. Crewe minute, 23 Apr 1916, FO 371/2804.
8. Leon O'Broin, *Dublin Castle and the 1916 Rising* (London, 1970) pp. 135–42.
9. *New York World*, 26 Apr and 2 May 1916; *New York Times*, 4 May 1916; *New York Herald*, 28 Apr 1916; S. Gwynn (ed.), *Spring-Rice*, II, 331.

10. Desmond Ryan, *The Rising. The Complete Story of Easter Week* (Dublin, 1949) pp. 260-1.
11. Coffey, *Agony at Easter*, p. 65.
12. Margaret Digby, *Horace Plunkett. An Anglo-American Irishman* (Oxford, 1949) pp. 210, 212.
13. Walter to Plunkett, 9 May 1916, Plunkett Papers; News Department to Irish Office, 9 May 1916, unsigned draft, FO 371/2844.
14. New York *Sun*, 27 Apr 1916; Leslie to Redmond, 16 May 1916, Redmond Papers, MS 15236(14).
15. D. Gwynn, *Redmond*, p. 481; APR, in FO 395/43; *The Times*, 2 May 1916.
16. Leslie to Redmond, 20 May 1916, Redmond Papers, MS 15236(14).
17. New York *Herald*, 26, 27 and 28 Apr 1916; APR, 25 May 1916, FO 395/43.
18. Parker to Montgomery, 6 Oct 1916, FO 395/7; Drummond to Grey, 25 May 1916, FO 395/6; Whigham to Parker, 28 Apr 1916, FO 371/2837; Long memorandum, 19 May 1916, Cab 37/148/11; Maxwell to Sir John French, 13 May 1916, WO 32/9574.
19. Spring-Rice to Plunkett, 4 May 1916, Plunkett Papers; Spring-Rice to Grey, telegram, 5 June 1916, FO 371/2793; Lord Eustace Percy, *Some Memories* (London, 1958) p. 49.
20. Sperling and Grey minutes, 15 and 20 May 1916, on Spring-Rice to Grey, 1 May, FO 371/2797.
21. Sperling and Malkin minutes, 7 and 10 June 1916, on Spring-Rice to Grey, 5 June, FO 371/2793.
22. New York *World*, 2 May 1916; Spring-Rice to Grey, 4 May 1916, FO 371/2792.
23. Redmond to Asquith, and Redmond to Dillon, both 3 May 1916, Redmond Papers, MSS 15165(6), 15182(22); *Hansard*, HC, 11 May 1916 (LXXX, 50).
24. *Daily Chronicle*, 10 May 1916; *Manchester Guardian*, 10 May 1916; Willert telegrams to *The Times*, 4, 6 and 9 May 1916; Dawson to Willert, 4 May 1916, Willert Papers.
25. Spring-Rice to Grey, telegram, 19 May 1916, Grey Papers, FO 800/86; Spring-Rice to Grey, 19 May 1916, FO 371/2793; Sherill P. Wells, 'The Influence of Sir Cecil Spring-Rice and Sir Edward Grey on the Shaping of Anglo-American Relations, 1913–16' (unpublished Ph.D. thesis, London University, 1978) pp. 9, 38, 162, 228–31, 243–4.
26. Hardinge minute, n.d., c. January 1917, FO 395/65; Curzon to Hardinge, 17 Sep 1916, Hardinge Papers, vol. 25; Cecil to Lord Milner, 25 Dec 1916 (copy), Cecil Papers, FO 800/198; Spring-Rice to his wife, 13 June 1916, Spring-Rice Papers, 2/12.
27. Owen Dudley Edwards and Fergus Pyle (eds), *1916. The Easter Rising* (London, 1968) p. 166; Spring-Rice to his wife, 14 June 1916, Spring-Rice Papers, 2/12; unsigned memorandum enclosed in Willert to Dawson, 28 Apr 1916, Willert Papers; Wells, 'The Influence of Spring-Rice and Grey', p. 268; Lady Barclay's views, as described by her son, Colville Herbert Barclay, in a letter to the author, 14 Mar 1979; Dudley Edwards and Pyle (eds), *1916*, p. 166.
28. Percy minute, 10 May 1916, FO 371/2793; Tansill, *America and the Fight*

for Irish Freedom, p. 219; Senate resolution and Lansing's reply, 2 and 7 June 1916, FO 371/2797.
29. Shane Leslie, *Long Shadows* (London, 1967) p. 203; Dudley Edwards and Pyle (eds), *1916*, p. 162; D. Gwynn, *Redmond*, p. 491; Asquith's Cabinet report to George V, 6 May 1916, Cab 37/147/13.
30. *New York Times*, 19 May 1916.
31. Maxwell to Bonham-Carter, 20 May 1916, Asquith Papers, vol. 42; WO to FO, 20 May, and Lampson minutes, 20 and 21 May 1916, FO 395/43; *New York Times*, 21 May 1916.
32. Dudley Edwards and Pyle, *1916*, p. 162.
33. Drummond to Bonham-Carter, 22 May 1916, transmitted to Dublin, and General Byrne's reply, 5 June, Asquith Papers, vol. 37.
34. Durant to Parker, 12 May 1916, FO 395/43; Whigham to Parker, 5 May 1916, FO 395/6.
35. Whigham to Parker, 16 June 1916, FO 395/6; Durant to Parker, 12 May 1916, FO 395/43; Munsterberg to Bethmann Hollweg, 12 May 1916, FO 395/6; Fuehr to Frau Rechtsanwalt (Wiesbaden, Germany), 30 May 1916, FO 371/2794. (Both the last two were intercepted by British Admiralty Intelligence.)
36. Frederick Dixon (Boston editor) to Guy Locock (on Lansing's warning), received 13 May 1916, Grey Papers, FO 800/108; Gaunt letter, no addressee given, 2 June 1916 (copy), Grey Papers, FO 800/107; Whigham to Parker, 12 May 1916, FO 395/6; Spring-Rice to Grey, 19 May 1916, FO 371/2793.
37. Lucy Masterman, *C. F. G. Masterman. A Biography* (London, 1939) pp. 290–1; Roxburgh minute, 25 May 1916, Parker to Whigham, 24 May 1916, FO 395/43.
38. *Gravesend Reporter*, 26 Nov 1910; Parker to Whigham, 24 May 1916, FO 395/43.
39. Butler minute, 5 June 1916, and Grey minute, n.d., c. 25 May, FO 395/6; Sperling minute, 31 May 1916, on Spring-Rice to FO, telegram, 30 May, FO 371/2797; Nicolson minutes, 30 May 1916, FO 371/2793, and 1 June, on Spring-Rice to Grey, telegram, 30 May, FO 371/2797.
40. James Pope-Hennessy, *Lord Crewe, 1858–1945. The Likeness of a Liberal* (London, 1955) p. 46; *Hansard*, HL, 10 May 1916 (xxv, 973); Crewe minute, 1 June 1916, FO 371/2797; Hardinge minute, n.d., c. 1 July 1916, FO 395/43; Hubert to Hugh Montgomery, 2 June 1916, Montgomery Papers, D 627/429/29.
41. Viscount Grey of Fallodon, *Twenty-Five Years*, 3 vols (London, 1928) II, 155.
42. V. H. Rothwell, 'War Aims, Peace Moves and Strategy in British Policy, 1916–18' (Ph.D. thesis, Leeds University, 1969) p. 42.
43. Wells, 'The Influence of Spring-Rice and Grey', p. 29.
44. Pope-Hennessy, *Lord Crewe*, p. 13; Crewe minute, 5 Oct 1916, FO 371/2796.
45. Durant to Parker, 12 May 1916, FO 395/43; New York *Herald*, 4 May 1916; Whigham to Parker, 19 May 1916, FO 395/6; Roxburgh minute, 25 May 1916, FO 395/43.

46. Sperling and Crewe minutes, 31 May and 1 June 1916, FO 371/2797. Strachey to Montgomery, 24 July 1916; Montgomery's reply, 25 July 1916 (copy); and Butler to Professor Firth, 31 July 1916 (copy): FO 395/6. Spring-Rice to Grey, 2 June 1916, FO 371/2794.
47. Whigham to Parker, 5 May 1916, FO 395/6; Elting E. Morison (ed.), *The Letters of Theodore Roosevelt*, 8 vols (Cambridge, Mass., 1951) VIII, 1054.
48. S. Gwynn (ed.), *Spring-Rice*, II, 298.
49. *Spectator*, 7 June 1916.
50. Plunkett's confidential report to George V on the Irish Convention, Apr 1918, Lloyd George Papers, F/179/5/3.
51. Whigham to Parker, 5 May 1916, FO 395/6; Durant to Parker, 12 May, and APR, 25 May 1916, FO 395/43.
52. Peterson, *Propaganda for War*, p. 13.
53. *Hansard*, HC, 26 Apr 1916 (LXXXI, 2434, 2579); *Belfast News Letter*, 1 May 1916; *Daily Mail*, 27 Apr 1916; Pound and Harmsworth, *Northcliffe*, pp. 468–9; Willert, *Road to Safety*, p. 74; *The Times*, 29 Apr 1916.
54. *The Times*, 15 May 1916; *Hansard*, HL, 29 June 1916 (XC, 504).
55. Newton, *Retrospection*, p. 221; Crewe to Kitchener, 26 Apr 1916, Grey Papers, FO 800/102.
56. Frederick Palmer, *With my Own Eyes* (New York, 1934) p. 332; Captain Butler to Montgomery, 29 and 30 Apr 1916, FO 371/2844.
57. Davies to Montgomery, and Montgomery's reply, both 1 May 1916, FO 371/2844.
58. Lampson minute, n.d., c. 2 May 1916, FO 371/2833.
59. Parker to Whigham, 24 May 1916, FO 395/43; *Hansard*, HL, 29 June 1916 (XXII, 502); Needham's notes, Nathan Papers, vol. 477; *New York Times*, magazine section, 28 May 1916.
60. Grey to Asquith, 30 May 1916, Asquith Papers, vol. 30; Maxwell statement, 3 June 1916, FO 395/43; Spring-Rice to Montgomery and to Grey, telegrams, both 2 June 1916, FO 395/43 and 371/2794; Butler minute, 5 June 1916, FO 395/6.
61. Montgomery memorandum, n.d., c. late June 1916; Newton minute, 1 July 1916; and Hardinge minute, n.d., c. early July 1916; FO 395/43. Montgomery minute, 25 July 1916, FO 371/2797.
62. Lampson and Newton minutes, 21 and 24 Aug 1916, FO 395/43; Lampson to Strachey, 25 Aug, and Strachey to Desart, 31 Aug 1916, Strachey Papers, S/21/1/24–5.
63. WO to Newton, 5 Sep 1916, FO 395/43; Derby to Lloyd George, 12 Nov 1916, Lloyd George Papers, E/1/1/9; War Cabinet minutes, 28 Feb 1917, Cab 23/1.
64. Percy and Montgomery minutes, 10 and 30 May, and Montgomery to Spring-Rice, telegram, 15 Aug 1916, FO 371/2793.
65. Lampson and Montgomery minutes, 6 and 8 May 1916, on Birrell to Lampson, 4 May; and Spring-Rice to FO, telegram, 10 June 1916: FO 371/2793.
66. Wells, 'The Influence of Spring-Rice and Grey', p. 33.
67. Lord Killearn to author, 6 Mar 1979.
68. Sperling minutes, 29 and 14 June 1916, FO 371/2794.

69. Sperling's daughter, Mrs Elizabeth Emery, to author, 17 Mar 1979.
70. Newton, *Retrospection*, p. 99; Newton minute, 21 July 1916, FO 371/2794.
71. Spring-Rice to Grey, 9 June 1916, Grey Papers, FO 800/86; Spring-Rice to Grey, 16 June 1916, FO 371/2794.

CHAPTER 5. SIR ROGER CASEMENT'S TRIAL AND EXECUTION

1. *New York Tribune*, 26 Apr 1916; *New York Times*, 27 Apr 1916, Boston *Evening Transcript*, 25 Apr 1916; Spring-Rice to FO, telegram, 26 Apr 1916, Grey Papers, FO 800/86; S. Gwynn (ed.), *Spring-Rice*, II, 335–6.
2. Percy memorandum, 13 May 1916, Cab 37/147/33; Spring-Rice to FO, telegram, 4 May 1916, FO 371/2851; Stamfordham to Asquith, 6 May 1916, Asquith Papers, vol. 4.
3. Minute by Oliphant, n.d., c. 5 May 1916, FO 371/2851; Bertie diary, 17 May 1916, quoted in Lennox (ed.), *Diary of Lord Bertie*, I, 346–7.
4. Minutes by Sperling, Nicolson, Lampson, Drummond and Butler, 11 May 1916, FO 371/2792.
5. Minutes by Drummond, 15 June 1916, on Gaunt letter (no addressee indicated), 2 June 1916, Grey Papers, FO 800/107; Admiral Sir Guy Gaunt, *The Yield of the Years* (London, 1940) p. 164.
6. Spring-Rice to Grey, 2 June 1916, FO 371/2794; minute by Langley, 31 May 1916, FO 371/2791; Willert to Dawson, 9 and 19 May 1916, Willert Papers.
7. *New York Herald*, 28 Apr 1916; Spring-Rice to FO, telegram, 8 May 1916, and Home Office view, cited in minute by Sperling, 14 June, FO 371/2792; Devoy, *Recollections*, pp. 477–8.
8. Ernest Marshall to his newspaper, the *New York Times*, 16 June 1916, FO 371/2792; Gaunt to Butler, 28 June 1916, FO 395/2; Ernley Blackwell (Home Office) to FO, 13 June 1916, FO 371/2797; Grey memorandum, 17 June 1916, Grey Papers, FO 800/86; Grey to Samuel, 16 June 1916, and Samuel's reply, 19 June 1916, Grey Papers, FO 800/212.
9. APR, 19 July 1916, Cab 37/152/3; Gregory, *On the Edge of Diplomacy*, p. 79; Hardinge to Spring-Rice, 30 June 1916 (copy), Hardinge Papers, vol. 22.
10. Henry Nevinson, *Last Change, Last Chances* (London, 1928) p. 114; Inglis, *Casement*, p. 374; Drummond to Grey, 13 May 1916, Grey Papers, FO 800/96; Inglis, *Casement*, pp. 365–6. Authenticity of the diaries has been accepted by MacColl and Inglis in their books on Casement, and rejected by Noyes and Denis Gwynn in theirs.
11. Spring-Rice to Grey, 15 May 1916, Grey Papers, FO 800/86; Leslie, *Long Shadows*, p. 188; Tansill, *America and the Fight for Irish Freedom*, p. 208.
12. Smith to Grey, 29 June 1916; draft telegram to Gaunt, 29 June 1916; and Grey to Smith, 29 June 1916: FO 395/43.
13. See, for example, Inglis, *Casement*, p. 374.

14. Minutes by Newton, Hardinge and Grey, 30 June 1916, FO 395/43; Newton to Spring-Rice, 30 June 1916, Spring-Rice Papers, 1/52.
15. Cab 41/37/25; Inglis, *Casement*, p. 373; Page to Lansing, 3 July 1916, quoted in Ward, *Ireland and Anglo-American Relations*, p. 122.
16. Murray to Grey, telegram, 2 Aug 1916, Grey Papers, FO 800/109; Quinn memorandum, 2 June 1916, Grey Papers, FO 800/110; negro petition, FO 371/2798; minute by Sperling, 1 Aug 1916, FO 371/2792.
17. Devlin to Asquith, 25 July, and Dillon to Asquith, 26 July 1916, Asquith Papers, vol. 37; Bryce to Lloyd George, 1 Aug 1916, Lloyd George Papers, E/2/5/1; Bryce to Samuel, n.d., c. July 1916, Samuel Papers, A55(10); Willert, *Road to Safety*, p. 75; Edwin Montagu (Minister of Munitions) to Curzon, 5 Aug 1916 (on latter's forecast), Curzon Papers, F 117/65; note by Long, n.d., Long Papers, WRO/147/176; *Boston Post*, 14 Jan 1918.
18. Asquith to George V, 5 July 1916, Cab 41/37/25.
19. Troup memorandum, 17 July, and Blackwell memorandum, 15 July 1916, Cab 37/151/35; Inglis, *Casement*, p. 375.
20. Newton, *Retrospection*, p. 226.
21. Spring-Rice to Newton, telegram, and Newton minute, both 20 July 1916; FO to Spring-Rice, telegram, 21 July 1916; Montgomery to Spring-Rice, 28 July 1916; Montgomery, Newton and Cecil minutes, 29 July 1916; and Newton to Spring-Rice, telegram, 30 July 1916: FO 395/43.
22. Ward, *Ireland and Anglo-American Relations*, p. 123.
23. Basil Thomson, *The Scene Changes* (London, 1937) p. 305.
24. Wilson to Tumulty, 30 July 1916, quoted in Tansill, *America and the Fight for Irish Freedom*, p. 210; Newton minute, n.d., and Sperling minute, 3 Aug 1916, on Spring-Rice to FO, telegram, 2 Aug 1916, FO 371/2798.
25. *The Times*, 31 July 1916; Spring-Rice to FO, telegram, 29 July 1916, FO 371/2797; Asquith's Cabinet report to George V, 2 Aug 1916, Cab 37/151/11.
26. Inglis, *Casement*, p. 381.
27. Samuel to his wife, 2 Aug 1916, Samuel Papers, A/157/844.
28. Hardinge to Chirol, 3 Aug 1916, Hardinge Papers, vol. 24.
29. Burton J. Hendrick, *The Life and Letters of Walter Hines Page, 1855–1918*, 2 vols (New York, 1927) II, 167–8.
30. *New York Times*, 17 Oct 1916.
31. Sperling minute, 3 Nov 1916, FO 371/2798; Grey to House, 28 Aug 1916, Cab 37/154/20.
32. Spring-Rice to Grey, 10 Aug 1916, Grey Papers, FO 800/86; Montagu to Curzon, 5 Aug 1916, Curzon Papers, F/117/65; Hardinge minute, n.d., c. mid August 1916, FO 371/2797; Sperling minute, 15 Aug 1916, FO 371/2798.
33. Grey to Spring-Rice, telegram, 4 Aug 1916, FO 395/43.
34. Grey to H. E. Duke (the new Chief Secretary), 15 Aug 1916, Grey Papers, FO 800/99.
35. Spring-Rice to Grey, 4 and 15 Aug 1916, FO 371/2798; Butler minute, 17 Aug 1916, on Spring-Rice to Newton, telegram, 16 Aug, FO 395/43; Spring-Rice to Montgomery, 4 Sep 1916, FO 395/6.

36. Noyes, *Two Worlds for Memory* (London, 1953) p. 127; Spring-Rice to FO, telegram, 2 Aug 1916, FO 371/2798.
37. Spring-Rice to FO, telegram, 14 Aug 1916, FO 395/3.
38. *Christian Science Monitor*, n.d., in FO 395/43; Dixon to Cecil, 18 Sep 1916, Cecil Papers, Add. MS 51092.
39. Gaselee minute, 3 Feb 1918, FO 395/43; Newton, *Retrospection*, p. 226; Vansittart, *The Mist Procession*, p. 56.

CHAPTER 6. THE HOME RULE NEGOTIATIONS; THE AMERICAN PRESIDENTIAL ELECTION

1. D. Gwynn, *Redmond*, pp. 500–1.
2. Barry to Redmond, 24 May 1916, Redmond Papers, MS 15236; Lloyd George Papers, D/14/2/3; Trevor Wilson (ed.), *The Political Diaries of C. P. Scott, 1911–28* (London, 1970) p. 207.
3. Spring-Rice to Grey, 16 June 1916, FO 371/2794.
4. Jenkins, *Asquith*, p. 294.
5. Asquith Cabinet report to George V, 27 June 1916, Cab 37/150/23.
6. Hubert to Hugh Montgomery, 29 May 1916, Montgomery Papers, D/627/429/10; Hardinge to Sir William Birdwood, 1 July, to Sir Harcourt Butler, 9 Aug, to Lord Bertie, 2 Aug, and to Lord Errington, 27 June 1916 (all copies), Hardinge Papers, vols 23, 24, 24, 22, respectively.
7. *Manchester Guardian*, 2 May 1916; *Daily Chronicle*, 22 June 1916; *Observer*, 2 July 1916, *Daily Express*, 17 May 1916; editorial and Willert despatch, *The Times*, 15 May 1916.
8. William O'Brien, *The Irish Revolution and How it Came About* (Dublin, 1923), p. 271.
9. Ronald McNeill, *Ulster's Stand for Union* (London, 1922) p. 247.
10. *The Times*, 24 Apr 1918.
11. Duffin to Miss Olive Duffin, 30 June 1916, Duffin Papers, Mic 127/20; Hugh to Hubert Montgomery, 9 June 1916, and Hubert to Hugh Montgomery, 29 May 1916, Montgomery Papers, D/627/429/26, 13.
12. Hugh to Hubert Montgomery, 30 June 1916, Montgomery Papers, D/627/429/49.
13. *Belfast News Letter*, 16 June 1916; Lloyd George to Lynn, 5 June 1916 (copy), Lloyd George Papers, D/14/2/13.
14. *The Times*, 24 June 1916.
15. Earl of Midleton, *Ireland, Dupe or Heroine* (London, 1932) pp. 101–4.
16. Southern Unionist statements: 26 June 1916, in Bonar Law Papers, 63/C/63; 27 June 1916, in Lloyd George Papers, D/15/1/20; and 22 June 1916, in *Belfast News Letter*. Midleton, *Ireland, Dupe or Heroine*, p. 104.
17. Jenkins, *Asquith*, p. 401.
18. F. S. L. Lyons, *John Dillon* (London, 1968) p. 394.
19. Charles Townshend, *The British Campaign in Ireland, 1919–21* (London, 1975) p. 12.
20. Long memorandum, 23 June 1916, Cab 37/150/15.

21. Eustace Percy minute, 23 Aug 1916, in FO memorandum on Brooks, FO 395/215; Brooks to Long, 7 June 1916, Long Papers, WRO 947/165.
22. Long to Asquith, 8 June 1916, Asquith Papers, vol. 16; Lloyd George's draft resignation to Asquith, 12 June 1916, Lloyd George Papers, D/14/2/29; Lyons, *Dillon*, p. 396; Lloyd George, *War Memoirs*, I, 422; Long memoranda to Cabinet Unionists, 15 June 1916, Chamberlain Papers, 14/5/13–14. See also Cabinet memorandum, 23 June 1916, Cab 37/150/15.
23. Long memorandum, n.d., c. June 1916, Long Papers, WRO 947/402, enclosure IV(15).
24. Lord Newton, *The Life of Lord Lansdowne* (London, 1929) p. 504; Lansdowne memorandum, 2 June 1916, Lloyd George Papers, D/15/1/10; Lansdowne to Long, 17 June 1916, Long Papers, WRO 947/268; Lansdowne memorandum, 21 June 1916, Cab 37/150/11.
25. Cecil to Strachey, 13 Sep 1916, Strachey Papers, S/4/4/18; Cecil memorandum, 26 June 1916, Cab 37/150/21.
26. Blackley to Carson, 13 July 1916, Carson Papers, D 1507/1/1916/44; Mackay Wilson to Irish Unionist Alliance, n.d., Ulster Unionist Council Papers, D 989/A/9/7; Colvin, *Carson*, III, 174; Lady Carson diary, 19 June 1916, Carson Papers, D 1507/6/2.
27. Watt, *Personalities and Policies*, p. 34.
28. Balfour memorandum, 24 June 1916, Cab 37/150/17; Asquith's Cabinet report to George V, 27 June 1916, Cab 41/37/24.
29. Bonar Law Papers, 63/C/64.
30. Ibid.
31. Robert Blake, *The Unknown Prime Minister. The Life and Times of Andrew Bonar Law, 1858–1923* (London, 1955) pp. 287–8; *Hansard*, HL, 11 July 1916 (LII, 646); Lloyd George, *War Memoirs*, I, 424–5.
32. Whigham to Parker, 28 July 1916, FO 395/11; House to Wilson, 30 July 1916, quoted in Arthur Link, *Wilson. Campaigns for Progressivism and Peace* (Princeton, NJ, 1965) p. 37; *Spectator*, 5 Aug 1916; O'Brien, *The Irish Revolution*, p. 283.
33. Sperling minute, 29 June 1916, on Spring-Rice to Grey, 16 June 1916, FO 371/2794.
34. Information from interview with de Bunsen's eldest daughter, Lady Salisbury-Jones, 22 Mar 1979.
35. De Bunsen minute, 3 July 1916, and Newton minute, 21 July 1916, FO 371/2794.
36. WO to Eric Drummond, 21 July 1916; Hardinge minute, n.d., on Spring-Rice to FO, telegram, 14 July 1916; and Clive Bayley to Grey, 27 July 1916: FO 371/2794.
37. Home Office to Drummond, 1 July 1916, FO 371/2794; *Hansard*, HC, 31 July 1916 (LXXXIV, 2055–6); General Macdonagh (DMI) to GHQ, Home Forces, 2 Sep 1916, WO 35/69/8.
38. Congressional resolution enclosed in Spring-Rice to Grey, 4 Aug 1916, FO 371/2794; Harrell memorandum, enclosed in Duke report, 16 Aug 1916, Cab 37/154/1; WO to DMI in Ireland, 5 Sep 1916, WO 35/69/8; Thomson to FO, 28 Sep, and de Bunsen minute, 7 Oct 1916, FO 371/2795.

39. Healy article, Los Angeles *Examiner*, 22 May 1916; MacNeill article, New York *Irish World*, 29 Apr. 1916; Jenkins, *Asquith*, p. 398; Birrell, *Things Past Redress*, p. 219; Wimborne to Lloyd George, 6 Nov 1916, Lloyd George Papers, E/2/9/2.
40. News Department to Irish Office, 9 May 1916, FO 371/2844; Parker to Whigham, 24 May 1916, FO 395/43; Spring-Rice to Hardinge, 14 July 1916, Hardinge Papers, vol. 23.
41. Butler minutes, 24 July and 22 Sep 1916, FO 371/2794 and 395/43; Montgomery minute, 22 Sep 1916, FO 395/43; Montgomery to his father, 28 Sep, and father's reply, 30 Sep 1916 (copy), Montgomery Papers, D 627/429/76-7; Irish Office to Montgomery, 30 Oct 1916 (enclosing copy of interview), FO 395/43.
42. Butler and Montgomery minutes, 21 Sep 1916; Newton minute, 28 Sep 1916; News Department to Parker, 27 Sep 1916 (copy); and Parker's reply, 4 Oct 1916: FO 395/43.
43. S. Gwynn (ed.), *Spring-Rice*, II, 331.
44. Spring-Rice to Grey, 20 June 1916, FO 371/2794.
45. Broderick memorandum, 16 June 1916 and Percy minute, 6 July 1916, FO 371/2794.
46. Ward, *Ireland and Anglo-American Relations*, p. 134.
47. War Trade Intelligence Department to FO, 28 Sep 1916, FO 371/2795.
48. *New York Times*, 23 Oct 1916.
49. Ward, *Ireland and Anglo-American Relations*, pp. 136-7; *New York Times*, 24 Oct 1916.
50. Crichton Stuart minute, 7 Nov 1916, FO 371/2796; Hardinge minute, c. July 1916, FO 371/2794; Hardinge to Spring-Rice, 8 Sep 1916 (copy), Hardinge Papers, vol. 25; Spring-Rice to Grey, 16 June 1916, FO 371/2794.
51. *Gaelic American*, 29 Apr 1916.
52. Dudley Edwards and Pyle (eds), *1916*, p. 175.
53. Link, *Campaigns for Progressivism*, p. 20.
54. Spring-Rice to Grey, 26 May 1916, FO 371/2848; S. Gwynn, *Spring-Rice* (ed.), II, 337.
55. Wilson to John D. Crimmins, quoted in Leslie, *The Irish Issue in its American Aspect* (New York, 1917) p. 202.
56. S. Gwynn (ed.), *Spring-Rice*, II, 341; Link, *Wilson and the Progressive Era*, p. 255 (on Lloyd George interview); Hardinge to Spring-Rice, 5 Oct 1916 (copy), Hardinge Papers, vol. 26; Grey to Lloyd George, 29 Sep, and Lloyd George's reply, 2 Oct 1916 (copy), Lloyd George Papers, E/2/13/5-6; Grey minute, n.d., c. late Oct 1916, FO 371/2796.
57. *Irish World*, 28 Oct 1916; Broderick memorandum, 19 Jan 1917, FO 371/3071; William M. Leary, Jr, 'Woodrow Wilson, Irish-Americans and the Election of 1916', *Journal of American History*, LIV (June 1967) 65-72.
58. Link, *Wilson and Progressive Era*, pp. 243-51.
59. W. B. Fowler, *British-American Relations, 1917-18. The Role of Sir William Wiseman* (Princeton, NJ, 1969) *passim*.
60. Spring-Rice to Balfour, 22 Jan 1917, enclosing Broderick memorandum, FO 371/3071.

CHAPTER 7. LLOYD GEORGE TAKES THE HELM

1. *Observer*, 17 Dec 1917; Spring-Rice to Grey, 5 Dec 1916, Balfour Papers, Add. MS 49731; Sperling minute, 5 Dec 1916, FO 371/2796.
2. Hankey memorandum, 8 Dec 1916, Cab 42/19/2; Hankey, *The Supreme Command*, II, 594; Redmond memorandum, 9 Dec 1916, Redmond Papers, MS 15189.
3. FOIF resolution, Dec 1916, quoted in Government memorandum, Dec 1920, Lloyd George Papers, F/180/5/19; Viereck's newspaper, the *Fatherland*, 27 Dec 1916.
4. Spring-Rice to Balfour, 29 Dec 1916, Balfour Papers, Add. MS 49740; Crowe and Cecil minutes, 26 Dec 1916, FO 371/2806.
5. War Cabinet minutes, 21 and 23 Dec 1916, Cab 23/1; Redmond to Asquith, 30 Nov 1916, Cab 1/21/1; Gill to Professor W. G. S. Adams, 12 July 1916 (copy), Gill Papers, MS 13488(18).
6. German communiqué, 11 Jan 1917, and FO reply, n.d., FO 395/132; *Belfast News Letter*, 13 Jan 1917.
7. Ward, *Ireland and Anglo-American Relations*, p. 131.
8. Sperling minute, 21 Dec 1916, FO 371/2806; Spring-Rice to Balfour, 11 Jan 1917, Balfour Papers, Add. MS 49740; Crichton Stuart minute, n.d., on Spring-Rice to Balfour, 8 Mar 1917, FO 371/3071.
9. New York *Herald*, 7 Jan 1917.
10. William O'Brien and Desmond Ryan, *Devoy's Post Bag, 1871–1928*, 2 vols (Dublin, 1953) II, 519–20.
11. Sperling minute, 19 Feb 1917, FO 371/3071.
12. Sperling and Crichton Stuart minutes, 2 Jan 1917, on Horace Nugent (Chicago Consul) to Spring-Rice, 15 Dec 1916, FO 371/3063; Chicago *Daily News*, 4 Dec 1916, FO 395/43; Montgomery to S. J. M. Power (Dublin Castle), 11 Jan 1917, FO 395/72.
13. Montgomery to Chief Secretary's Office, 8 and 14 Dec, and reply, 19 Dec 1916; Basil Thomson (Metropolitan Police chief) to Montgomery, and Gleason to Butler, both 27 Dec 1916: FO 395/5.
14. Montgomery to Chief Secretary's Office, 8 Feb 1917; Hapgood to Butler, 28 Feb, and Butler's reply, 1 Mar 1917; and Censor to Butler, 19 Mar 1917: FO 395/66.
15. Spring-Rice to Balfour, 5 Jan 1917, FO 395/65; Newton, *Retrospection*, p. 227.
16. Beith to Lord Beaverbrook, 10 Aug 1918, Beaverbrook Papers, E/8/192.
17. Noyes, *Two Worlds for Memory*, pp. 128–9; Noyes to Butler, 8 Mar 1917, FO 395/66.
18. Duke to Masterman, 16 Jan 1917 (copy); Whitton to Masterman, 22 Jan 1917; Masterman to Duke, 23 Jan 1917: FO 395/72.
19. Dawson to Horace Plunkett, 16 Feb 1916, *Times* Irish Papers; Gwynn to Bonar Law, 15 Mar 1916, Bonar Law Papers, 52/4/15; Northcliffe to Lloyd George, 23 Jan 1917, Lloyd George Papers, F/41/7/4; M. L. Sanders, 'Wellington House and British Propaganda during the First World War', *Historical Journal*, XVIII, no. 1 (1975) 123–4.
20. Masterman report, 16 Sep 1916, Cab 37/156/6; Hardinge minute, 4 Feb

1917, and Cecil minute, n.d., Balfour Papers, FO 800/211; Montgomery memorandum, 5 Feb 1917, FO 395/65.
21. War Cabinet minutes (75/13), 20 Feb 1917, Cab 23/1.
22. Whibley minute, 8 Mar 1917, on Noyes to Butler, 14 Feb 1917, FO 395/66.
23. *Hansard*, HC, 22 Mar 1917 (xci, 2139), and 26 Feb 1917 (xc, 1787); Leslie to Dillon, 2 Mar 1917, Redmond Papers, MS 15182(24).
24. Wimborne memorandum, 11 Feb 1917, and Adams memorandum, n.d., c. Mar 1917, Lloyd George Papers, F/47/7 and 66/5; *The Times*, 7 Mar 1917; *Hansard*, HC, 22 Mar 1917 (xci, 2125).
25. *Hansard*, HC, 7 Mar 1917 (xci, 463, 476, 510–12).
26. *The Times*, 9 Mar 1917.
27. *Belfast News Letter*, 9 and 10 Mar 1917.
28. Roxburgh minute, 9 Mar 1917, FO 395/72; Broderick memorandum, 19 Jan 1917, FO 371/3071. Spring-Rice to Balfour, telegram, 8 Mar and letter, 9 Mar 1917; and Balfour minute, n.d.: Balfour Papers, Add. MS 49740.
29. Whibley minute and Tanner article, n.d., c. mid March 1917, FO 395/72.
30. Butler minute, 12 Mar 1917, FO 395/66.
31. Extract of Butler letter (no addressee) enclosed in Butler to Drummond, 16 July 1918 (copy), Lloyd George Papers, F/60/2/79.
32. Entry in the *Dictionary of National Biography: 1922–30*, by William Spens, a friend and FO colleague.
33. G. Butler, *The Tory Tradition* (London, 1914).
34. In addition to lecturing in America, he married the daughter of a Philadelphia lawyer in 1916.
35. Montgomery minute, 12 Mar 1917, FO 395/66; John Buchan, *Memory Hold the Door* (London, 1940) pp. 145–6; Janet Adam Smith, *John Buchan* (London, 1965) p. 184.
36. Buchan, *Memory Hold the Door*, pp. 145–6; Buchan minute, 14 Mar 1917, FO 395/66.
37. Lucy Masterman, *C. F. G. Masterman*, pp. 309, 288; Masterman to Magill, 23 Jan 1917, FO 395/72.
38. Fowler, *British–American Relations, 1917–18*, pp. 22–4.
39. Hendrick, *Page*, II, 251.
40. Leo Amery, *My Political Life*, 2 vols (London, 1953) II, 112–13.
41. Spring-Rice to Balfour, 9 Mar 1917, FO 371/3109.
42. *The Times*, 30 Mar 1917.
43. Baker to Balfour, 2 Apr 1917, Lloyd George Papers, F/3/2/16; Lloyd George, *War Memoirs*, I, 416.

CHAPTER 8. AMERICA ENTERS THE WAR; THE BALFOUR MISSION

1. Alison W. Phillips, *The Revolution in Ireland, 1910–23* (London, 1926) p. 114.
2. *Hansard*, HC, 18 Apr 1917 (xcii, 1674); Gwynn to Redmond, 17 Nov

1917, Redmond Papers, MS 15192(9); Plunkett to George V, Apr 1918, Lloyd George Papers, F/179/5/3.
3. War Cabinet minutes (120/1–2), 17 Apr 1917, Cab 23/2; *Irish Independent*, 23 Apr 1917; Wilson (ed.), *Political Diaries of C. P. Scott*, p. 273.
4. Wrench, *Dawson*, p. 149; *The Times*, 24 and 26 Apr 1917.
5. *The Times*, 11 Apr 1917; Northcliffe communiqué, 11 Apr 1917, Northcliffe Papers.
6. Leslie to Redmond, 18 May 1917, Redmond Papers, MS 15236(14).
7. Mayor Mitchel in *The Times*, 26 Apr 1917.
8. See Theodore Roosevelt and Dr Charles Eliot of Harvard, ibid.
9. *Belfast News Letter*, 27 Apr 1917; Montgomery to Sir James Stronge, 5 May 1917 (copy), Montgomery Papers, D/627/430/4; *Hansard*, HC, 26 Apr 1917 (xcii, 2722).
10. Bagwell to Hugh Montgomery, 19 May 1917, Montgomery Papers, D/627/431/44; Wilson to Bonar Law, 28 Apr 1917 (copy), Ulster Unionist Council Papers, D/989/A/8/7/30; *Irish Times*, 1 May 1917; Phillips, *The Revolution in Ireland*, Preface to 1st edn, p. xi.
11. *Observer*, 22 and 29 Apr 1917; *Daily Express*, 26 Apr 1917; *Morning Post*, 27 Apr 1917.
12. Salisbury to Curzon, 1 May 1917, Curzon Papers, F/112/120(66–7).
13. *Belfast News Letter*, 4 May 1917.
14. Lloyd George, *War Memoirs*, ii, 995; Bonar Law to Gershom Stewart, 11 Apr 1917 (copy), Bonar Law Papers, 84/6/73.
15. Ward, *Ireland and Anglo-American Relations*, pp. 146–7.
16. Hendrick, *Page*, ii, pp. 259–60.
17. Phillips, *The Revolution in Ireland*, pp. 121–2; Alfred Gollin, *Proconsul in Politics. A Study of Lord Milner* (London, 1964) p. 428; *The Times*, 28 Apr 1917.
18. Robert Lansing, *War Memoirs* (Indianapolis, 1935) p. 277.
19. Leslie, *The Irish Issue*, p. 200.
20. Interview transcript, Balfour Papers, FO 800/208.
21. Balfour to Lloyd George, telegram, 5 May 1917, and Dormer to Theodore Russell, 6 May 1917, Lloyd George Papers, F/60/2/15–17; Willert, *Road to Safety*, p. 76; Leslie to Redmond, 6 May 1917, Redmond Papers, MS 236(14).
22. *The Times*, 28 Apr 1917.
23. Willert, *Road to Safety*, p. 76, and *Washington*, pp. 98–9.
24. *The Times*, 14 May 1917; Charles Hanson Towne (ed.), *The Balfour Visit* (New York, 1917) p. 66; Balfour to Lloyd George, 23 June 1917, FO 371/3073.
25. Dixon to Cecil, 9 May 1917, enclosing Boston *Christian Science Monitor*, 27 Apr 1917, Cecil Papers, Add. MS 51092; Cecil minute to Lloyd George, n.d., c. 1 May 1917, Lloyd George Papers, F/60/2/13.
26. *Croydon Express*, 26 Nov 1910; Malcolm to Cecil, 6 May 1917 (copy), Balfour Papers, Add. MS 49738.
27. Dormer to Theodore Russell, 6 May 1917, Lloyd George Papers, F/60/2/17; Dormer to author, 5 Nov 1975.
28. Lt Gen. Sir Thomas Bridges, *Alarms and Excursions* (London, 1938) p. 171; Balfour to Lloyd George, 23 June 1917, FO 371/3073.

29. Noyes to Butler, 5 Apr 1917, FO 395/66.
30. J. St Loe Strachey, *The Adventure of Living* (London, 1922) p. 189.
31. Fisher to Butler, 24 and 29 May 1917, and Fisher to Buchan, 18 June 1917, FO 395/68.
32. Buchan to Duke, 26 Apr 1917, Lloyd George Papers, F/37/4/22; F. S. Oliver (D of I) to Pemberton Wicks, 12 June 1917, Carson Papers, D 1507/1/1917/58; Plunkett to Buchan, 19 June 1917 (copy), Plunkett Papers.
33. Oliver to Wicks, 12 June 1917, and Dawson-Bates to Wicks, 28 June 1917, Carson Papers, D 1507/1/1917/58, 64.
34. Hutchinson minute, n.d., and Montgomery minute, 5 June 1917, FO 395/67.
35. *The Times*, 30 Apr, 26 Apr and 19 May 1917; War Cabinet minutes 140, 16 May 1917, Cab 23/2.
36. *Hansard*, HC, 21 May 1917 (xcIII, 1995–9), and HL, 21 May 1917 (xxv, 199–200).
37. *Hansard*, HL, 21 May 1917 (xxv, 228).
38. *Hansard*, HL, 21 May 1917, (xxv, 243, 217); Midleton, *Ireland, Dupe or Heroine*, pp. 134–41; Wilson to Hugh Montgomery, 20 May 1917, Montgomery Papers, D 627/431/47.
39. *Belfast News Letter*, 29 May 1917.
40. William Coote (Ulster businessman) to Hugh Montgomery, Montgomery Papers, D 627/429/19.
41. McNeill, *Ulster's Stand for Union*, pp. 257–9.
42. O'Brien to Duke, 24 May 1917, O'Brien Papers, MS 8506/2; O'Brien to Lloyd George, 18 June 1917, Lloyd George Papers, F/41/91.
43. *Irish Times*, 21 and 19 May 1917.
44. Balfour to Lloyd George, 23 June 1917, FO 371/3073; Fisher to Buchan, 18 June 1917, FO 395/68.
45. See Tansill, *America and the Fight for Irish Freedom*, p. 231; D. Gwynn, *Redmond*, p. 544.
46. Northcliffe communiqué, 22 May 1917, Northcliffe Papers; *Irish Times*, 18 May 1917; Frances Stevenson, *Lloyd George. A Diary*, ed. A. J. P. Taylor (London, 1971) p. 158; R. B. McDowell, *The Irish Convention, 1917–18* (London, 1970) p. 77.

CHAPTER 9. THE NORTHCLIFFE MISSION; THE IRISH CONVENTION AND BRITISH PROPAGANDA IN THE UNITED STATES

1. Watt, *Personalities and Policies*, p. 4.
2. Cecil to Maurice Hankey, 17 May 1917, Cecil Papers, FO 800/198; Drummond to FO and to Hankey, telegrams, 21 May 1917, Balfour Papers, FO 800/208.
3. Drummond to Spring-Rice, 14 June 1917 (copy), Drummond Papers, FO 800/383; Willert, *Washington*, p. 100.

4. Pound and Harmsworth, *Northcliffe*, p. 546; Cecil to Hankey, 17 May 1917, Cecil Papers, FO 800/198; Pound and Harmsworth, *Northcliffe*, p. 546; Northcliffe to Lloyd George, 20 June 1917, Lloyd George Papers, F/41/7/8.
5. Fowler, *British–American Relations, 1917–18*, p. 33.
6. Spring-Rice letter (no addressee given), 14 June 1917, Spring-Rice Papers, FO 800/242; Spring-Rice to Balfour, 5 July 1917, Balfour Papers, Add. MS 49740.
7. See *Hansard*, HC, 4 and 19 Apr 1917 (xcii, 455, 1847); Plunkett to Lloyd George, 11 June 1917, Lloyd George Papers, F/69/12; Lord Wimborne to Bonar Law, 13 Oct 1917, J. C. C. Davidson Papers, C/2; *The Times*, 16 June 1917.
8. McNeill, *Ulster's Stand for Union*, p. 256; *Belfast News Letter*, 16 June 1917; *Freeman's Journal*, 10 July, 26 Oct and 16 Aug 1917; Plunkett's Convention report to George V, Apr 1918, Lloyd George Papers, F/179/5/3; O'Brien to Moreton Frewen, 23 June 1917, O'Brien Papers, MS 8551/5.
9. Roxburgh, Cecil and Montgomery minutes, 27, 31 and 27 July 1917, on Spring-Rice to FO, telegram, 26 July 1917, FO 371/3071; Hubert to Hugh Montgomery, n.d., c. July 1917, Montgomery Papers, D 627/430/75.
10. Spring-Rice to FO, telegram, 2 Aug, and Montgomery and Buchan minutes, 7 Aug 1917, FO 371/3071; Buchan to Fisher, 9 Aug, and Fisher's reply, 13 Aug 1917, FO 395/72.
11. Tom Spring-Rice (an Embassy Secretary) to Butler, 25 July 1917, FO 395/72.
12. Butler to Buchan, 8 June 1917, FO 395/68.
13. Roxburgh, Montgomery and Buchan minutes, 25 June 1917, on Butler to Buchan, telegram, 22 June, FO 395/67.
14. Fooks, Arnold and Chadwick (law firm) to Balfour, 7 June 1917; Sperling and Drummond minutes, 9 and 15 June 1917; Thomson to Crichton Stuart, 13 June 1917: FO 371/3072.
15. Shane Leslie obituary, *The Times*, 21 Aug 1971.
16. Willert, *Road to Safety*, pp. 90, 92.
17. Leslie to Monsignor Arthur Barnes, 23 Oct 1917, FO 395/215; Spring-Rice to Drummond, 13 July 1917, Drummond Papers, FO 800/83; Dixon to Cecil, 18 Aug 1917, Cecil Papers, Add. MS 51092.
18. Roxburgh and Willson minutes, 6 Sep and Randall minute, 7 Sep 1917, on Butler to Buchan, 17 Aug, FO 395/80; Watts to Randall, 12 Sep and 16 Oct, and Watts to Montgomery, 24 Aug 1917, FO 395/83.
19. Edward F. Roberts, *Ireland in America* (London, 1931) pp. 195–6; Tom to Mary Spring-Rice, 31 Aug 1917, Monteagle Papers, Mic 284 D/9.
20. Tansill, *America and the Fight for Irish Freedom*, p. 236; Spring-Rice to his wife, 23 Sep 1917, Spring-Rice Papers, 2/13; Devoy, *Recollections*, p. 463.
21. Ward, *Ireland and Anglo-American Relations*, p. 156; Willert to Northcliffe, 15 Nov 1917 (copy), Willert Papers.
22. Barclay to D of I, telegram, 7 Nov, and Montgomery to *The Times*, 15 Nov 1917, FO 395/85.
23. Duke to Buchan, 13 Nov 1917, FO 395/85.
24. Butler to Buchan, telegram, 5 Nov 1917, FO 395/85; Montgomery to

John Baptist Crozier, 6 Sep 1917, Montgomery Papers, D 627/430/90; Spring-Rice to his wife, 23 Sep 1917, Spring-Rice Papers, 2/13; Morison (ed.), *Letters of Roosevelt*, VIII, 1403.
25. Spring-Rice to his wife, 23 Sep 1917, Spring-Rice Papers, 2/13; Hubert to Hugh Montgomery, c. July 1917, Montgomery Papers, D 627/430/75.
26. Minute by H. A. Goode (New York Publicity Bureau), 8 Jan 1918, FO 395/86.
27. FO memorandum, 13 Oct 1919, Lloyd George Papers, F/180/1/3.
28. Smith, *Buchan*, p. 202.
29. Northcliffe to Lloyd George, telegram, 19 Sep 1917, FO 395/83; Northcliffe to *Times* editorial staff, 22 Sep 1917, Northcliffe Papers.
30. Northcliffe to War Cabinet, telegram, 8 Sep 1917, Lloyd George Papers, F/41/7/21.
31. Fowler, *British–American Relations, 1917–18*, p. 64; Willert, *Washington*, pp. 104–5.
32. Pound and Harmsworth, *Northcliffe*, p. 597.
33. Northcliffe to Lloyd George, 11 Dec, and Buchan to Lloyd George, 12 Dec 1917, Lloyd George Papers, F/41/7/34 and F/3/2/39.
34. Frewen to Balfour, 13 Jan 1918, Balfour Papers, FO 800/211; *Boston Post*, 14 Jan 1918.
35. *Boston Post*, 25 Jan 1918; Butler to Buchan, 6 Feb 1918, Balfour Papers, FO 800/211; Spring-Rice to Tom Spring-Rice, 8 Feb 1918, Monteagle Papers, Mic 284 C/2; Murray to Drummond, 25 Jan 1918, Drummond Papers, FO 800/329.
36. J. Tuohy's telegram to New York *World*, 5 Feb 1918; Roxburgh minute, 6 Feb 1918; Buchan to Tuohy, 6 Feb 1918; Tuohy's reply, 7 Feb 1918; and Cecil minute, n.d.: FO 395/213.
37. See *New York Times*, 28 Apr and 28 May 1916.
38. Aberdeen to Reading, 21 Oct, and Aberdeen to Montgomery (now on Reading's staff), 19 Sep 1918, Reading Papers, FO 800/222; Gaselee minute, 7 June 1918, FO 371/3430.
39. Leslie, *The Irish Issue*, p. 198.
40. Hamilton Fyfe, *T. P. O'Connor* (London, 1935) pp. 266–7.
41. See Spring-Rice to Eric Drummond, telegram, 9 July 1917, Drummond Papers, FO 800/383.
42. Murray to Drummond, 17 Oct 1917, Drummond Papers, FO 800/384.
43. Hazleton to Redmond, 5 Dec 1917, Redmond Papers, MS 15236(10); Fyfe, *O'Connor*, pp. 268–69; *Hansard*, HC, 23 Oct 1917 (XCVIII, 723).
44. Fyfe, *O'Connor*, p. 274; Spring-Rice to Butler, 2 Aug 1917, FO 395/72; O'Connor to Redmond, 6 Aug 1917, Redmond Papers, MS 15215(2).
45. Montgomery to Crozier, 11 Sep 1917, Montgomery Papers, D 627/430/94; Hankey to Strachey, 9 Aug 1917, Strachey Papers, S/8/6/6.
46. Redmond's speech, 4 Sep 1917, Redmond Papers, MS 15265(3); *Belfast News Letter*, 5 Sep 1917.
47. Lord Granard to Asquith, 23 Jan 1918, Asquith Papers, vol. 37.
48. *Freeman's Journal*, 4 Jan 1918.
49. War Cabinet minutes (308A), 31 Dec 1917, Cab 23/13; Cecil's draft, 3 Jan 1918, Balfour Papers, FO 800/214.
50. War Cabinet minutes (313/3), 3 Jan 1918, Cab 23/5; Stephen Roskill, *Hankey. Man of Secrets*, 3 vols (London, 1970–4) I, 478–9; *The Times*, 7 Jan

1918; Duke memorandum, 19 Feb 1918, Milner Papers, C 696/2.
51. *Daily Chronicle*, 14 Jan 1918; *Observer*, 13 Jan 1918; Northcliffe's views cited in Plunkett to Professor Adams, 13 Jan 1918, Lloyd George Papers, F/41/8/3; *The Times*, 23 Jan 1918; Northcliffe communiqué to *Times* editorial staff, 23 Jan 1918, Northcliffe Papers.
52. J. Mackay Wilson to the *Irish Times*, 29 Jan 1918; Belfast *Evening Telegraph*, 25 Jan 1918; *Belfast News Letter*, 24 Jan 1918.
53. Butler to Buchan, telegram, 17 Jan, and Murray to Buchan, 14 Jan 1918, FO 395/211; Willert memorandum, n.d., c. 18 Jan 1918, FO 395/215; Barclay to FO, telegram, 17 Jan 1918, FO 371/3429; Spring-Rice to Hardinge, 25 Jan 1918, Hardinge Papers, vol. 36.
54. Drummond minute, 15 Jan 1918, and Cecil minute, n.d., c. 25 Jan 1918, FO 395/215; Malcolm to Buchan, 8 Feb 1918, and Sperling minute, 25 Jan 1918, FO 395/211.
55. Plunkett to Balfour, 3 Aug, 17 and 28 Sep 1917, Balfour Papers, FO 800/211.
56. Roxburgh minute, 1 Feb 1918, FO 395/215; Roxburgh minute, 22 Jan 1918, and Cecil minute, n.d., FO 395/211.
57. *Freeman's Journal*, 28 Jan 1918; Plunkett to Karl Walter, 28 Jan 1918, Plunkett Papers.
58. *Morning Post*, 26 Jan 1918; Belfast *Northern Whig*, 11 Feb 1918; *Belfast News Letter*, 12 Feb 1918.
59. *Manchester Guardian*, 15 Feb 1918; Roxburgh to Scott via G. H. Mair (D of I censorship section and former *Guardian* journalist), 19 Feb, and Lindsay to Buchan, 21 Feb 1918, FO 395/220.
60. *Hansard*, HC, 29 July 1918 (CIX, 186); *Freeman's Journal*, 7 Aug 1918.
61. Smith, *Buchan*, p. 211.
62. De Valera in *Freeman's Journal*, 16 Jan 1918; Lord Southborough to H. E. Duke, 16 Jan 1918, Lloyd George Papers, F/65/6/4.
63. Plunkett to Raphoe, 2 Mar 1918 (copy), Lloyd George Papers, F/64/7/9.
64. Plunkett to Professor Adams, 12 Jan 1918; Duke to Adams, 27 Jan 1918; and Plunkett to Adams, 15 Jan 1918: Lloyd George Papers, F/64/6/5, F/65/6/1 and F/64/6/10.
65. *Belfast News Letter*, 23 Jan 1918; Fisher to Montgomery, 4 Mar 1918, Montgomery Papers, D/627/433/68.
66. See *Belfast News Letter*, 7 Jan 1918.
67. Montgomery to Fisher, 11 Feb 1918, Montgomery Papers, D 627/433/53.
68. *Spectator*, 23 Mar 1918; *Belfast News Letter*, 15 Mar 1918.
69. Plunkett's Convention report to George V, Apr 1918, Lloyd George Papers, F/179/5/3.
70. Lloyd George to Bonar Law, 12 Jan 1918, Bonar Law Papers, 82/8/4.
71. McDowell, *The Irish Convention*, p. 161; Lloyd George to Barrie, 21 Feb 1918 (copy), Bonar Law Papers.
72. Wiseman to Balfour, telegram, 4 Feb 1918, Balfour Papers, Add. MS 49741.
73. C. P. Scott, conversation with Smuts, 20 Mar 1918, and Lloyd George, 21 Mar 1918, in Wilson (ed.), *Political Diaries of C. P. Scott*, p. 328.
74. Roxburgh minutes, 21 Dec 1917, 1 and 7 Jan 1918, FO 395/86 and 215; Plunkett to Professor Adams, 26 and 30 Mar 1918, Lloyd George Papers, F/64/8/18 and 22.

CHAPTER 10. THE CONSCRIPTION CRISIS; THE LAST MONTHS OF THE WAR

1. *Hansard*, HC, 21 Dec 1915 (LXXXVII, 268); Asquith Cabinet report to George V, 4, 6 and 11 Oct 1916, Cab 37/157/10 and 19; Maxwell memorandum, 28 Sep, and Duke memorandum, 9 Oct 1916, Cab 37/155/40; *Lord Riddell's War Diary*, p. 239.
2. *Irish Times*, 7 and 5 Apr 1917.
3. Reading to FO, telegram, 30 Mar 1918, FO 371/3441; Callwell, (ed.) *Diaries of Field Marshal Sir Henry Wilson*, pp. 82, 85.
4. War Cabinet minutes (379a), 1 Apr 1918, Cab 23/14; Balfour to House via Wiseman, telegram, 2 Apr 1918, Reading Papers, FO 800/222.
5. Oliver to Chamberlain, 2 and 3 Apr 1918, Chamberlain Papers, 14/6/90; Oliver to Milner, 2 Apr 1918, Milner Papers, vol. 145.
6. Ward, *Ireland and Anglo-American Relations*, p. 159.
7. Wiseman to Drummond, 5 Apr 1918, Reading Papers, FO 800/222; Balfour to Lloyd George, 5 Apr 1918 (copy), Balfour Papers, FO 800/199; War Cabinet minutes 383/16, 5 Apr 1918, Cab 23/6.
8. *Hansard*, HC, 10 Apr 1918 (c, 1536–7); Fisher to *The Times*, 16 Apr 1918; *Spectator*, 6 Apr 1918.
9. Entry for 28–9 October 1921, in Wilson (ed.) *Political Diaries of C. P. Scott*, p. 405.
10. See John Dillon and Joseph Devlin speeches in *Hansard*, HC, 9, 10 and 12 Apr 1918 (CIV, 1398, 1502, 1929).
11. Murray to Reading, telegram, 12 Apr 1918, Reading Papers, FO 800/222; Reading to Murray, telegram, 14 Apr 1918, Balfour Papers, FO 800/209.
12. Montgomery to Reading, telegram, 14 Apr 1918, Balfour Papers, FO 800/209; Hubert to Hugh Montgomery (copy), 1 Aug 1917, Montgomery Papers, D 627/430/75.
13. Cecil minute, n.d., Balfour Papers, FO 800/209; Murray to Reading, telegram, 17 Apr 1918, Reading Papers, FO 800/222.
14. War Cabinet minutes 392/13, 16 Apr 1918, Cab 23/6; *Hansard*, HC, 16 Apr 1918 (CV, 346–8).
15. Dixon to Reading, 17 Apr 1918, Reading Papers, FO 800/222; Vincent to H. A. Goode (New York Publicity Bureau), forwarded to M of I, 23 May 1918, FO 395/224.
16. *The Times*, 20 and 24 Apr 1918.
17. *Hansard*, HL, 17 Apr 1918 (XXIX, 743); Belfast *Northern Whig*, 24 Apr 1918; Archdale to Hugh Montgomery, 6 and 20 Apr 1918, Montgomery Papers, D 627/432/48 and 127.
18. Reading to Lloyd George and Murray, telegrams, 5 and 6 May 1918, and minute by Murray, n.d., on former, Lloyd George Papers, F/60/2/59–60; Fisher to Lord Willoughby de Broke, 24 Aug 1918, Willoughby de Broke Papers, 11/62.
19. McDowell, *The Irish Convention*, p. 161.
20. Oliver to Austen Chamberlain, n.d., Austen Chamberlain Papers, 12/28; Oliver to Philip Kerr, Good Friday, and Long to Lloyd George, 7 May and 20 July 1918, Lloyd George Papers, F/91/7/3, F/32/5/31 and F/33/1/11.

21. Balfour to Carson, 2 Mar 1918 (copy), Balfour Papers, Add. MS 49709; War Cabinet minutes (453/7), 29 July 1918, Cab 23/7; Salisbury to Strachey, 27 May 1918, Strachey Papers, S/13/2/6; Murray to Reading, telegram, 15 May 1918, Reading Papers, FO 800/222.
22. Memorandum by Irish Attorney General Arthur Samuels to Lloyd George, n.d. (copy), Drummond Papers, FO 800/385.
23. Reading to Murray (for Hall), telegram, 23 Apr 1918, Reading Papers, FO 800/222; Chamberlain to Lloyd George, 3 May 1918, Lloyd George Papers, F/7/2/11; War Cabinet minutes (408A), 10 May 1918, Cab 23/14.
24. Tansill, *America and the Fight for Irish Freedom*, pp. 265–6.
25. Long to Reading, telegram, 16 May 1918 (copy), Balfour Papers, Add. MS 49741.
26. Dorothy Macardle, *The Irish Republic* (London, 1968) pp. 236–67.
27. Lansing–Wilson correspondence quoted in Tansill, *America and the Fight for Irish Freedom*, pp. 266–7; Reading to Long and FO, telegrams, 20 and 22 May 1918, Balfour Papers, Add. MS 49741; Thomson to Lord French (via Long), 21 May 1918, Long Papers, WRO 947/223.
28. *The Times*, 21 May 1918; Goode to M of I, 23 May 1918, Reading Papers, FO 800/222; War Cabinet minutes (414A), 22 May 1918, Cab 23/14; Hankey diary entry, quoted in Roskill, *Hankey*, II, 554; Tansill, *America and the Fight for Irish Freedom*, p. 261.
29. Lowell to Plunkett, 28 May 1918, Plunkett Papers; *New York Times*, 28 May 1918; Philadelphia *Public Ledger*, 27 May 1918; Reading to Balfour, 29 June 1918, FO 371/3430.
30. *Saturday Review*, 1 June 1918; *Spectator*, 22 June 1918; *Hansard*, HC, 5 Aug 1918 (CIX, 96, 1033).
31. *The Times*, 24 Apr 1918; *New York Times*, 23 Apr 1918; Plunkett to Cruise O'Brien, 24 Apr 1918, and to Karl Walter, 24 May 1918, Plunkett Papers.
32. Long to Reading, telegram, 17 May 1918, Balfour Papers, Add. MS 49741; Wilson to State Department, 4 May 1918, quoted in Francis M. Carroll, *American Opinion on the Irish Question, 1910–23* (Dublin, 1978) p. 110; O'Neill to Balfour, 15 May 1918 (copy), Long Papers, WRO 947/142(e); Plunkett to Karl Walter, 24 May 1918, Plunkett Papers.
33. Nationalist Manifesto, 18 June 1918, FO 371/3430.
34. Ward, *Ireland and Anglo-American Relations*, p. 164.
35. DMI–FO correspondence, July 1918, and Gaselee minute, 23 July 1918, FO 371/3430.
36. Ronald McNeill, *Ulster's Stand for Union*, pp. 296–99.
37. Fisher to Carson, n.d., c. Aug 1918, Carson Papers, D 1507/1/1919/52; Fisher to Hugh Montgomery, 27 Aug 1918, Montgomery Papers, D 627/436/32.
38. See *Hansard*, HC, 12 Apr 1918 (CIV, 1960); and Hugh Law's article 'Ireland 1918', *Contemporary Review*, June 1918, pp. 601–9.
39. Ridgeway to Carson, 30 Aug 1918, Carson Papers, D 1507/1/1918/77A; Robert T. Nightingale, 'The Personnel of the British Foreign Office and Diplomatic Service, 1851–1929', *Fabian Tracts*, no 232 (Feb 1930); Crichton Stuart election appeal, suplied by Mount Stuart Archives, Rothesay, to author, 8 Dec 1977.
40. *Hansard*, HC, 5 Aug 1918 (CIX, 1031); Hay to Beaverbrook, 10 Aug 1918, Beaverbrook Papers, E/8(192).

41. *The Journals of Arnold Bennett, 1892–1921*, 2 vols (London, 1932) II, 224–5.
42. Cecil to Tom Spring-Rice, 8 Feb 1918, Monteagle Papers, Mic 284 C/2; Beaverbrook memorandum, 'Criticism of M of I', n.d., c. summer 1918, Beaverbrook Papers, E/6 (33); A. J. P. Taylor, *Beaverbrook* (London, 1974) pp. 111, 569.
43. Beaverbrook memorandum, 15 Feb 1918 (copy), Beaverbrook Papers, E/10 (271); War Cabinet minutes (398/10 and 412/8), 24 Apr and 15 May 1918, Cab 23/6; Beaverbrook minute, 13 May 1918, Beaverbrook Papers, E/13.
44. Lt Col. Arthur Murray, *At Close Quarters. A Sidelight on Anglo-American Diplomatic Relations* (London, 1946) pp. 81–4; Campbell Stuart (Northcliffe's assistant) to Shortt, 5 June 1918 (copy), Long Papers, WRO 947/354(1); Plunkett to Professor Adams, 9 July 1918, Lloyd George Papers, F/69/28.
45. Milner to Long, 25 June 1918, Long Papers, WRO 947/312; DMI to War Department, Washington, 16 June 1918, Reading Papers, FO 800/222.
46. Murray, *At Close Quarters*, p. 83.
47. *Hansard*, HL, 20 June 1918 (xxx, 289–341); Reading to Murray, telegram, 24 June 1918 (copy), Reading Papers, FO 800/222; Leay to Reading, 30 June 1918, FO 371/3490.
48. Willert to Dawson, 30 Oct 1918, Willert Papers; Wiseman memorandum to Balfour, n.d., c. Nov 1918, Balfour Papers, FO 800/214; Reading to Long, 22 Oct 1918, Long Papers, WRO 947/330.
49. *Hansard*, HC, 29 July (CIX, 85–6, 106–7) and 5 Nov 1918 (CX, 1974, 1996).
50. Salisbury to St Loe Strachey, 27 May 1918, Strachey Papers, S/13/2/5; Campbell to Bonar Law, 10 Oct 1918, Bonar Law Papers, 84/2/7; Sperling minute, 12 Nov 1918, on Barclay to FO, telegram, 11 Nov 1918, FO 371/3430.
51. *Hansard*, HC, 5 Nov 1918 (CX, 1985–9, 2008–22); Long to French, 19 July 1918 (copy), Long Papers, WRO 947/230; Long to Reading, 24 Oct 1918, Reading Papers, F/118/49 (India Office Library).
52. *The Times*, 22 Nov 1918.
53. Macardle, *The Irish Republic*, pp. 253–4.
54. Barclay to Balfour, 12 Nov and 12 Dec 1918. FO 371/3430.
55. Nicholas Mansergh, *Ireland in the Age of Reform and Revolution* (London, 1940) p. 278.
56. Lansing diary quoted in Ward, *Ireland and Anglo-American Relations* pp. 170–1.
57. Carroll, *American Opinion on the Irish Question*, chs 5–6; Ward, *Ireland and Anglo-American Relations*, chs 8–9.
58. J. L. Hammond, *C. P. Scott and the 'Manchester Guardian'* (London, 1934) p. 271.

CHAPTER 11. CONCLUSION

1. Hankey, *The Supreme Command*, II, 867; Asquith, *Memories and Reflections*, II, 251; Zara Steiner, 'The Foreign Office under Sir Edward

Grey' in F. H. Hinsley (ed.), *British Foreign Policy under Sir Edward Grey* (Cambridge, 1977) p. 68; Stephen Gwynn, *The Last Years of John Redmond* (London, 1919), p. 107.
2. Kevin Leys to W. G. S. Adams, 31 Oct 1918, and Balfour to Lloyd George, 10 Feb 1920, Lloyd George Papers, F/69/2/8 and F/3/5/2; Leslie to Moreton Frewen, 1 Aug 1919, Strachey Papers, S/6/4/20.
3. Birrell, *Things Past Redress*, p. 229; Butler to H. A. Goode, 21 Nov 1918, FO 395/312.
4. *Hansard*, HL, 14 Dec 1921, XLVIII, (30).
5. *Daily Telegraph*, 24 Aug 1979.
6. Address to Congress, 20 Feb 1985.
7. *Daily Telegraph*, 25 Sep 1979.
8. *Daily Telegraph*, 27 Feb 1985.
9. Ibid.
10. *Observer*, 2 Sep 1979.
11. *Daily Telegraph*, 6 Sep 1979.
12. Television interview on BBC *Newsweek*, 27 Sep 1979.
13. *Daily Telegraph*, 20 Aug 1974, 6 and 21 Sep 1979.
14. *Daily Telegraph*, 6 Sep 1979; *Observer*, 12 Aug 1979.
15. Television interview, BBC *Panorama*, 12 Feb 1979.
16. *Daily Telegraph*, 24 Aug 1979.

Bibliography and Sources

PRIMARY SOURCES

OFFICIAL PAPERS, UNPUBLISHED

Public Record Office, London

Cabinet Papers
Cab 37   Cabinet memoranda (to Dec 1916)
Cab 41/37   Asquith's Cabinet reports to King George V
Cab 23   War Cabinet minutes (Dec 1916–1918)
Cab 24   Cabinet memoranda (Dec 1916–1918)

Foreign Office Departmental Papers
FO 371   Political Series
FO 395   News Series

OFFICIAL PAPERS, PUBLISHED

Hansard House of Commons/Lords
Report of the Royal Commission on the Rebellion in Ireland, Cmd 8279 (1916).

PRIVATE PAPERS

Public Record Office, London (FO 800 Series)
    Balfour Papers
    Cecil Papers
    Drummond Papers
    Grey Papers
    Nicolson Papers
    Reading Papers
    Spring-Rice Papers

House of Lords Record Office, London
  Beaverbrook Papers
  Bonar Law Papers
  J. C. C. Davidson Papers
  Lloyd George Papers
  St Loe Strachey Papers
  Samuel Papers
  Willoughby de Broke Papers

British Library, London
  Balfour Papers
  Cecil Papers
  C. P. Scott Papers

The *Times* Archive, London
  Northcliffe Papers
  Times Irish Papers (1917–18)
  Willert Papers

India Office Library, London
  Curzon Papers
  Reading Papers

National Library of Ireland, Dublin
  T. P. Gill Papers
  William O'Brien Papers
  Redmond Papers

Northern Ireland Public Record Office, Belfast
  Carson Papers
  Adam Duffin Papers
  Monteagle Papers
  Hugh Montgomery Papers
  Ulster Unionist Council Papers

Cambridge University Library
  Hardinge Papers

Churchill College Archive, Cambridge
  Spring-Rice Papers

Bodleian Library, Oxford
 Asquith Papers
 Milner Papers
 Nathan Papers

The Plunkett Foundation, Oxford
 The Plunkett Papers

Wiltshire Record Office, Trowbridge
 Long Papers

Kent County Council Archives, Maidstone
 Hardinge Family Papers

Birmingham University Library
 Austen Chamberlain Papers
 Joseph Chamberlain Papers

NEWSPAPERS AND PERIODICALS

English
Croydon Express	1910
Daily Chronicle	1914–18
Daily Express	1916–18
Daily Mail	1916–18
Daily News	1916
Gravesend Reporter	1910
Manchester Guardian	1914–18
Morning Post	1914–18
Observer	1915–18
Punch	1914–18
Spectator	1914–18
The Times	1910–18

Irish
Belfast *Evening Telegraph*	1918
Belfast *News Letter*	1914–18
Belfast *Northern Whig*	1914–18
Freeman's Journal	1915–18
Irish Times	1915–18

American
Boston American	1917
Boston Christian Science Monitor	1916–18
Gaelic American (New York)	1916
New York Herald	1916
New York Sun	1916
New York Times	1916–18
New York Tribune	1916
New York World	1916–18
Fatherland (New York)	1916
Irish World (New York)	1914–18

Reviews
Contemporary Review	1914–18
National Review	1914–18
Saturday Review	1916–18

CONTEMPORARY WORKS, COLLECTED CORRESPONDENCE AND MEMOIRS

Amery, Leo, *My Political Life*, 2 vols (London, 1953).
Asquith and Oxford, Lord, *Memories and Reflections, 1857–1927*, 2 vols (London, 1928).
Beaverbrook, Lord, *Politicians and the War, 1914–16* (New York, 1928).
Bennett, Arnold, *The Journals of Arnold Bennett, 1892–1921*, 2 vols (London, 1932).
Birrell, Augustine, *Things Past Redress* (London, 1937).
Bridges, Lt Gen. Sir Thomas, *Alarms and Excursions* (London, 1938).
Buchan, John, *Memory Hold the Door* (London, 1940).
Butler, Geoffrey, *The Tory Tradition* (London, 1914).
Callwell, Sir C. E. (ed.), *The Diaries of Field Marshal Sir Henry Wilson*, 2 vols (London, 1927).
Cambray, Philip G., *Irish Affairs and the Home Rule Question*, 2nd edn (London, 1911).
Devoy, John, *Recollections of an Irish Rebel* (New York, 1929).
Fitzroy, Sir Almeric, *Memoirs*, 2 vols (London, 1925).
Gaunt, Admiral Sir Guy, *The Yield of the Years* (London, 1940).
Gerard, James W., *My Four Years in Germany* (New York, 1917).
Gregory, J. D., *On the Edge of Diplomacy* (London, 1928).
Grey of Fallodon, Viscount, *Twenty-Five Years*, 3 vols (London, 1928).

Gwynn, Stephen, *The Last Years of John Redmond* (London, 1919).
—— (ed.), *The Letters and Friendships of Sir Cecil Spring-Rice*, 2 vols (London, 1929).
Hankey, Maurice, *The Supreme Command*, 2 vols (London, 1961).
Hardinge of Penshurst, Lord, *Old Diplomacy* (London, 1947).
Healy, Timothy, *Letters and Leaders of my Day*, 2 vols (London, 1928).
Hendrick, Burton J., *The Life and Letters of Walter Hines Page, 1855–1918*, 2 vols (New York, 1927).
Lansing, Robert, *War Memoirs* (Indianapolis, 1935).
Lennox, Lady Algernon Gordon (ed.), *The Diary of Lord Bertie of Thame, 1914–18*, 2 vols (London, 1924).
Leslie, Shane, *Long Shadows* (London, 1967).
——, *The Irish Issue in its American Aspect* (New York, 1917).
Lloyd George, David, *War Memoirs*, 2 vols (London, 1938).
Long, Walter, *Memories* (London, 1923).
McGuire, James K., *The King, the Kaiser and Irish Freedom* (New York, 1915).
McNeill, Ronald, *Ulster's Stand for Union* (London, 1922).
Midleton, Earl of, *Ireland, Dupe or Heroine* (London, 1932).
Monteith, Robert, *Casement's Last Adventure* (Dublin, 1953).
Morison, Elting E. (ed.), *The Letters of Theodore Roosevelt*, 8 vols (Cambridge, Mass., 1951).
Murray, Lt Col. Arthur, *At Close Quarters. A Sidelight on Anglo-American Diplomatic Relations* (London, 1946).
Nevinson, Henry W., *Last Changes, Last Chances* (London, 1928).
Newton, Lord, *Retrospection* (London, 1941).
Noyes, Alfred, *Two Worlds for Memory* (London, 1953).
O'Brien, William, *The Irish Revolution and How it Came About* (London, 1923).
Percy, Lord Eustace, *Some Memories* (London, 1958).
Riddell, George, Baron, *Lord Riddell's War Diary, 1914–18* (London, 1933).
St Loe Strachey, J., *The Adventure of Living* (London, 1922).
Seymour, Charles (ed.), *The Intimate Papers of Colonel House*, 2 vols (Boston, Mass., 1926).
Smith, F. E., *My American Visit* (London, 1918).
Spender, J. A., *Life, Journalism and Politics*, 2 vols (London, 1927).
Spindler, Captain Karl, *The Mystery of the Casement Ship* (Tralee, 1965).
Stevenson, Frances, *Lloyd George. A Diary*, ed. A. J. P. Taylor (London, 1971).

Thomson, Basil, *The Scene Changes* (London, 1937).
Towne, Charles Hanson (ed.), *The Balfour Visit* (New York, 1917).
Vansittart, Robert, *The Mist Procession* (London, 1958).
Viereck, George Sylvester, *Spreading Germs of Hate* (London, 1931).
Wickham Steed, Henry, *Through Thirty Years 1892–1922*, 2 vols (London, 1924).
Willert, Sir Arthur, *The Road to Safety* (London, 1952).
——, *Washington and Other Memories* (Boston, Mass., 1972).
Wilson, Trevor (ed.), *The Political Diaries of C. P. Scott, 1911–28* (London, 1970).

SECONDARY SOURCES
BOOKS

Birkenhead, Frederick, Second Earl of, *F. E. Smith, First Earl of Birkenhead* (London, 1960).
Blake, Robert, *The Unknown Prime Minister. The Life and Times of Andrew Bonar Law, 1858–1923* (London, 1955).
Calder, Kenneth J., *Britain and the Origins of the New Europe, 1914–18* (London, 1976).
Carroll, Francis M., *American Opinion on the Irish Question, 1910–23* (Dublin, 1978).
Churchill, Winston, *The World Crisis, 1911–18* (London, 1923).
Coffey, Thomas M., *Agony at Easter* (London, 1971).
Colvin, Ian, *The Life of Lord Carson*, 3 vols (London, 1932–6).
Dangerfield, George, *The Strange Death of Liberal England* (London, 1966).
Digby, Margaret, *Horace Plunkett. An Anglo-American Irishman* (Oxford, 1949).
Dudley Edwards, Owen, and Pyle, Fergus (eds), *1916. The Easter Rising* (London, 1968).
Dugdale, Blanche, *Arthur James Balfour*, 2 vols (London, 1936).
Fowler, Wilton B., *British–American Relations, 1917–18. The Role of Sir William Wiseman* (Princeton, NJ, 1969).
Fyfe, Hamilton, *T. P. O'Connor* (London, 1935).
Gollin, Alfred, *Pro-Consul in Politics. A Study of Lord Milner* (London, 1964).
Gwynn, Denis, *The Life and Death of Roger Casement* (London, 1931).
——, *The Life of John Redmond* (London, 1932).
Hammond, J. L., *C. P. Scott and the 'Manchester Guardian'* (London, 1934).

Hinsley, F. H. (ed.), *British Foreign Policy under Sir Edward Grey* (Cambridge, 1977).
Inglis, Brian, *Roger Casement* (London, 1974).
Jenkins, Roy, *Asquith* (London, 1964).
Keatinge, Patrick, *A Place Among the Nations. Issues of Irish Foreign Policy* (Dublin, 1978).
Leopold, Richard, *The Development of American Foreign Policy* (New York, 1962).
Leslie, Anita, *Mr Frewen of England. A Victorian Adventurer* (London, 1966).
Link, Arthur S., *Woodrow Wilson and the Progressive Era, 1910–17* (Princeton, NJ, 1954).
——, *Wilson. Campaigns for Progressivism and Peace* (Princeton, NJ, 1965).
Lyons, F. S. L., *John Dillon* (London, 1968).
Macardle, Dorothy, *The Irish Republic* (London, 1968).
MacColl, Rene, *Roger Casement* (London, 1960).
McDowell, R. B., *The Irish Convention, 1917–18* (London, 1970).
Mansergh, Nicholas, *Ireland in the Age of Reform and Revolution* (London, 1940).
Masterman, Lucy, *C. F. G. Masterman. A Biography* (London, 1939).
Newton, Lord, *The Life of Lord Lansdowne* (London, 1929).
Nicolson, Harold, *Sir Arthur Nicolson. A Study in Old Diplomacy* (London, 1930).
Noyes, Alfred, *The Accusing Ghost or Justice for Casement* (London, 1957).
O'Broin, Leon, *Dublin Castle and the Rising* (London, 1970).
——, *The Chief Secretary. Augustine Birrell in Ireland* (London, 1969).
Parmiter, Geoffrey de C., *Roger Casement* (London, 1936).
Peterson, Horace, *Propaganda for War* (Norman, Okla, 1939).
Petrie, Sir Charles, *The Life and Letters of Sir Austen Chamberlain*, 2 vols (London, 1939–40).
Phillips, Alison W., *The Revolution in Ireland, 1910–23* (London, 1926).
Pope-Hennessy, James, *Lord Crewe, 1858–1945. The Likeness of a Liberal* (London, 1955).
Pound, Reginald, and Harmsworth, Geoffrey, *Northcliffe* (London, 1959).
Prill, Felician, *Ireland, Britain and Germany, 1871–1914* (Dublin, 1975).
Roberts, Edward F., *Ireland in America* (London, 1931).
Roskill, Stephen, *Hankey. Man of Secrets*, 3 vols (London, 1970–4).

Ryan, Desmond, *The Rising. The Complete Story of Easter Week* (Dublin, 1949).
Singleton-Gates, Peter, and Girodias, Maurice, *The Black Diaries* (London, 1959).
Smith, Janet Adam, *John Buchan. A Biography* (London, 1965).
Steiner, Zara, *Britain and the Origins of the First World War* (London, 1977).
——, *The Foreign Office and Foreign Policy, 1898–1914* (Cambridge, 1969).
Stewart, A. T. Q., *The Ulster Crisis* (London, 1967).
Tansill, Charles C., *America and the Fight for Irish Freedom, 1886–1921* (New York, 1957).
Taylor, A. J. P., *Beaverbrook* (London, 1974).
Townshend, Charles, *The British Campaign in Ireland, 1919–21* (London, 1975).
Ward, Alan J., *Ireland and Anglo-American Relations, 1899–1921* (London, 1969).
Watt, D. C., *Personalities and Policies. Studies in the Formulation of British Foreign Policy in the Twentieth Century* (London, 1965).
Wrench, John Evelyn, *Geoffrey Dawson and our Times* (London, 1955).

ARTICLES

Leary, William M., Jr, 'Woodrow Wilson, Irish-Americans and the Election of 1916', *Journal of American History*, LIV (June 1967).
Nightingale, Robert T., 'The Personnel of the British Foreign Office and Diplomatic Service, 1851–1929', *Fabian Tracts*, no. 232 (Feb 1930).
Sanders, M. L., 'Wellington House and British Propaganda during the First World War', *Historical Journal*, XVIII, no. 1 (Mar 1975).

UNPUBLISHED THESES

Rothwell, V. H., 'War Aims, Peace Moves and Strategy in British Policy, 1916–18' (Ph.D. thesis, Leeds University, 1969).
Wells, Sherrill P., 'The Influence of Sir Cecil Spring-Rice and Sir Edward Grey on the Shaping of Anglo-American Relations, 1913–16' (Ph.D. thesis, London University, 1978).

PRIVATE INFORMATION TO THE AUTHOR

Sir Colville Herbert Barclay – regarding his father, Colville Barclay.
Sir Cecil Dormer.
Mrs C. E. Emery – regarding her father, Rowland Sperling.
Major Graham Curtis Lampson – regarding his father, Miles Lampson.
Mount Stuart Archives – regarding Lord Colum Crichton Stuart.
Lady Salisbury-Jones – regarding her father, Sir Maurice de Bunsen.

Index

Aberdeen, Lord, 162–3
Adams, Edward L., 61–2
Adams Newspaper Service, 122
Adams, Professor W. G. S., 126, 130
All for Ireland League, 100, 149
Allen, Ben, 85
America (Jesuit newspaper), 156
American Civil War, 135, 152, 171–2, 177, 184
American Embargo Conference, 113
American Independence Union, 30
American Press Résumé, 55, 70, 104
American Truth Society, 30
Amery, Leo, 131
Amette, Cardinal, 24
Archdale, Edward, 179–80
Asquith, Herbert Henry, 14, 16–17, 19, 23, 33, 37, 58, 62, 85–7, 89, 97, 101–2, 106–7, 110, 117, 129, 137, 193–4
Associated Press, 119, 122, 185
Atkins, Humphrey, 199
Australia, 129
Austria, 16

Bagwell, Richard, 136
Baker, J. Allen, 132
Balfour, Arthur J., 2, 11, 14, 17, 33, 35–7, 54, 101–2, 105, 117–18, 128, 131–2, 137–44, 146, 149–50, 161, 168, 175–6, 180, 184–5, 195–7, 199
Balfour Mission, 137–43
Barclay, Colville, 38, 40, 48, 60, 158, 168, 189, 191

Barrie, Sir Hugh, 172
Barry, P. T., 96
Bates, Richard Dawson, 145
Bayly, Admiral Sir Lewis, 53
Beaverbrook, Lord, 186–7, 202
Belfast *Evening Telegraph*, 167
Belfast *News Letter*, 25, 34, 70, 99–100, 119, 135, 137, 148, 152, 165, 167, 169, 170–1, 197–8
Belfast *Northern Whig*, 100, 144, 169, 179
Belgium, 16, 17, 41, 126
Bennet, Courtenay, 12, 44–7
Bennett, Arnold, 74, 128, 187
Bernstorff, Count von, 27, 47, 52, 120
Bertie, Sir Francis, 24–5, 80
Bethman Hollweg, Theodore von, 27, 63
Beyens, Baron, 16
Birrell, Augustine, 12, 18–19, 27–8, 38, 70, 72, 77, 97, 110, 196
Blackley, Travers, 105
Blackwell, Ernley, 83, 87–8, 90
Boers, 47
Boston *Christian Science Monitor*, 94, 140
Boston Post, 161–2
Bridges, General Sir Thomas, 142
British Publicity Bureau (New York), 154, 160, 179, 183, 196
British War Mission, 137–43, 150–2, 158
Broderick, Joyce, 39–40, 112, 116, 127
Brogan, Anthony, 44–5
Brooks, Sydney, 102
Bryan, William Jennings, 4, 12

237

Index

Bryce, Lord, 86
Buchan, John, 76, 125, 129–30, 145, 154–5, 161
Buchanan, Sir George, 8
Buckingham Palace Conference, 15, 101
Bullock, W. F., 46
Butler, Geoffrey, 38, 42, 65, 74, 80, 82, 93, 110–11, 122, 125, 180–30, 143, 154, 156, 159, 161–2, 167–8, 179, 183, 194–6
Butler, Captain Ralph, 72
Byrne, Alfred, 109

'C' (Indian revolutionary), 46
Callaghan, James, 199
Cambray, Philip, 3
Campbell, J. H., 33–7, 189
Canada, 43–5
Carlton Club, 20, 106
Carson, Sir Edward, 5–7, 9, 15–16, 20–1, 33, 35, 37, 69, 79, 98, 101, 105, 130, 137–8, 161, 169–70, 186, 195, 201
Carter, Jimmy, 198
Casement, Sir Roger, 1–2, 26–30, 45, 50–3, Ch. 5 (*passim*), 118, 155, 161, 181, 194
Catholic Publicity Bureau, 156
Catholics, 40–2, 129, 154–6, 158, 168, 191
Cavell, Nurse Edith, 63, 65
Cecil, Lord Robert, 20, 38, 59, 88–9, 94–5, 102, 104–7, 119, 124, 140–1, 151, 153, 162, 166, 168–9, 178, 194–5, 200
Censor, 122
Chamberlain, Austen, 4, 10, 20, 33, 36, 105–7, 176, 180–1, 195
Chaplin, Charlie, 162–3
Chicago *Daily News*, 145
Chicago *Tribune*, 170
Chirol, Valentine, 9, 91
Christensen, Adler, 28–9
Churchill, Winston, 5–6, 11, 16–17, 18–20, 187
Cla na Gael, 11–13, 19, 22, 44–5, 47, 50, 55–6, 82, 188
Clarke, Thomas, 62

Clerk, George Russell, 32
Cochrane, Bourke, 79
Cohalan, Daniel F., 56, 157–8
Colum, Padraic, 27
Conscription for Ireland, 173, 174–80, 184–6, 188
Cork incident, 159–60
Craig, James, 5–6
Crawford, Major Frederick, 5, 10
Crewe, Lord, 34, 52, 66–8, 72, 74, 150
Crichton Stuart, Lord Colum, 113, 120–1, 186, 200
Cromer, Lord, 10
Crowe, Eyre, 26, 67, 118–19
Cunard Shipping Co., 45
Curragh Mutiny, 8–11
Curzon, Lord, 20, 33, 59, 86, 92, 136–7, 147, 180, 183, 196–7

Daily Chronicle, 19, 24, 33, 97–8, 124
Daily Express, 98, 136
Daily Mail, 70, 102, 151
Daily Telegraph, 197, 199
Dallas Morning News, 55
Davies, Colonel Warburton, 72–3
Dawson, Geoffrey, 15, 21, 30–1, 59, 71–2, 81, 98, 124, 134, 149
De Bunsen, Sir Maurice, 108, 110, 191, 200
Democrat Party, 12, 35, 112
Department of Information, 125, 127–31, 144–6, 154–6, 158–62, 168–70, 173, 195, 201
Derby, Lord, 76
Desart, Lord, 76
De Valera, Eamon, 61–2, 170, 182–3
Devlin, Joseph, 3, 171, 184, 186
Devonshire, Duke of, 17
Devoy, John, 11, 13, 29, 44–5, 48, 51–2, 56, 157–8
Dillon, John, 3, 58–9, 96, 102, 125–6, 133, 153, 174, 189
Dixon, Frederick, 94, 140–1, 156, 179
Dominions, 127, 165, 174
Donald, Robert, 19, 124
Dormer, Cecil, 139, 141–2

Doyle, Michael, 81–2
Drummond, Eric, 34, 38, 56, 80–1, 83–4, 155, 163, 168, 176, 186, 195, 200
Dublin Castle, 53, 111, 122–3, 131
Dudley Edwards, Owen, 60
Duffin, Adam, 98–9
Duke, H. E., 109, 122–3, 167, 174, 181
Dunraven, Lord, 46
Durant, Kenneth, 62–3, 67–8, 70

Easter Rising, 13, 39, 43, 49, Ch. 4 (*passim*), 157, 174, 183, 193–5, 197
Egan, Patrick, 22, 27, 40
Egypt, 166, 191
Eighty Club, 137
Embargo threat, 30–2, 113–14, 117

Farley, Cardinal, 108, 121
Federalism, 10, 180–1
Findlay, Mansfeldt, 28–9
Finland, 166
Fisher, Joseph, 130, 144–5, 149, 154, 171, 177, 180, 185–6
Fitzroy, Sir Almeric, 4–5
France, 8, 17, 24–5
Free Hindustan, 46
Freeman, George, 46–7
Freeman's Journal, 152, 159, 169–70
French, Field Marshal Lord, 181, 190
Frewen, Moreton, 161
Friend, General L. B., 28, 53
Friends of Irish Freedom, 68, 116, 118, 122
Fuehr, Dr Alexander, 63

Gaelic American, 39, 46–7, 114
Garvin, J. L., 3–5, 10, 98, 106, 117, 180
Gaselee, Stephen, 94, 163, 185, 200–2
Gaunt, Captain Guy, 63, 81–2, 84, 92–4
George V, 15, 80, 85, 168
Gerard, James W., 15–16
German-Americans, 3, 30–2, 34–5, 37–9, 44–6, 48–9, 59, 64, 71, 80, 92, 102, 112–15, 117–18, 132, 162–3
'German Plot' (1918), 181–4, 186, 188–9
Germany and Irish Question, 1–2, 5–7, 10, 15–16, 26–9, 39, 43, 45, 47–8, 50–6, 58–9, 63–4, 72, 79, 114, 118–20, 157, 159–60, 163
Germany and the United States, 4, 35, 39–41, 43–9, 63–4, 112–15, 120, 132, 143, 156–9, 161–4
Ghadr, 46
Gibbons, Cardinal, 35, 58, 80, 108, 135
Gill, John, 108, 110
Gill, T. P., 25, 119
Ginnell, Lawrence, 125
Gleason, Arthur, 122
Gollin, Alfred, 138
Goode, H. A., 183, 201
Goschen, Sir Edward, 6, 10
Grant-Duff, Evelyn, 29
Gregory, J. D., 41–2, 83
Grey, Sir Edward, 8–11, 18–19, 23–9, 34, 38, 41, 51, 54, 56–7, 62, 65–7, 74–5, 79, 81–2, 84–7, 89, 91–3, 96–7, 99, 101, 104, 107, 115, 138, 193, 195–6, 200
Griffiths, Arthur, 145, 152, 182
Guest, Frederick, 127
Gupta, H. L., 47
Gwynn, Denis, 61
Gwynn, Stephen, 134, 194
Gwynne, H. A., 21, 124

Hall, Henry Noble, 167, 183
Hall, Captain (later Admiral) Reginald, 85, 181–3
Hamburg, 10
Hankey, Maurice, 118, 164–6, 183, 194
Hapgood, Norman, 122
Harbison, T. J., 170
Hardinge Lord, 9, 59, 66–7, 75, 83, 85, 88, 91–2, 95, 97, 107, 113–14, 124, 194, 200
Harrell, Commander W. V., 109
Hay Beith, Ian, 123, 186, 201
Hazleton, Richard, 164, 189

Healy, Tim, 7, 23–4, 100, 110, 184
Henry, Prince of Prussia, 15
Herbert, Sir Arthur, 37
Hitler, Adolf, 197
Home Office and Casement trial, 82–3, 85, 87–8, 90–2, 95
House, Colonel E. M., 92, 107, 113, 132, 175–6
Hughes, Charles Evan, 112–13
Hurst, Charles B., 200
Hutchinson, Colonel, 146
Hutchison, General, 61
Hyland, John F., 158

Igel, Wolf von, 50–3, 57, 157–8, 181
Imperialist Unionist Association, 136
India, 9, 44–8, 166, 191
Inglis, Brian, 83, 87, 95
Ireland (newspaper), 40, 55, 77
Irish-American (newspaper), 44
Irish Brigade scheme (Casement), 26–8
Irish Brigade scheme (under American command), 188
Irish Churchman, 6
Irish Convention, 99, 131–2, 146–50, 152–3, 159–61, 164–73, 175, 178, 181, 190, 195
Irish Independent, 26, 100, 134
Irish Relief Fund, 108–12
Irish Republican Army, 197
Irish Republican Brotherhood, 11
Irish Times, 136, 174
Irish Volunteers, 11–13, 22, 26, 50
Irish War Aims Committee, 196
Irish World, 11–12, 22, 39, 116

Jay, Peter, 198
Jellicoe, Admiral Sir John, 138
Jenkins, Roy, 101
Jewish influence in United States, 142
Jodh Singh, 47
Jones, Sir Roderick, 202
Justice, Edmund, 44

Kelly, Thomas H., 109
Kerr, Philip, 131

Kerr, S. Parnell, 43
Kettle, Thomas, 154–5
Killearn, Lord, 77
Kilpatrick, General, 68–9
Kingston, Lady, 111
Kitchener, Lord, 19, 27, 72
König, Paul, 44
Krupps arms supply, 44

Lampson, Miles, 61, 73, 75–7, 129, 195, 200
Lane, Franklin K., 152
Langley, Walter, 14, 81
Lansdowne, Lord, 15, 87, 102–4, 106–7, 147–8, 195
Lansing, Robert, 61, 63, 120, 138, 144, 182, 191
Larne gun-running, 10–11
Law, Andrew Bonar, 5, 16–17, 20–1, 33, 101, 105–7, 136–7, 172, 177, 180–1, 187, 190, 195
Law, Hugh, 186, 201
League of Nations, 189
Leay, Cornelius, 44, 188
Leays, Kevin, 195–6
Lee, General Robert E., 68
Leslie, Shane, 40, 42, 54–5, 84, 96, 126, 139, 154–5, 157, 163, 186, 195–6
Lincoln, Abraham, 69, 130, 136, 172, 177
Lindsay, Nigel, 169–70
Lloyd George, David, 3, 16, 19, 60, 76, 86, 97–107, 115, 117–19, 124, 126, 130–4, 136–43, 147, 149–50, 152, 166, 170, 172–80, 182–3, 190, 195–7, 199, 201
Locock, Guy, 43, 200
Lodge, Henry Cabot, 90
Londonderry, Lord, 179
Long, Walter, 20, 56, 86–7, 102–6, 166, 178, 180–2, 184, 187, 190, 195
Lowell, Lawrence, 183
Lusitania, 34, 45
Lynch, Arthur, 134
Lynch, Jeremiah, 61–2
Lynn, R. J., 100

McCarthy, Dr, 44
McCormick, Medill, 140, 144
MacDonagh, Michael, 43
MacDonagh, Thomas, 68
McDowell, Alexander, 105
McGuire, James K., 39
MacNeill, Eoin, 110
McNeill, Ronald, 70, 135–6, 152
Magill, A. P., 131
Malcolm, Ian, 141, 144, 168
Malkin, Herbert, 57–8, 200
Mallet, Sir Louis, 7
Mallon (Cunard Security Police), 45
Maloney, William, 157
Manchester Guardian, 25, 33–4, 97, 170
Masefield, John, 41
Mason, Roy, 199
Masterman, Charles, 64, 123–4, 130–1, 187, 201
Maxwell, General Sir John, 54, 56, 61, 74–5, 97, 109, 174
Meyer, Kuno, 15
Midleton Lord, 71, 100–1, 148, 165, 171–3
Milner, Lord, 10, 137, 176, 188
Ministry of Information, 125, 186–7, 202
Mitchel, John P., 135, 144, 158
Monday Club, 198
Montagu, Edwin, 92
Montgomery, Hubert, 23, 29–30, 43, 66, 68, 72–3, 75–8, 88, 97, 99, 107, 111, 122, 124, 129, 146, 153–4, 158–9, 164, 178, 194, 200
Montgomery, Hugh, 10, 66, 99, 111, 135, 171
Moore, John D., 68
Morley, Lord, 4–5, 18
Morning Post, 21, 30, 77–8, 136, 169
Mountsier, Robert, 122
Munsterberg, Hugo, 63
Murphy, John D., 108
Murray, Colonel Arthur, 162–4, 167–8, 177, 180–1, 186, 195
Murray Gilbert, 86

Nathan, Sir Matthew, 28, 46, 53

Nation (newspaper), 83
National Volunteers, 22
Navy League, 160, 198
Needham, Raymond, 74, 128, 202
Negro Fellowship League, 86
Nevinson, Henry W., 83
New York draft riots, 177
New York *Herald*, 55
New York Times, 53, 73–4, 113, 159, 170, 183–4
New York *Tribune*, 122, 159
New York *World*, 49, 53, 58, 144, 162
Newton, Lord, 14, 23, 72, 75, 78, 85, 88–9, 94, 104, 108, 111, 129, 194, 200
Nicholas II, Tsar of Russia, 8
Nicolson, Arthur, 7–10, 14, 26–8, 59, 65–7, 80, 129, 194, 200
Norddeutsche Allgemeine Zeitung, 26
Northcliffe, Lord, 15, 31, 70–1, 98, 100–1, 124, 135–6, 138, 141, 143, 149–52, 155, 158, 160–1, 167, 197
Norway, 28–9
Noyes, Alfred, 6, 93, 123, 125, 143–4, 200
Nugent, Horace, 179

O'Brien, Fred Burns, 197
O'Brien, William, 98, 100, 107, 149, 153, 164
Observer, 3, 98, 117, 137, 199
O'Connell, Cardinal, 156, 161–2, 191
O'Connor, T. P., 19, 24–5, 40, 77, 163–4, 179–80, 185, 189
O'Donnell, Bryan, 130
O'Gorman, Senator J. A., 13–14
O'Leary, Jeremiah, 30, 113
Oliphant, Lancelot, 80
Oliver, F. S., 130, 145, 176, 180
O'Neill, Laurence, 184–5

Page, Walter Hines, 61, 89, 91–3, 131, 137–8, 176–7, 182
Palmer, Frederick, 72
Panama Canal Tolls, 13
Papen, Franz von, 27

Parker, Gilbert, 41, 56, 62, 64–6, 68, 73–4, 107, 110–11, 124, 141, 194
Peace Conference, 125–6, 133–4, 147, 149, 152–3, 172–3, 188–92
Pearse, Padraic, 54, 68
Peel, Arthur, 29
Percy, Lord Eustace, 11–13, 28, 31–2, 35–7, 40–1, 56, 58, 60, 76–7, 79, 112, 129, 157, 161, 195, 200
Peterson, H. C., 70
Philadelphia *Public Ledger*, 183
Philippines, 68
Phillips, W. Alison, 136, 138
Plunkett, Sir Horace, 54, 56, 69, 134, 152–3, 168–9, 171, 173, 184
Poincaré, Raymond, President of France, 24–5
Poland, 126
Polk, Frank, 57, 91
Press Bureau, 124
Prill Felician, 16
Primrose, Neil, 200

Quinn, John, 79, 84, 86, 135, 138–9

Randall, Alec, 156, 201
Raphoe, Bishop of, 165, 171
Reading, Lord, 161, 175–85, 188–91
Redmond, John, 3, 5, 11–12, 18–19, 21–3, 25, 31, 34–5, 38–40, 55, 58, 61, 96, 107, 118–19, 127, 147, 150, 155, 163–6, 173, 193
Reuters, 119
Riddell, Lord, 174
Ridder, Hermann, 28
Ridgeway, Professor, 186
Ridgeway, William, 46
Roberts, Edward, 157
Roosevelt, Theodore, 69, 135, 159
Rothermere, Lord, 187, 202
Roxburgh, Ronald, 64, 68, 127, 153–4, 156, 168, 200–1
Royal Commission on Easter Rising, 66
Runciman, Walter, 19
Russia, 8–9, 17, 106, 126, 134, 152, 165
Ryan, Michael, 96

Salisbury, Lord, 136, 180–1, 189
Samuel, Sir Herbert, 18, 82, 86–7, 90, 109
Sazonov, Sergei, 8
Schiemann, Professor, 15
Scott, C. P., 96–7, 134
Seely, Colonel J. E. B., 8
Selborne, Lord, 148
Self-determination, 114, 126, 128, 133–4, 153, 166–7, 170–1, 178, 181, 185, 189–91, 195–6, 198
Shortt, Edward, 181, 190
Sinn Fein, 11, 110, 117, 125, 128, 133, 144–5, 149, 152, 159, 163, 170, 172, 174, 181–3, 185, 190–1
Skeffington, Hannah Sheehy, 121
Sloss, Robert, 145
Smith, F. E., 82, 84–5, 87, 101, 161–3
Smith, Joseph, 109
Smuts, General Jan, 172–3, 181, 183
South Africa, 197
Soviet Union, 198
Spectator, 68–9, 76, 107, 177, 183–4
Sperling, Rowland, 41, 51, 57–8, 65, 68, 77–8, 80, 90, 91–2, 108, 117–18, 120–1, 168, 189–90, 194, 200
Sprindler, Captain Karl, 47–8
Spring-Rice, Sir Cecil, 11–15, 17, 23, 27, 31–2, 34–5, 37–42, 48–9, 51–2, 54, 56–60, 64–6, 68–9, 74, 77, 79–82, 84–5, 88–96, 102, 108–10, 112–18, 120, 126, 128, 152–7, 159, 161–2, 164, 168, 175, 180, 187, 194, 196, 198
Spring-Rice, Tom, 157
Stalin, Joseph, 197
Stamfordham, Lord, 80
Steed, Henry Wickham, 15
Strachey, St Loe, 68–9, 76, 104, 107, 177
Stronge, Sir James, 6
Switzerland, 29

Taft, William Howard, 135
Tanner, Dr Joseph, 128
Tansill, Charles, 49, 183

Thatcher, Margaret, 197–8
Thomson, Basil, 93, 110, 155, 182–3
Times, The, 10, 12, 15, 18, 21, 30–1, 43, 46, 55, 59, 71, 90, 98, 126, 134–7, 140, 146, 149, 151, 158, 167, 170, 184
Tower, Reginald, 29
Trades Union Congress, 166
Trotsky, Leon, 166
Troup, Sir Edward, 87, 90
Tumulty, Joseph, 89

Ukraine, 166
Ulster Unionist Council, 98, 105, 149
Ulster Volunteers, 5, 10–11
United Irish League of America, 22, 58
United States Congress, 34, 117, 144, 167

Vance, Cyrus, 198
Vansittart, Robert, 28, 94
Vatican, 29, 41–2, 141
Viereck, George, 39, 118
Vincent, Arthur, 179, 201

Walter, Karl, 54
War Aims, 166–7, 170
War Office, 38, 61, 72–6, 193
Ward, Wilfred, 23–4
Washington, George, 79
Watts, H. Christopher, 156

Welland Canal, 44
Wellington House, 41–3, 55–6, 62, 64, 67, 69, 110, 123–4, 194
Whibley, Laurence, 125, 128, 201
Whigham, H. J., 55–6, 62–5, 68–70, 73–4, 107
White, Henry, 2–3
Whitten, H. M., 123
Wicks, Pemberton, 145
Willert, Arthur, 12, 14, 21–2, 30–1, 38, 59–60, 71, 81, 86, 98, 139–40, 146, 155, 158, 161, 167–8, 188, 201
Wilhelm II, German Emperor, 5–7, 15–16, 19, 28
Willson, P. F., 156
Wilson, General Sir Henry, 8, 175
Wilson, J. Mackay, 105, 136, 148
Wilson, Woodrow, 13–14, 30, 32, 34–5, 37–8, 48, 51–2, 56–7, 59–61, 69, 81–2, 89–92, 99–100, 107, 112–22, 126–7, 131–5, 137–8, 140, 149, 151, 158, 161, 166–8, 170–2, 175–7, 179, 182–5, 189–92, 195–6, 198
Wimborne, Lord, 54, 72, 110, 126, 181, 188
Wiseman, William, 131, 158, 161, 166, 176–7, 188–9
Wrench, Evelyn, 202

Yeats, W. B., 93

Zulus, 47

GPSR Compliance

The European Union's (EU) General Product Safety Regulation (GPSR) is a set of rules that requires consumer products to be safe and our obligations to ensure this.

If you have any concerns about our products, you can contact us on

ProductSafety@springernature.com

In case Publisher is established outside the EU, the EU authorized representative is:

Springer Nature Customer Service Center GmbH
Europaplatz 3
69115 Heidelberg, Germany

www.ingramcontent.com/pod-product-compliance
Lightning Source LLC
Chambersburg PA
CBHW031519100426
42873CB00013B/134